Collins

Latin

Language

— and —

Roman Culture

HarperCollins Publishers
Westerhill Road
Bishopbriggs
Glasgow
G64 2QT
Great Britain

First Edition 2012

Reprint 10 9 8 7 6 5 4 3 2 1 0

ISBN 978-0-00-745007-7

www.collinslanguage.com

A catalogue record for this book is available from the British Library

Typesetting by Davidson Publishing Solutions, Glasgow

Printed in Great Britain by Clays Ltd, St Ives plc

Acknowledgements
We would like to thank those authors and publishers who kindly gave permission for copyright material to be used in the Collins Word Web. We would also like to thank Times Newspapers Ltd for providing valuable data.

WRITTEN BY
Ben Harris

FOR THE PUBLISHER
Freddy Chick
Lucy Cooper
Elaine Higgleton
Susanne Reichert
Lisa Sutherland

Contents

Introduction **v**

Latin pronunciation **viii**

Latin Language **1**

Nouns **2**

Using nouns 2

Gender 3

Forming plurals 6

Cases 7

Declensions 9

Adjectives **16**

Using adjectives 16

Declensions 17

Comparison of adjectives 22

Pronouns **27**

Personal pronouns 28

Possessive pronouns 30

Reflexive pronouns 31

Determinative pronouns 32

Demonstrative pronouns 34

Relative pronouns 36

Interrogative pronouns 38

Verbs **42**

The four conjugations 42

The present tense 45

The present tense: regular ***-āre*** (first conjugation) verbs 45

The present tense: regular ***-ēre*** (second conjugation) verbs 47

The present tense: regular ***-ere*** (third conjugation) verbs 48

The present tense: regular ***-īre*** (fourth conjugation) verbs 49

The present tense: irregular verbs 50

The imperative 55

The imperfect tense 57

The future tense 63

The perfect tenses 68

The passive 77

The present participle 87

Future participles 91

Impersonal verbs 93

The subjunctive 95

The infinitives 110

Deponent verbs 115

Defective verbs 117

Contents

Negatives		**119**
	Using negatives	119
Questions		**123**
	How to ask a question in Latin	123
Adverbs		**127**
	Using adverbs	127
	Comparison of adverbs	129
Prepositions		**132**
	Using prepositions	132
	Prepositions followed by the ablative case	133
	Prepositions followed by the accusative case	135
Conjunctions		**139**
	Using conjunctions	139
	and, but, or, however and *therefore*	140
	Some other common conjunctions	141
Numbers		**146**
	Cardinal numbers	146
	Ordinal numbers	148
	Distributive numbers	149
	Numeral adverbs	150
Time and date		**152**
	Expressing time	152
	Calculating dates	153
Latin Literature		**157**
Cicero	*The last advocate of the Republic*	158
Caesar	*The legendary chronicler of war*	166
Catullus	*The true father of the epigram*	174
Virgil	*The national poet of Rome*	182
Horace	*The lyrical songster of life*	190
Livy	*The epic poet of history*	198
Ovid	*The soft philosopher of love*	206
Martial	*The unforgiving observer of the world*	214
Tacitus	*The scathing judge of empire*	222
Pliny	*The cultured man of letters*	229
Latin Legacy		**237**
A-Z of Latin words and phrases		238
Reference Section		**277**
Common uses of the cases		278
Common principal parts of verbs		283
Answer key		**299**
Sources and Index		**303**
About the author		**310**

Introduction

Whether you are starting to learn Latin for the very first time, brushing up on topics you have studied with a tutor, or revising for public exams, *Collins Latin Language and Roman Culture* is here to help. This easy-to-use guide takes you through all the basics you will need to read and understand classical Latin.

Collins Latin Language and Roman Culture is made up of three main parts: 1) **Latin Language**; 2) **Latin Literature**; and 3) **Latin Legacy**.

Newcomers can sometimes struggle with the technical terms they come across when they start to explore the grammar of a new language. **Latin Language** explains how to get to grips with all the parts of speech you will need to know, using simple language and cutting out jargon.

This part of the book is divided into sections, each dealing with a particular area of grammar. Each section can be studied individually, as numerous cross-references in the text point you to other relevant sections of the book for further information. Exercises (with answers at the back of the book) are included with all the sections to help you practise what you have learnt.

Every major section begins with a brief explanation of the area of grammar covered on the following pages.

What is a verb?
A verb is a 'doing' word which describes what someone or something does, what someone or something is, or what happens to them (for example, *write*, *is*, *be eaten*).

Each grammar point is followed by simple Latin examples, complete with English translations, helping you understand the rules. Bold and underlined text has been used throughout to highlight the grammatical point being explained.

If you are telling somebody **NOT TO DO** something, you use the imperative form of **nōlle** followed by the infinitive.

puerī, istum poētam <u>audīre nōlīte</u>!
Boys, do not listen to that scandalous poet!

In Latin, as with any foreign language, there are certain pitfalls which have to be avoided. **Tips** throughout the sections are useful reminders of the things that often trip learners up.

> ✔ **TIP**
> Remember that you **NEVER** use the verb **esse** to translate *was* or *were* in forms like *was reading* or *were walking* and so on. You change the Latin verb ending instead.

Key points sum up all the important facts about a particular area of grammar, to save you time when you are revising and help you focus on the main grammatical points.

> **KEY POINTS**
> - Negatives indicate when something is not happening or is not true. Latin uses adverbs like **nōn** (or **haud**) to indicate this, as well as certain nouns and adjectives.
> - Two negatives used in the same sentence make it affirmative.
> - Latin does not use **et nōn** but **nec**.
> - Latin does not generally use **nōn** with the subjunctive but **nē**.

The literature that survives from Roman times allows us to appreciate what was so special about Roman civilisation and how it has had such an enormous influence on our own world. **Latin Literature** is made up of ten units, each illustrating the work of a particular Latin writer.

Each unit gives a flavour of the best of this remarkable literature in the original Latin, grouped into themes under English headings to help you navigate through them. Short introductions and numbered English translations of every extract help you understand the original Latin. These translations are deliberately quite literal and for every extract there is a section headed **Nota Bene** which explains the most important grammatical features. For further help with understanding the literature, a free download with all the original Latin extracts recorded is available on **www.collinslanguage.com/latin-audio**.

Appreciating Roman civilisation isn't just about linguistic competence – it's also about cultural knowledge. For you to get a feel for what life was like in the Roman world, at the end of each unit the **Culture Vulture** will give you the information you need to gain a deeper insight into the Roman world and its people.

The huge influence of the Latin language continues to be felt in many areas of our lives today. An alphabetical list of over 300 Latin words and phrases that are still used in current English is provided in **Latin Legacy**. Each expression comes with an English translation and any necessary explanation about its background, as well as a real English example of it being used.

Finally, the supplement at the end of the book contains a summary of the **Common uses of the cases** and a useful list of over 400 **Common principal parts of verbs**. As well as a general index, there is also a list of references for the original Latin extracts.

We hope that you will enjoy using *Collins Latin Language and Roman Culture* and find it useful in the course of your study.

Latin pronunciation

There are some sounds in Latin which need a bit of practice, such as the Latin **r**, which is much more noticeable than an English *r*, and the long **ō** sound to be heard in words like **mōns** and **pōns**, which is different from the *oo* sound in an English word like *moon*.

Silent letters

In English, not all letters are pronounced – for example, the *b* at the end of the word *lamb* or the *e* at the end of the word *complete*. In Latin, there are no silent letters.

Latin vowels

These are the main ways in which Latin vowels are pronounced:

- **a** - closer to *u* as in *tut* than *a* as in *tat* (**amō**, **canis**)
- **ā** - *ar* as in *cart* (**amāre**, **māter**)
- **e** - *e* as in *net* (**centum**, **facile**)
- **ē** - closer to *ai* as in *aim* than *ay* as in *day* (**cēna**, **spērāre**)
- **i** - *i* as in *sip* (**liber**, **mittere**)
- **ī** - *ee* as in *keen* (**dīcere**, **sīcut**)
- **o** - *o* as in *hot* (**forum**, **rogāre**)
- **ō** - closer to *oa* as in *moat* than *o* as in *mobile* (**adeō**, **nōmen**)
- **u** - *u* as in *put* (**bellum**, **epistula**)
- **ū** - *oo* as in *tool* (**lūdere**, **mūrus**)
- **y** - *u* as in the French *plume* (**Olympia**, **Pyrrhus**) – this is a sound borrowed from Greek

Vowel combinations

- **ae** - *i* as in *hi* (**aeger**, **puellae**)
- **au** - *ow* as in *cow* (**autem**, **nauta**)
- **ei** - *ay* as in *hay* (**deinde**) – this is a rare sound in Latin
- **eu** - something like *e* as in *net* + *oo* as in *tool* (**ēheu**, **Orpheus**) – another rare sound
- **oe** - *oy* as in *toy* (**coepī**, **foedus**)
- **ui** - something like *u* as in *put* + *i* as in *sip* (**alicui**, **huic**)

Latin consonants

Many Latin consonants are pronounced the same as their English equivalents. Some consonants, however, vary in their pronunciation in the following ways:

- **c** - always *c* as in *cat* (**capere**, **cibus**)
- **ch** - *c* as in *cat* but with extra emphasis (**Achātēs**, **chorus**)
- **g** - always *g* as in *get* (**gladius**, **legiō**)
- **gn** - *ngn* as in *wrongness* (**agnus**, **magnopere**)
- **i** - *y* as in *yet* (**iānua**, **iam**)
- **n** - *n* as in *angry* when it comes before 'c', 'g', or 'q' (**ingēns**, **relinquere**)
- **ph** - *p* as in *pig* but with extra emphasis (**nympha**, **Pharsālus**)
- **r** - *rr* as in the French *rouge* (**rēx**, **trēs**)
- **s** - always *s* as in *sat* (**studium**, **urbs**)
- **th** - *t* as in *time* but with extra emphasis (**Thalīa**, **theātrum**)
- **v** - *w* as in *weed* (**amāvērunt**, **via**) – this consonant is traditionally written in Latin as **u**

Nota bene
Two sounds that you will **NEVER** hear in classical Latin are the consonant sounds associated with the English letters *j* as in *jam* and *v* as in *vote*.

Stress

In English words, a particular syllable is stressed – for example, *beau*ty, con*cer*to, *den*tistry. In Latin, stress usually depends on the number of syllables in a word.

In words of two syllables, the stress falls on the first syllable (**amō, amās, amat**).

In words of three or more syllables, the stress falls on the third syllable from the end (**amīcitia**, **imperium**, **suspicit**). But the stress falls on the second syllable from the end if that syllable contains a long vowel (**labōrāmus**), a vowel combination (**incautē**) or a short vowel followed by two consonants (**dēspērandum**).

Part One

Latin Language

Nouns

What is a noun?
A noun is a 'naming' word for:
- a living being (for example, *girl*, *Hercules*, *dog*)
- a place or a thing (for example, *house*, *Pompeii*, *table*)
- an activity, an event, or an idea (for example, *sleep*, *dinner party*, *anger*)

Using nouns

In Latin, all nouns are ***masculine***, ***feminine***, or ***neuter***. This is called their ***gender***. Even words for things have a gender.

Whenever you are using a noun, you need to know whether it is masculine, feminine, or neuter as this affects the form of other words used with it, such as:
- adjectives that describe it
- pronouns (such as **hic** and **ille**) that replace it

For more information on Adjectives or Pronouns, see pages 16 and 27.

You can find information about gender by looking the word up in a dictionary. When you come across a new noun, always learn its gender as well as its meaning. Unlike English, Latin nouns do not have articles (such as *the* or *a*) that go before them.

We refer to something as ***singular*** when we are talking about just one, and as ***plural*** when we are talking about more than one. The singular is the form of the noun you will usually find when you look a noun up in the dictionary. As in English, nouns in Latin change their form in the plural.

Adjectives and pronouns are also affected by whether a noun is singular or plural.

In Latin, all nouns also change form by taking different endings in order to reflect their function in a sentence. This is called their ***case***. The six main cases are the ***nominative*** case, the ***vocative***, the ***accusative***, the ***genitive***, the ***dative***, and the ***ablative***. When you look up a noun in the dictionary, its nominative and genitive singular case endings will usually be given.

Again, adjectives and pronouns are affected by a noun's case.

> ✔ **TIP**
> In North America, it is still common practice to list the Latin cases after the nominative and vocative in the following order of priority: genitive, dative, accusative, ablative.

Finally, in Latin, all nouns are divided into five main groups. These are called **declensions**. Each declension has its own set of case endings for the nouns that belong to it. The genitive singular ending of a noun will enable you to identify its declension, and therefore the pattern that the noun's different case endings will follow. When you come across a new noun, always learn its genitive singular case ending, too.

Adjectives also follow the same declension patterns as nouns.

> ✔ **TIP**
> Remember to learn the gender and genitive singular case of each new noun you come across, as well as the meaning of the noun.

Gender

Nouns referring to people

All nouns referring to men and boys are ***masculine***.

dominus	*a master*
rēx	*a king*

All nouns referring to women and girls are ***feminine***.

māter	*a mother*
rēgīna	*a queen*

When the same word is used to refer to either men/boys or women/girls, its gender changes depending on the sex of the person it refers to.

cīvis	*a citizen*
sacerdōs	*a priest/priestess*

4 Nouns

In English, we can sometimes make a word masculine or feminine by changing the ending – for example, *Englishman* and *Englishwoman*, or *prince* and *princess*. In Latin, the ending of a noun can sometimes change depending on whether it refers to a man/boy or a woman/girl.

fīlius	*a son*
fīlia	*a daughter*
Lūcius	*Lucius*
Lūcia	*Lucia*
deus	*a god*
dea	*a goddess*

Nouns referring to animals

In English, we can choose between words like *bull* or *cow*, depending on the sex of the animal we are referring to. In Latin, too, there are sometimes separate words for male and female animals.

taurus	*a bull*
vacca	*a cow*

Sometimes, the same word with different endings is used for male and female animals.

cervus	*a stag*
cerva	*a doe/hind*

Words for some animals do not change according to the sex of the animal, and their gender can be either masculine or feminine.

canis	*a dog*
serpēns	*a snake*

Words for some other animals also do not change according to the sex of the animal, but their gender is always the same.

columba	*a dove* (***feminine***)
passer	*a sparrow* (***masculine***)

Nouns referring to things

In English, we call things – for example, *table*, *car*, *apple* – 'it'. In Latin, however, things as well as places, events, and ideas have a gender, which is sometimes decided by the ending of the noun. But always try to learn the gender as you learn the word.

These endings are often found on ***masculine*** nouns:

-us	**cibus**	*food*
-er	**pater**	*a father*
-or	**mercātor**	*a merchant*

These endings are often found on ***feminine*** nouns:

-a	**puella**	*a girl*
-tās	**vēritās**	*truth*
-tūdō	**pulchritūdō**	*beauty*
-iō	**regiō**	*a region*
-ēs	**fidēs**	*faith*

These endings are often found on ***neuter*** nouns:

-um	**templum**	*a temple*
-men	**nōmen**	*a name*
-e	**cubīle**	*a couch/bed*
-al	**tribūnal**	*a tribunal*
-ū	**cornū**	*a horn*

✔ Tip

The ending of a noun can help you identify its gender. The **-us**, **-a**, and **-um** endings are the most common clues – for example, **ānulus** (meaning *a ring*) is ***masculine***, **barba** (meaning *a beard*) is ***feminine***, and **imperium** (meaning *empire*) is ***neuter***.

However, there are exceptions to these rules, so it is best to check in a dictionary if you are unsure. For example, **manus** (meaning *a hand*) and **domus** (meaning *a house*) are both feminine, and **tempus** (meaning *time*) is neuter; **nauta** (meaning *a sailor*) and **diēs** (meaning *a day*) are both masculine.

Key points

- Most nouns referring to men, boys, and male animals are ***masculine***; most nouns referring to women, girls, and female animals are ***feminine***. The ending of a Latin noun sometimes changes depending on whether it refers to a male or a female.
- These endings are often found on masculine nouns: **-us**, **-er**, **-or**.
- These endings are often found on feminine nouns: **-a**, **-tās**, **-tūdō**, **-iō**, **-ēs**.
- These endings are often found on neuter nouns: **-um**, **-men**, **-e**, **-al**, **-ū**.

Forming plurals

In English, we usually make nouns plural by adding an *-s* or *-es* to the end (*garden – gardens*; *kiss – kisses*), although we do have some nouns which are irregular and do not follow this pattern (*mouse – mice*; *child – children*). In Latin, most nouns form their plural by changing their ending. The ending is determined by what declension the noun belongs to.

For more information on Declensions, see page 9.

Most ***feminine*** nouns change the ending **-a** to **-ae**. (These nouns are in the ***first*** declension.)

fēmina	*a woman*
fēminae	*women*

Most ***masculine*** nouns change the ending **-us** to **-ī**. (These nouns are in the ***second*** declension.)

servus	*a slave*
servī	*slaves*

However, most ***masculine*** nouns in the second declension ending in **-er** add an **-ī**.

puer	*a boy*
puerī	*boys*

Most ***neuter*** nouns change the ending **-um** to **-a**. (These nouns are also in the ***second*** declension.)

bellum	*war*
bella	*wars*

The following nouns are all from the ***third*** declension. Notice the different ways that the plural is formed.

cōnsul	*a consul* (**masculine**)
cōnsulēs	*consuls*
legiō	*a legion* (**feminine**)
legiōnēs	*legions*
flūmen	*a river* (**neuter**)
flūmina	*rivers*
cīvis	*a citizen* (**masculine/feminine**)
cīvēs	*citizens*
mare	*the sea* (**neuter**)
maria	*seas*
animal	*an animal* (**neuter**)
animālia	*animals*

These nouns are both from the ***fourth*** declension.

exercitus	*an army (**masculine**)*
exercit<u>ūs</u>	*armies*
genū	*a knee (**neuter**)*
gen<u>ua</u>	*knees*

This noun is from the ***fifth*** declension. Notice how the plural form is the same as the singular.

diēs	*a day (**masculine**)*
diēs	*days*

KEY POINTS

- Latin nouns almost always change their ending in order to form their plural, but sometimes they change internally as well.
- Remember to check what declension the noun belongs to, so that you can follow the correct pattern for forming its plural.

Cases

In English, we change the form of some words to reflect their function in a sentence. For example, in the sentence *I see the sun*, '*I*' is the subject of the verb (i.e. doing the action). But '*I*' changes to '*me*' if we want it to become the object of the verb (i.e. having the action done to it): *The sun sees me*.

Notice that in English it is only the pronoun that changes its form to reflect a change of function (*I* – *me*), and not the noun (*the sun* – *the sun*). In Latin, nouns and adjectives as well as pronouns change their form to reflect their function. This is what we call their ***case***.

There are six regular cases in Latin. Each case indicates that a word is performing a specific function in a sentence, and the form of the word in each case depends on which declension it belongs to.

The ***nominative*** case is mainly used to show that the word is the subject of a verb, or to describe the subject of the verb.

__The master__ died.
The cook is __a slave__.

The ***vocative*** case is used to show that someone or something is being spoken to.

Welcome, ***Alexander****.*

The ***accusative*** case is mainly used to show that the word is the direct object of a verb, and after some prepositions.

The dog ate ***the food****.*

The dog jumped onto ***the table****.*

For more information on Prepositions, see page 132.

The ***genitive*** case is mainly used to show possession, like 'of' in English.

He is the owner ***of the shop****.*

The ***dative*** case is mainly like 'to' in English, to show that the word is what we call the indirect object of a verb.

She gave the present ***to the boy****.*

The ***ablative*** case is mainly like 'by' or 'with' in English, to show how something was done, and is used after some prepositions.

The friend was woken ***by the shouts****.*

The girls ran away from ***the theatre****.*

For Common uses of the cases, see supplement.

✔ TIP

You can remember all the singular and plural case endings of Latin nouns if you memorise the patterns of the five declensions.

KEY POINTS

- The nominative case is used for the subject in a sentence.
- The vocative case is used to address someone.
- The accusative case is used for the direct object in a sentence.
- The genitive case is used to show possession.
- The dative case is used for the indirect object in a sentence.
- The ablative case is used to show how something was done.

Declensions

In Latin, all nouns are divided into five groups or ***declensions***. Each declension has the six cases, both singular and plural, indicated by different endings.

The ending of the genitive singular case helps to identify which declension a noun belongs to.

Declension	Nominative singular case	Genitive singular case	Genitive singular case ending
1st Declension	**fēmina**	**fēminae**	**-ae**
2nd Declension	**puer, bellum**	**puerī, bellī**	**-ī**
3rd Declension	**cōnsul, legiō, flūmen, cīvis, mare, animal**	**cōnsulis, legiōnis, flūminis, cīvis, maris, animālis**	**-is**
4th Declension	**exercitus, genū**	**exercitūs, genūs**	**-ūs**
5th Declension	**diēs**	**diēī**	**-ēī**

✔ **TIP**

To help you remember the correct singular and plural case endings for a noun in any declension, take the genitive singular case of the noun and remove the ending. This gives you a 'stem' to which the other case endings in that declension are attached.

For example, the genitive singular case of **fēmina** is **fēminae**. Remove the ending **-ae**, and you are left with the 'stem', **fēmin-**.

Always remember to take care. With **legiō**, for example, the genitive singular case is **legiōnis**. When you have removed the ending **-is**, the 'stem' you are left with is **legiōn-**. With **flūmen**, it is **flūmin-**, and with **animal**, it is **animāl-**.

First Declension

All Latin nouns in the first declension end in **-a** in the nominative case, and they are all feminine except when the context indicates a man/boy – for example, **poēta** (meaning *a poet*) or **agricola** (meaning *a farmer*).

Case	Singular	Plural
Nominative (and Vocative)	**fēmina**	**fēminae**
Accusative	**fēminam**	**fēminās**
Genitive	**fēminae**	**fēminārum**
Dative	**fēminae**	**fēminīs**
Ablative	**fēminā**	**fēminīs**

Note that **dea** (meaning *a goddess*) and **fīlia** (meaning *a daughter*) have their dative and ablative plural endings as **deābus** and **fīliābus**.

Second Declension

Most nouns of this declension end in **-us** in the nominative case, with a few ending in **-er** or **-r**. All of them are masculine. Those few nouns which end in **-um** are all neuter.

Case	Singular	Plural
Nominative (and Vocative)	**servus (serve)**	**servī**
Accusative	**servum**	**servōs**
Genitive	**servī**	**servōrum**
Dative	**servō**	**servīs**
Ablative	**servō**	**servīs**

Case	Singular	Plural
Nominative (and Vocative)	**puer**	**puerī**
Accusative	**puerum**	**puerōs**
Genitive	**puerī**	**puerōrum**
Dative	**puerō**	**puerīs**
Ablative	**puerō**	**puerīs**

Case	Singular	Plural
Nominative (and Vocative)	**bellum**	**bella**
Accusative	**bellum**	**bella**
Genitive	**bellī**	**bellōrum**
Dative	**bellō**	**bellīs**
Ablative	**bellō**	**bellīs**

Note that nouns with a nominative singular ending in **-ius** have a vocative singular ending in **-ī**. For example, **fīlius** (meaning *a son*) becomes **fīlī**.

The noun **deus** (meaning *a god*) keeps the same ending in the vocative singular, and has some irregular plural forms: **dī** in the nominative, **deum** in the genitive, and **dīs** in the dative and ablative. The noun **vir** (meaning *a man*) can also have the form **virum** in the genitive plural.

Some nouns with a nominative and vocative singular ending in **-er** drop the 'e' in their other case endings. For example, **magister** (meaning *a teacher*) becomes **magistrum** in the accusative singular, and **ager** (meaning *a field*) becomes **agrōrum** in the genitive plural.

Third Declension

The third declension is the largest group of Latin nouns. The gender of the nouns in this declension has to be learnt.

Nouns like **cōnsul** (meaning *a consul*), **legiō** (meaning *a legion*) and **flūmen** (meaning *a river*) have a genitive plural case ending in **-um**.

Case	Singular	Plural
Nominative (and Vocative)	**cōnsul**	**cōnsulēs**
Accusative	**cōnsulem**	**cōnsulēs**
Genitive	**cōnsulis**	**cōnsulum**
Dative	**cōnsulī**	**cōnsulibus**
Ablative	**cōnsule**	**cōnsulibus**

Case	Singular	Plural
Nominative (and Vocative)	**legiō**	**legiōnēs**
Accusative	**legiōnem**	**legiōnēs**
Genitive	**legiōnis**	**legiōnum**
Dative	**legiōnī**	**legiōnibus**
Ablative	**legiōne**	**legiōnibus**

Case	Singular	Plural
Nominative (and Vocative)	**flūmen**	**flūmina**
Accusative	**flūmen**	**flūmina**
Genitive	**flūminis**	**flūminum**
Dative	**flūminī**	**flūminibus**
Ablative	**flūmine**	**flūminibus**

It is well worth learning the following nouns which are like **legiō** but which are made up of only one syllable in the nominative case, because their genitive plural case ends in **-ium**:

arx, arcis (*feminine*) — *a citadel*
gēns, gentis (*feminine*) — *a nation / a people*
mōns, montis (*masculine*) — *a mountain*
nox, noctis (*feminine*) — *a night*
pōns, pontis (*masculine*) — *a bridge*
urbs, urbis (*feminine*) — *a city*

Nouns like **cīvis** (meaning *a citizen*) have a genitive plural case ending in **-ium**.

Case	Singular	Plural
Nominative (and Vocative)	**cīvis**	**cīvēs**
Accusative	**cīvem**	**cīvēs**
Genitive	**cīvis**	**cīvium**
Dative	**cīvī**	**cīvibus**
Ablative	**cīve**	**cīvibus**

It is also worth learning the following nouns which are like **cīvis**, but whose genitive plural case ends in **-um**:

pater, patris (*masculine*) — *a father*
māter, mātris (*feminine*) — *a mother*
frāter, frātris (*masculine*) — *a brother*
senex, senis (*masculine*) — *an old man*

iuvenis, iuvenis (*masculine*) *a young man*
canis, canis (*masculine/feminine*) *a dog*

Neuter nouns like **mare** (meaning *the sea*) and **animal** (meaning *an animal*) have an ablative singular case ending in **-ī**.

Case	Singular	Plural
Nominative (and Vocative)	**mare**	**maria**
Accusative	**mare**	**maria**
Genitive	**maris**	**marium**
Dative	**marī**	**maribus**
Ablative	**marī**	**maribus**

Case	Singular	Plural
Nominative (and Vocative)	**animal**	**animālia**
Accusative	**animal**	**animālia**
Genitive	**animālis**	**animālium**
Dative	**animālī**	**animālibus**
Ablative	**animālī**	**animālibus**

Fourth Declension

Nouns in this declension end in **-us** in the nominative singular and are mainly masculine. A few are neuter nouns and end in **-ū**.

Case	Singular	Plural
Nominative (and Vocative)	**exercitus**	**exercitūs**
Accusative	**exercitum**	**exercitūs**
Genitive	**exercitūs**	**exercituum**
Dative	**exercituī**	**exercitibus**
Ablative	**exercitū**	**exercitibus**

Case	Singular	Plural
Nominative (and Vocative)	**genū**	**genua**
Accusative	**genū**	**genua**
Genitive	**genūs**	**genuum**
Dative	**genū**	**genibus**
Ablative	**genū**	**genibus**

The noun **domus** (meaning *a house*) belongs to the fourth declension and is feminine. It has a number of irregular forms, including the ablative singular **domō**, the accusative plural **domōs** and the genitive plural **domōrum**. It is also a rare example of a noun with a locative case – **domī** – meaning *at home*.

For more information on the Locative case, see page 134.

Fifth Declension

There are only a few nouns in the fifth declension. All of them end in **-ēs** in the nominative case. Most are feminine, but **diēs** (meaning *a day*) and **meridiēs** (meaning *midday*) are both masculine.

Case	Singular	Plural
Nominative (and Vocative)	**diēs**	**diēs**
Accusative	**diem**	**diēs**
Genitive	**diēī**	**diērum**
Dative	**diēī**	**diēbus**
Ablative	**diē**	**diēbus**

Key points

- All first declension nouns ending in **-a** follow the pattern of **fēmina, fēminae**.
- Most second declension nouns follow the pattern of **servus, servī** or **puer, puerī** or **bellum, bellī**.
- Most third declension nouns follow the pattern of **cōnsul, cōnsulis** and **legiō, legiōnis**, and **flūmen, flūminis**; or of **cīvis, cīvis** and **mare, maris**, and **animal, animālis**.
- Fourth declension nouns follow the pattern of **exercitus, exercitūs** or of **genū, genūs**.
- Fifth declension nouns follow the pattern of **diēs, diēī**.

Exercise 1

Use all the information on nouns so far, and the examples used, to work out the Latin for *the words in italics* in the following sentences:

a *The woman* walked to the theatre.

....

b A merchant saw *the slaves* in the street.

....

c The teacher found a book *for the boy*.

....

d The size *of the temples* in Rome is legendary.

....

e The Senate was deceived by *the consuls*.

....

f 'I have done my best, *master*,' replied the cook.

....

g *The nations* of the East are in revolt.

....

h They ran away from *the bridge* before it collapsed.

....

i '*Citizens!*' shouted the king, 'stand and fight!'

....

j No one gave any food *to the animals*.

....

k Hannibal led his *army* over the Alps into Italy.

....

l She left at the final hour *of the day*.

....

Adjectives

What is an adjective?
An adjective is a 'describing' word that tells you about a person or thing, such as their appearance, colour, size, or other qualities (for example, *pretty*, *brown*, *large*, *happy*).

Using adjectives

Adjectives can tell you more about a noun (a living being, a place or thing, an event, or idea). They can also tell you more about a pronoun, such as *she* or *they*. They can be used right next to the noun or pronoun they are describing, or can be separated from it by a verb like *be*, *look*, or *feel*.

- a ***pretty*** girl
- the ***brown*** dog
- The house is ***large***.
- He does not look ***happy***.

For more information on Nouns or Pronouns, see pages 2 and 27.

In English, we put adjectives ***before*** the nouns they describe (for example, *the brown dog*). In Latin, adjectives that indicate size or quantity – for example, **magnus** (meaning *large*) – are usually also placed before the noun; but other adjectives like **laetus** (meaning *happy*) are usually placed ***after***.

In English, the only time an adjective changes its form is when you are making a comparison:

*He is **happier** than his wife.*
*That's the **largest** house I've ever seen.*

In Latin, however, all adjectives ***agree*** with what they are describing. This means that their endings change depending on whether the person or thing you are referring to is masculine, feminine, or neuter, whether it is singular or plural, and what case it is in:

magnus servus (*nominative singular masculine*)	*a large slave*
magnam urbem (*accusative singular feminine*)	*a large city*
magnīs flūminibus (*dative or ablative plural neuter*)	*by large rivers*
cīvium laetōrum (*genitive plural masculine*)	*of the happy citizens*

Finally, in Latin, adjectives follow the same declension patterns as nouns and are arranged in two main groups:

- those with endings like nouns of the first and second declensions
- those with endings likes nouns of the third declension

✔ **Tip**

Remember to learn the masculine, feminine, and neuter endings of the nominative singular case of each new adjective you come across, as well as the meaning of the adjective. Sometimes the endings are the same for more than one gender.

Key points

- Latin adjectives change their form depending on the gender and case of the person or thing they are describing, and whether it is singular or plural.
- In Latin adjectives usually go after the noun they describe.

Declensions

First and second declensions

Adjectives like **bonus**, **bona**, **bonum** (meaning *good*) follow second declension nouns like **servus** to form their masculine endings; first declension nouns (for example, **fēmina**) to form their feminine endings; and second declension nouns like **bellum** to form their neuter.

Singular

Case	Masculine	Feminine	Neuter
Nominative (and Vocative)	**bonus (bone)**	**bona**	**bonum**
Accusative	**bonum**	**bonam**	**bonum**
Genitive	**bonī**	**bonae**	**bonī**
Dative	**bonō**	**bonā**	**bonō**
Ablative	**bonō**	**bonā**	**bonō**

Plural

Case	Masculine	Feminine	Neuter
Nominative (and Vocative)	**bonī**	**bonae**	**bona**
Accusative	**bonōs**	**bonās**	**bona**
Genitive	**bonōrum**	**bonārum**	**bonōrum**
Dative	**bonīs**	**bonīs**	**bonīs**
Ablative	**bonīs**	**bonīs**	**bonīs**

Note that when it comes to adjectives ending in **-er**, some of them like **miser**, **misera**, **miserum** (meaning *unhappy*) keep the 'e' like the second declension noun **puer**; but others like **pulcher**, **pulchra**, **pulchrum** (meaning *beautiful*) drop the 'e' like **magister** and **ager**.

It is worth learning the following adjectives which end in **-us** or **-er** but whose genitive singular case ends in **-īus** and dative singular in **-ī**:

alius, alia, aliud	*another*
alter, altera, alterum	*one* or *the other (of two)*
neuter, neutra, neutrum	*neither*
nūllus, nūlla, nūllum	*none*
sōlus, sōla, sōlum	*alone*
tōtus, tōta, tōtum	*whole*
ūllus, ūlla, ūllum	*any*
ūnus, ūna, ūnum	*one*
uter?, utra?, utrum?	*which (of two)?*

The word **nēmō** (meaning *nobody*) has an accusative form **nēminem** and a dative **nēminī**, but takes its genitive and ablative forms from **nūllus**.

Third declension

There are several types of adjective in this group.

Adjectives like **prūdēns** (meaning *shrewd*) have the same nominative singular case ending in all three genders.

Singular

Case	Masculine	Feminine	Neuter
Nominative (and Vocative)	**prūdēns**	**prūdēns**	**prūdēns**
Accusative	**prūdentem**	**prūdēntem**	**prūdēns**
Genitive	**prūdentis**	**prūdentis**	**prūdentis**
Dative	**prūdentī**	**prūdentī**	**prūdentī**
Ablative	**prūdentī**	**prūdentī**	**prūdentī**

Plural

Case	Masculine	Feminine	Neuter
Nominative (and Vocative)	**prūdentēs**	**prūdentēs**	**prūdentia**
Accusative	**prūdentēs**	**prūdentēs**	**prūdentia**
Genitive	**prūdentium**	**prūdentium**	**prūdentium**
Dative	**prūdentibus**	**prūdentibus**	**prūdentibus**
Ablative	**prūdentibus**	**prūdentibus**	**prūdentibus**

Note that a few adjectives, like **vetus** (meaning *old*), **dīves** (meaning *rich*), and **pauper** (meaning *poor*), have an ablative singular case ending in **-e**, nominative, vocative, and accusative plural case endings for the neuter in **-a**, and a genitive plural ending in **-um**.

> ✔ **TIP**
> Remember that all present participles of verbs follow the same pattern of case endings as **prūdēns** when used as adjectives. If not, their ablative singular case ending is **-e**.

For more information on Present participles, see page 87.

Adjectives like **fēlīx** (meaning *lucky*) have the same case endings in all three genders apart from the accusative singular and the nominative, vocative, and accusative plural of the neuter.

Singular

Case	Masculine	Feminine	Neuter
Nominative (and Vocative)	fēlīx	fēlīx	fēlīx
Accusative	fēlīcem	fēlīcem	fēlīx
Genitive	fēlīcis	fēlīcis	fēlīcis
Dative	fēlīcī	fēlīcī	fēlīcī
Ablative	fēlīcī	fēlīcī	fēlīcī

Plural

Case	Masculine	Feminine	Neuter
Nominative (and Vocative)	fēlīcēs	fēlīcēs	fēlīcia
Accusative	fēlīcēs	fēlīcēs	fēlīcia
Genitive	fēlīcium	fēlīcium	fēlīcium
Dative	fēlīcibus	fēlīcibus	fēlīcibus
Ablative	fēlīcibus	fēlīcibus	fēlīcibus

Adjectives like **fortis, forte** (meaning *brave*) have two nominative singular case endings, one for the masculine and feminine and one for the neuter.

Singular

Case	Masculine	Feminine	Neuter
Nominative (and Vocative)	fortis	fortis	forte
Accusative	fortem	fortem	forte
Genitive	fortis	fortis	fortis
Dative	fortī	fortī	fortī
Ablative	fortī	fortī	fortī

Plural

Case	Masculine	Feminine	Neuter
Nominative (and Vocative)	fortēs	fortēs	fortia
Accusative	fortēs	fortēs	fortia
Genitive	fortium	fortium	fortium
Dative	fortibus	fortibus	fortibus
Ablative	fortibus	fortibus	fortibus

Adjectives like **ācer**, **ācris**, **ācre** (meaning *keen* or *sharp*) have a different ending for each gender in the nominative singular case.

Singular

Case	Masculine	Feminine	Neuter
Nominative (and Vocative)	ācer	ācris	ācre
Accusative	ācrem	ācrem	ācre
Genitive	ācris	ācris	ācris
Dative	ācrī	ācrī	ācrī
Ablative	ācrī	ācrī	ācrī

Plural

Case	Masculine	Feminine	Neuter
Nominative (and Vocative)	ācrēs	ācrēs	ācria
Accusative	ācrēs	ācrēs	ācria
Genitive	ācrium	ācrium	ācrium
Dative	ācribus	ācribus	ācribus
Ablative	ācribus	ācribus	ācribus

Note that some adjectives that end in **-er** and follow the pattern of third declension nouns, like **celer**, **celeris**, **celere** (meaning *fast*), keep the 'e' throughout.

✔ **TIP**

As with nouns, to help you remember the correct singular and plural case endings for an adjective in any declension, take the genitive singular case of the adjective and remove the ending. This gives you a 'stem' to which the other case endings in that declension are attached.

For example, the genitive singular case of **fortis** is **fortis**. Remove the ending **-is**, and you are left with the 'stem', **fort-**.

Always remember to take care. With **prūdēns**, for example, the genitive singular case is **prūdentis**. When you have removed the ending **-is**, the 'stem' you are left with is **prūdent-**. With **vetus**, it is **veter-**, and with **dīves**, it is **dīvit-**.

Key points

- Adjectives ending in **-us** follow the pattern of first or second declension nouns depending on the gender of the person or thing they are describing.
- Some adjectives ending in **-er** follow the pattern of **puer** and some **magister**.
- Most third declension nouns follow the pattern of **prūdēns**, **fēlīx**, **fortis**, or **ācer**.

Exercise 2

Use all the information on adjectives so far, and the examples used, to work out the Latin for *the words in italics* in the following sentences:

a The *lucky* woman walked to the theatre.

....

b The teacher found a book for the *other* boy.

....

c The size of the *beautiful* temples in Rome is legendary.

....

d The Senate was deceived by the *shrewd* consuls.

....

e '*Brave* citizens!' shouted the king, 'stand and fight!'

....

f Hannibal led his *unhappy* army over the Alps into Italy.

....

Comparison of adjectives

In English, when we want to compare people or things we can add *-er* or *-est* to the end of an adjective that describes them. For example, *prettier* is what we call the ***comparative*** form of *pretty*, and *prettiest* the ***superlative*** form; *larger* is the ***comparative*** form of *large*, and *largest* the ***superlative*** form. We can also add words like *more* or *most* and *quite* or *very* in front of an adjective (for example, *brown – more brown*, *happy – very happy*).

Forming comparatives and superlatives

Adjectives in Latin also change their ending, to **-ior** for the comparative form and usually to **-issimus** for the superlative. If the nominative singular masculine of the adjective ends in **-er**, then the superlative form ends **-errimus**.

Adjective	Meaning	Comparative	Meaning	Superlative	Meaning
laetus	happy	**laetior**	happier	**laetissimus**	happiest, very happy
prūdēns	shrewd	**prūdentior**	shrewder	**prūdentissimus**	shrewdest, very shrewd
fēlīx	lucky	**fēlīcior**	luckier	**fēlīcissimus**	luckiest, very lucky
fortis	brave	**fortior**	braver	**fortissimus**	bravest, very brave
ācer	keen	**ācrior**	keener	**ācerrimus**	keenest, very keen

Note that six adjectives with a nominative singular masculine ending in **-ilis** have a superlative ending **-illimus**. These are **facilis** and **difficilis** (meaning *easy* and *difficult*), **similis** and **dissimilis** (meaning *like* and *unlike*), and **gracilis** and **humilis** (meaning *slender* and *low*).

Irregular comparatives and superlatives

Just as English has some irregular comparative and superlative forms – *better* instead of 'more good', and *worst* instead of 'most bad' – several common adjectives in Latin also have irregular forms.

Adjective	Meaning	Comparative	Meaning	Superlative	Meaning
bonus	good	**melior**	better	**optimus**	best, very good
malus	bad	**peior**	worse	**pessimus**	worst, very bad
parvus	small	**minor**	smaller	**minimus**	smallest, very small
magnus	large	**maior**	larger	**maximus**	largest, very large
multus	much	**plūs**	more	**plūrimus**	most, very much
multī	many	**plūrēs**	more	**plūrimī**	most, very many

Note that **plūs**, the comparative form of **multus**, is actually a neuter singular noun and is often used with the genitive case – for example, **plūs cibī** means *more* (of) *food*.

Unless they end in **-quus**, all adjectives with a nominative singular masculine ending in **-us**, preceded by a vowel – for example, **idōneus** (meaning *suitable*) – place adverbs in front to form the comparative and superlative, instead of changing their ending.

magis idōneus	*more suitable*
maximē idōneus	*most suitable*

For more information on Adverbs, see page 127.

It is worth learning these adjectives. They only exist in comparative and superlative forms:

Comparative	Meaning	Superlative	Meaning
exterior	outer	**extrēmus**	furthest, very far
inferior	lower	**infimus** or **īmus**	lowest, very low
superior	higher	**suprēmus** or **summus**	highest, very high
posterior	later	**postrēmus**	last, very late

Declining comparatives and superlatives

The case endings of a comparative – for example, **altior**, **altius** from the adjective **altus**, **alta**, **altum** (meaning *high*) – follow the pattern of adjectives in the third declension, with the ablative singular case ending in **-e**.

Singular

Case	Masculine	Feminine	Neuter
Nominative (and Vocative)	**altior**	**altior**	**altius**
Accusative	**altiōrem**	**altiōrem**	**altius**
Genitive	**altiōris**	**altiōris**	**altiōris**
Dative	**altiōrī**	**altiōrī**	**altiōrī**
Ablative	**altiōre**	**altiōre**	**altiōre**

Plural

Case	Masculine	Feminine	Neuter
Nominative (and Vocative)	**altiōrēs**	**altiōrēs**	**altiōra**
Accusative	**altiōrēs**	**altiōrēs**	**altiōra**
Genitive	**altiōrum**	**altiōrum**	**altiōrum**
Dative	**altiōribus**	**altiōribus**	**altiōribus**
Ablative	**altiōribus**	**altiōribus**	**altiōribus**

All superlatives follow the pattern of **bonus**, **bona**, **bonum** (i.e. adjectives in the first and second declensions).

Special uses of comparatives and superlatives

In the same way that you can sometimes use the superlative form in Latin to mean *very*, you can sometimes use the comparative form to mean *rather* or *quite*.

facillimus *very easy*
fortior *quite brave*

To compare a person or thing, use a comparative adjective followed by the conjunction **quam** (meaning *than*), or simply use the ablative case.

altior quam monte *higher than a mountain*
altior monte *higher than a mountain*

For more information on Conjunctions, see page 139.

To say that someone or something is *as ... as possible*, use **quam** followed by a superlative adjective.

quam minimus *as small as possible*
quam celerrimus *as fast as possible*

Key points

- The ending of the comparative form of an adjective in Latin is usually **-ior**.
- The ending of the superlative form is usually **-issimus**, but sometimes **-errimus** or **-illimus**.
- Some common adjectives like **bonus**, **malus**, **parvus**, and **magnus** have irregular comparative and superlative forms.
- *than* in comparatives corresponds to **quam**.

Exercise 3

Use all the information on comparatives and superlatives so far, and the examples used, to work out the Latin for *the words in italics* in the following sentences:

a A merchant saw the *rather unhappy* slaves in the street.

....

b 'I have done my best, *most shrewd* master,' replied the cook.

....

c The *larger* nations of the East are in revolt.

....

d They ran away from the *very high* bridge before it collapsed.

....

e No one gave any food to the *smaller* animals.

....

f She left at the final hour of the *last* day.

....

Pronouns

> **What is a pronoun?**
> A pronoun is a word you use instead of a noun when you do not need or want to name someone or something directly – for example, *you*, *she*, *it*.

There are several different types of pronoun:

- ***Personal pronouns*** such as *I*, *you*, *we*, *her* and *them*, which are used to refer to yourself, the person you are talking to, or other people and things. They can be either ***subject pronouns*** (*I*, *you*, *we*, and so on) or ***object pronouns*** (*her*, *him*, *them*, to *me*, for *it*, with *us*, and so on).
- ***Possessive pronouns*** such as *mine*, *yours*, and *theirs*, which show who or what someone or something belongs to.
- ***Reflexive pronouns*** such as *myself* and *themselves*, which refer back to the subject of the sentence.
- ***Determinative pronouns*** such as *the same* or *itself*, which refer to people or things in an emphatic way.
- ***Demonstrative pronouns*** such as *this* or *those*, which point out people or things.
- ***Relative pronouns*** such as *who* or *that*, which link two parts of a sentence together.
- ***Interrogative pronouns*** such as *who?* or *what?*, which are used in asking questions.

For more information on Questions, see page 123.

Indefinite pronouns such as *someone* or *anything*, which refer to people or things in a general way without saying exactly who or what they are.

Pronouns often stand in for a noun to save repeating it.

Word order with personal pronouns is usually different in Latin and English.

Personal pronouns

You use the personal pronouns **ego** (meaning *I*) and **nōs** (meaning *we*) when you want to refer to yourself or others with you. Remember that the forms of the pronoun will change depending on its function in the sentence.

Case	Singular	Plural
Nominative	**ego**	**nōs**
Accusative	**mē**	**nōs**
Genitive	**meī**	**nostrum / nostrī**
Dative	**mihi**	**nōbīs**
Ablative	**mē**	**nōbīs**

In English, we have only ***one*** word to refer to the person or people we are talking to, but in Latin there are ***two*** words: the personal pronouns **tū** and **vōs** (both meaning *you*). The word you use depends on whether you are talking to one person or more than one person.

Case	Singular	Plural
Nominative	**tū**	**vōs**
Accusative	**tē**	**vōs**
Genitive	**tuī**	**vestrum / vestrī**
Dative	**tibi**	**vōbīs**
Ablative	**tē**	**vōbīs**

✔ TIP

The forms **nostrum** and **vestrum** are used to indicate what we call the ***partitive*** genitive.

multī <u>nostrum</u> many of us

The forms **nostrī** and **vestrī** are used for ***objective*** genitives.

īnscius <u>vestrī</u> unaware of you (plural)

For Common uses of the cases, see supplement.

The pronoun **is**, **ea**, **id** (meaning *he*, *she*, *it*) is used to refer to other people or things.

Singular

Case	Masculine	Feminine	Neuter
Nominative	**is**	**ea**	**id**
Accusative	**eum**	**eam**	**id**
Genitive	**eius**	**eius**	**eius**
Dative	**eī**	**eī**	**eī**
Ablative	**eō**	**eā**	**eō**

Plural

Case	Masculine	Feminine	Neuter
Nominative	**eī / iī**	**eae**	**ea**
Accusative	**eōs**	**eās**	**ea**
Genitive	**eōrum**	**eārum**	**eōrum**
Dative	**eīs / iīs**	**eīs / iīs**	**eīs / iīs**
Ablative	**eīs / iīs**	**eīs / iīs**	**eīs / iīs**

✔ Tip

In English, when we use a personal pronoun as the subject of a sentence it shows who is doing the action (for example, *I see the sun*). In Latin, however, when a personal pronoun is the subject of a sentence it is only there for emphasis because the ending of the verb in Latin is all that is needed to show who is doing the action.

For more information on Verbs, see page 42.

Key points

- The Latin personal pronouns are: **ego**, **tū**, and **is**, **ea**, **id** in the singular, and **nōs**, **vōs**, and **eī/iī**, **eae**, **ea** in the plural.
- To say *you* in Latin, use **tū** if you are referring to one person and **vōs** if more than one.
- **is** and **eī/iī** (masculine singular and plural) and **ea** and **eae** (feminine singular and plural) are used to refer to things if the Latin noun is masculine or feminine.
- If there is a mixture of masculine and feminine nouns, use **eī/iī**.

Possessive pronouns

In English, when you want to show that someone or something belongs to another, this is what we call 'possession' and you can express it in two ways. For example, if someone picks up a book that belongs to you and asks, 'Whose book is this?', you can reply either 'That book is ***mine***' or 'That is ***my*** book'.

In Latin, when you want to say that something belongs to you or to others with you, you can use **meus**, **mea**, **meum** (meaning *my* or *mine*) and **noster**, **nostra**, **nostrum** (meaning *our* or *ours*). Because these words are adjectives, they will change their ending depending on the case and gender of the noun they are describing, and whether it is singular or plural.

meus ānulus	*my ring, a ring of mine*
nostrae ancillae	*our slave-girl's, of our slave-girl* OR *our slave-girls, slave-girls of ours*

For more information on Adjectives, see page 16.

For a person or people you are talking to, you can use **tuus**, **tua**, **tuum** and **vester**, **vestra**, **vestrum** (both meaning *your* or *yours*) depending on whether there is one person or more than one.

You can also use the ***dative case*** of the personal pronoun to show possession in Latin.

ānulus mihi	*my ring, a ring of mine*
ancillae nōbīs	*our slave-girls, slave-girls of ours*

For Common uses of the cases, see supplement.

When you are talking about another person or other people who are doing the action in a sentence, use **suus**, **sua**, **suum** (meaning *his*, *her* or *hers*, *its*, *their* or *theirs*).

suum tablīnum	*his/her/their (i.e. his/her/their own) study*
suae cōpiae	*his/her/their (i.e. his/her/their own) troops*

The genitive singular and plural forms of **is**, **ea**, **id** can also be used to mean *his*, *her*, *its*, and *their*, but only when you are talking about someone or something that is ***not*** doing the action in a sentence.

eōrum dolor	*their (i.e. other people's) grief*
eius aula	*his/her (i.e. someone else's) palace*

The case endings of the possessive adjectives follow the pattern of first and second declension adjectives like **bonus**, **bona**, **bonum**. The only exception is that the vocative singular masculine of **meus** is **mī**. Notice that **noster**, **nostra**, **nostrum** and **vester**, **vestra**, **vestrum** drop the 'e' like **pulcher**, **pulchra**, **pulchrum**.

✔ **Tip**

Be careful because sometimes a possessive adjective in Latin can make a sentence mean two quite different things. For example, **odium tuum** can mean either *your hatred* or *hatred of you*. Always check the context!

Key points

- The Latin possessives are **meus**, **tuus**, **suus**, **noster**, and **vester**. Their forms change depending on the gender and case of the noun they describe, and whether it is singular or plural.
- **suus** only refers to the subject of a sentence; otherwise the genitive of **is**, **ea**, **id** is used.
- You can also use the dative case of the personal pronouns to express possession.

Reflexive pronouns

In English, when someone or something is both doing the action in a sentence and having the action done to them – in other words, they are both subject and object of the verb – we add *-self* or *-selves* to the second reference to that person or thing. For example: *I saw myself in the mirror*.

The correct form of the reflexive pronoun when you are talking about yourself is *myself* and not *me*. In English, we do not say *I saw me in the mirror*.

In Latin, however, when you want to use a reflexive pronoun to refer to yourself or others with you, or to a person or people you are talking to, you use the same forms as the ***personal pronoun***. For example, in the sentences *I saw myself in the mirror* and *She saw me in the mirror* the word in Latin for both *myself* and *me* is **mē**.

If you want to refer to another person or thing or to other people, like *himself, herself, itself*, or *themselves*, you use this special reflexive pronoun:

Case	Singular	Plural
Nominative	—	—
Accusative	**sē**	**sē**
Genitive	**suī**	**suī**
Dative	**sibi**	**sibi**
Ablative	**sē**	**sē**

There is no nominative case, and the same forms are used whether you are talking about one person or more than one.

> ✔ **Tip**
> When you use the preposition **cum** (meaning *with*) with a personal or reflexive pronoun, take the ablative form of the pronoun and join it to the beginning of the preposition to make one word.
>
> **mēcum** *with me, with myself*
> **vōbiscum** *with you (plural), with yourselves*
> **sēcum** *with him(self), with her(self), with it(self), with them(selves)*

For more information on Prepositions, see page 132.

> **Key points**
> - In Latin, personal pronouns are also used as reflexive pronouns.
> - **sē**, **suī**, **sibi**, **sē** is used as the reflexive pronoun, *himself, herself, itself*, or *themselves*.

Determinative pronouns

You use the pronoun **īdem**, **eadem**, **idem** (meaning *the same*) if you want to emphasise that the person or thing you are talking about is identical. When it is being used to describe a noun – i.e. as an adjective – remember that the ending will change according to the case and gender of the noun, and whether it is singular or plural.

mīles eīsdem armīs *the soldier with the same weapons*
hasta eiusdem mīlitis *the same soldier's spear*

Notice that the pattern of the cases is very close to **is**, **ea**, **id** with **-dem** on the end.

Singular

Case	Masculine	Feminine	Neuter
Nominative	**īdem**	**eadem**	**idem**
Accusative	**eundem**	**eandem**	**idem**
Genitive	**eiusdem**	**eiusdem**	**eiusdem**
Dative	**eīdem**	**eīdem**	**eīdem**
Ablative	**eōdem**	**eādem**	**eōdem**

Plural

Case	Masculine	Feminine	Neuter
Nominative	**eīdem / īdem**	**eaedem**	**eadem**
Accusative	**eōsdem**	**eāsdem**	**eadem**
Genitive	**eōrundem**	**eārundem**	**eōrundem**
Dative	**eīsdem / īsdem**	**eīsdem / īsdem**	**eīsdem / īsdem**
Ablative	**eīsdem / īsdem**	**eīsdem / īsdem**	**eīsdem / īsdem**

You use the pronoun **ipse**, **ipsa**, **ipsum** (meaning *self*) if you want to underline a reference you are making to someone or something. Again, be careful how the ending will change when it is being used as an adjective.

fabrō ipsī *for the craftsman himself*
gēns ipsa *the family itself*

Singular

Case	Masculine	Feminine	Neuter
Nominative	**ipse**	**ipsa**	**ipsum**
Accusative	**ipsum**	**ipsam**	**ipsum**
Genitive	**ipsīus**	**ipsīus**	**ipsīus**
Dative	**ipsī**	**ipsī**	**ipsī**
Ablative	**ipsō**	**ipsā**	**ipsō**

Plural

Case	Masculine	Feminine	Neuter
Nominative	**ipsī**	**ipsae**	**ipsa**
Accusative	**ipsōs**	**ipsās**	**ipsa**
Genitive	**ipsōrum**	**ipsārum**	**ipsōrum**
Dative	**ipsīs**	**ipsīs**	**ipsīs**
Ablative	**ipsīs**	**ipsīs**	**ipsīs**

KEY POINTS
- **īdem, eadem, idem** is used to refer to *the same* person or thing.
- **ipse, ipsa, ipsum** is used to refer to the person or thing *itself*.

Demonstrative pronouns

If you want to refer to someone or something near you, you use the pronoun **hic, haec, hoc** (meaning *this*).

Singular

Case	Masculine	Feminine	Neuter
Nominative	**hic**	**haec**	**hoc**
Accusative	**hunc**	**hanc**	**hoc**
Genitive	**huius**	**huius**	**huius**
Dative	**huic**	**huic**	**huic**
Ablative	**hōc**	**hāc**	**hōc**

Plural

Case	Masculine	Feminine	Neuter
Nominative	**hī**	**hae**	**haec**
Accusative	**hōs**	**hās**	**haec**
Genitive	**hōrum**	**hārum**	**hōrum**
Dative	**hīs**	**hīs**	**hīs**
Ablative	**hīs**	**hīs**	**hīs**

If you want to refer to someone or something at a distance from you, you use the pronoun **ille**, **illa**, **illud** (meaning *that*).

Singular

Case	Masculine	Feminine	Neuter
Nominative	**ille**	**illa**	**illud**
Accusative	**illum**	**illam**	**illud**
Genitive	**illīus**	**illīus**	**illīus**
Dative	**illī**	**illī**	**illī**
Ablative	**illō**	**illā**	**illō**

Plural

Case	Masculine	Feminine	Neuter
Nominative	**illī**	**illae**	**illa**
Accusative	**illōs**	**illās**	**illa**
Genitive	**illōrum**	**illārum**	**illōrum**
Dative	**illīs**	**illīs**	**illīs**
Ablative	**illīs**	**illīs**	**illīs**

Both **hic**, **haec**, **hoc** and **ille**, **illa**, **illud** can also be used to mean *he*, *she*, *it*, and *they*.

The pronoun **iste**, **ista**, **istud** (meaning *that ... of yours*) follows the same pattern of case endings as **ille** and is sometimes used to talk about something in a dismissive way.

<u>iste</u> medicus — *that doctor of yours*
<u>istī</u> custōdī — *to that useless guard*

> ✔ **TIP**
> When you are using a pronoun, make sure that you always look carefully at the noun it is replacing or describing – its case, its gender, and whether it is singular or plural – so that the pronoun agrees with the noun.

Key points
- **hic**, **haec**, **hoc** is used to refer to someone or something nearby, and also to a person or thing just mentioned in a story.
- **ille**, **illa**, **illud** is used to refer to someone or something further away, and also to a person or thing mentioned in a story.
- **iste**, **ista**, **istud** is used to refer to someone or something dismissively.

Relative pronouns

In English, if you want to introduce additional information about someone or to make it clear which person is being talked about, you use the words *who*, *whose* or the more formal *whom* to link the two parts of the sentence together – for example: *They met a woman who was walking to the theatre; I know the merchant whose ring has disappeared*.

If it is a thing you are talking about, you use the words *that* or *which* – for example: *She found a ring that had been lost; I don't know the book which you are reading*.

In Latin, however, you use the relative pronoun **quī**, **quae**, **quod** (meaning *who* or *which*) whether you are talking about a person or a thing.

Singular

Case	Masculine	Feminine	Neuter
Nominative	**quī**	**quae**	**quod**
Accusative	**quem**	**quam**	**quod**
Genitive	**cuius**	**cuius**	**cuius**
Dative	**cui**	**cui**	**cui**
Ablative	**quō**	**quā**	**quō**

Plural

Case	Masculine	Feminine	Neuter
Nominative	**quī**	**quae**	**quae**
Accusative	**quōs**	**quās**	**quae**
Genitive	**quōrum**	**quārum**	**quōrum**
Dative	**quibus / quīs**	**quibus / quīs**	**quibus / quīs**
Ablative	**quibus / quīs**	**quibus / quīs**	**quibus / quīs**

Relative pronouns agree with the gender of the noun they are replacing, and whether it is singular or plural. Their case ending, however, will depend on their function in the second part of the sentence.

fābulam <u>quae</u> — *a story/play* ***which***
fūrem <u>cuius</u> — *the thief* ***whose***
dōnum <u>quod</u> — *a gift* ***that***
gladium <u>quem</u> — *the sword* ***which***

> ✔ **TIP**
> In English we often miss out the pronouns *who*, *which* and *that*. For example, *I don't know the book <u>which</u> you are reading* can sometimes sound more natural as *I don't know the book you are reading*. In Latin you can **NEVER** miss out **quī**, **quae**, **quod** in this way.

There are a few indefinite pronouns like **aliquī**, **aliqua**, **aliquod** (meaning *some*) and **quīcumque**, **quaecumque**, **quodcumque** (meaning *whoever* or *whichever*), and the interrogative adjective **quī**, **quae**, **quod?** (meaning *which?*), that change their **quī / qua(e) / quod** endings in the same way as the relative pronoun.

ali<u>quī</u> sapiēns — *some wise person*
<u>cui</u>cumque scelere — *for whichever crime*
<u>quae</u> taberna? — *which shop?*

The pronoun **quīdam**, **quaedam**, **quoddam** (meaning *a certain*) does the same thing apart from in the accusative singular case and the genitive plural where the 'm' of **quem / quam** and **quōrum / quārum / quōrum** changes to 'n'.

<u>quae</u>dam porta — *a certain gate*
<u>quōrun</u>dam sacerdōtum — *of certain priests*

Singular

Case	Masculine	Feminine	Neuter
Nominative	**quīdam**	**quaedam**	**quoddam**
Accusative	**quendam**	**quandam**	**quoddam**
Genitive	**cuiusdam**	**cuiusdam**	**cuiusdam**
Dative	**cuidam**	**cuidam**	**cuidam**
Ablative	**quōdam**	**quādam**	**quōdam**

Plural

Case	Masculine	Feminine	Neuter
Nominative	**quīdam**	**quaedam**	**quaedam**
Accusative	**quōsdam**	**quāsdam**	**quaedam**
Genitive	**quōrundam**	**quārundam**	**quōrundam**
Dative	**quibusdam**	**quibusdam**	**quibusdam**
Ablative	**quibusdam**	**quibusdam**	**quibusdam**

Key points
- **quī**, **quae**, **quod** can refer to both people and things; it agrees with the gender of the noun it is replacing and whether it is singular or plural, but its case depends on its own function in the sentence.
- In English we often miss out the object pronouns *who*, *which*, and *that*, but in Latin you can **NEVER** miss out **quī**, **quae**, **quod**.

Interrogative pronouns

In English, when you want to ask a question about a person or a thing, you often introduce it with an interrogative pronoun like *who*, *what*, *whose*, or the more formal *whom* – for example: *Who is reading this book?* or *What is that slave-girl doing?*

In Latin, you use the interrogative pronoun **quis?**, **quid?** (meaning *who?* or *what?*). You'll notice how most of the case endings are the same as the relative pronoun.

Singular

Case	Masculine	Feminine	Neuter
Nominative	**quis**	**quis**	**quid**
Accusative	**quem**	**quam**	**quod**
Genitive	**cuius**	**cuius**	**cuius**
Dative	**cui**	**cui**	**cui**
Ablative	**quō**	**quā**	**quō**

Plural

Case	Masculine	Feminine	Neuter
Nominative	**quī**	**quae**	**quae**
Accusative	**quōs**	**quās**	**quae**
Genitive	**quōrum**	**quārum**	**quōrum**
Dative	**quibus / quīs**	**quibus / quīs**	**quibus / quīs**
Ablative	**quibus / quīs**	**quibus / quīs**	**quibus / quīs**

Be careful to remember that the interrogative pronoun will agree with the answer to the question it is expecting: **quis?** indicates that the answer to the question is either masculine or feminine and singular; **quae?** that the answer is either feminine, or neuter and plural.

For more information on Questions, see page 123.

> ✔ **TIP**
> In English, the question *To whom does that book belong?* is usually expressed less formally as *Who does that book belong to?* In Latin, there is only one way of saying *To whom ...?* or *Who ... to?*, and that is **cui?**

There are some indefinite pronouns – like **aliquis**, **aliqua**, **aliquid** (meaning *someone* or *something*); **quisquam**, **quidquam** (meaning *anyone* or *anything* after a negative); **quisque**, **quaeque**, **quidque** (meaning *each*); and **quisquis**, **quidquid** (meaning *whoever* or *whatever*) – that change their **quis / qua(e) / quid** endings in the same way as the interrogative pronoun **quis?**, **quid?**.

sententia alicuius	*someone's opinion*
nōn cuiquam	*not to anyone*
cuiusque senis	*of each old man*
quaequis testēs	*whichever witnesses*

> ✔ **Tip**
> If you use the pronoun **quisque** with a superlative adjective, it has a special meaning:
>
> | | |
> |---|---|
> | **optimus <u>quisque</u>** | all the best men (*literally* each very good man) |
> | **pulcherrima <u>quaeque</u>** | all the most beautiful women (*literally* each very beautiful woman) |

For more information on the Comparison of adjectives, see page 22.

> **Key points**
> - **quis?**, **quid?** is the pronoun used in Latin questions; it agrees with the answer that is expected to the question.
> - Remember that the questions in English *To whom...?* and *Who ... to?* mean the same thing and can only be expressed in Latin in one way.

Exercise 4

Use all the information on pronouns so far, and the examples used, to work out the Latin for *the words in italics* in the following sentences:

a *That* woman walked to the theatre.

....

b A merchant saw *some* slaves in the street.

....

c The teacher found *this* book for the boy *who* had arrived late.

....

d The size of *certain* temples in Rome is legendary.

....

e The Senate was deceived by the consuls *themselves*.

....

f '*I myself* have done my best *for you*, master,' replied *that useless* cook.

....

g *The same* nations of the East are in revolt.

....

h They ran away from *which* bridge before it collapsed?

....

i 'Citizens *whom* I cherish!' shouted *our* king, 'stand and fight *with me*!'

....

j No one gave any food *to them*.

....

k Hannibal, *whose* courage was limitless, led *his* army over the Alps into Italy.

....

l *Who* left at the final hour of the day?

....

Verbs

What is a verb?
A verb is a 'doing' word which describes what someone or something does, what someone or something is, or what happens to them (for example, *write, is, be eaten*).

The four conjugations

Verbs are generally used with a noun, with a pronoun such as *I, you*, or *she*, or with somebody's name. They can relate to the present, the past, and the future; this is called their ***tense***.

For more information on Nouns or Pronouns, see pages 2 and 27.

Verbs are either ***regular*** and their forms follow the normal rules, or ***irregular*** and their forms do not follow the normal rules.

In English, regular verbs have a ***base form*** (the form of the verb without any endings added to it – for example, *walk*). The base form can have *to* in front of it – for example, *to walk*. This is called the ***infinitive***. You will find the base or infinitive form when you look up a verb in your dictionary.

In Latin, verbs also have an infinitive. The infinitive ends in **-āre**, **-ēre**, **-ere**, or **-īre** – for example, **amāre** (meaning *to love*), **habēre** (meaning *to have*), **mittere** (meaning *to send*), **audīre** (meaning *to hear*). ***Regular*** Latin verbs belong to one of these four verb groups, which are called ***conjugations***. We will look at each of these four conjugations in turn over the following pages.

For more information on Infinitives, see page 110.

In English, verbs usually have three other forms apart from the base form and infinitive: a form ending in '-s' (*walks*), a form ending in '-ing' (*walking*), and a form ending in '-ed' (*walked*). Instead of the form ending in '-ed', many verbs change internally (for example, *sit – sat, drink – drank, write – wrote*).

In Latin, verbs have many more forms, which refer to the present, past, or future. These forms are made up of endings added to a ***root*** or a ***stem***. Each regular verb has one root and two stems.

The ***verb root*** can be worked out by removing the **-āre**, **-ēre**, **-ere**, or **-īre** ending from the infinitive – for example, **amāre – am-**, **habēre – hab-**, **mittere – mitt-**, **audīre – aud-**). The ***present***, ***imperfect***, and ***future*** tenses can be formed from the root of the verb.

The ***perfect stem*** can be worked out by replacing the **-re** of the infinitive in the first conjugation, and usually in the fourth conjugation, with **-v-** (for example, **amāre – amāv-**, **audīre – audīv-**), and by replacing the **-ēre** of the infinitive of the second conjugation with **-u** (for example, **habēre – habu-**). However, in the third conjugation (and sometimes in the other conjugations) there are a number of different possible endings (for example, **mittere – mīs-**) and you will have to learn them as you come across them. The ***perfect***, ***pluperfect***, and ***future perfect*** tenses are formed from the perfect stem.

The ***supine stem*** can be worked out by removing the **-um** ending from the supine form (for example, **amātum – amāt-**, **habitum – habit-**, **missum – miss-**, **audītum – audīt-**). The ***perfect participle*** and ***future participle*** are formed from the supine stem.

> ✔ **TIP**
> When you look up a verb in a Latin dictionary, you will always find the present tense and the infinitive and (unless the verb is from the first conjugation) the perfect tense and the supine. These four forms are what we call a verb's ***principal parts*** and they help you to work out the correct endings for most other forms of the verb, so it is worth learning them whenever you come across a new verb.

For Common principal parts of verbs, see supplement.

In English, when verbs are used with personal pronouns (*I*, *you*, *he*, *she*, or *it* in the singular, and *we*, *you*, *they* in the plural), it shows who you are talking about – for example: *I sit*, *she drinks*, *they are writing*.

In Latin, however, it is the verb endings that show who you are talking about. Personal pronouns are only used for emphasis.

scrīb<u>ō</u>	*I am writing*
ego scrīb<u>ō</u>	*I myself am writing*

For more information on Personal pronouns, see page 28.

✔ Tip

As you become familiar with the endings for the different tenses of verbs in Latin, you will notice that most of them follow a pattern like this:

-ō *or* **-m**	*I*
-s	*you (in the singular)*
-t	*he, she or it*
-mus	*we*
-tis	*you (in the plural)*
-nt	*they*

Some verbs in Latin do not follow the normal rules, and are called ***irregular*** verbs. These include some very common and important verbs like **esse** (meaning *to be*), **posse** (meaning *to be able*), **ferre** (meaning *to carry*), **fierī** (meaning *to become, to be made*), **īre** (meaning *to go*), **velle** (meaning *to be willing, to want*), **nōlle** (meaning *to be unwilling, to not want*), and **mālle** (meaning *to prefer*). There is information on all these irregular verbs in the following sections.

Key points

- Latin verbs have different forms depending on what noun (or pronoun) they are used with, and on their tense.
- They are made up of a root or stem and an ending.
- The present, imperfect and future tenses are based on the verb root.
- The perfect, pluperfect and future perfect tenses are based on the perfect stem.
- The perfect and future participles are based on the supine stem.
- Regular verbs fit into one of four patterns or conjugations: **-āre**, **-ēre**, **-ere**, or **-īre** verbs.
- Irregular verbs do not follow the normal rules.

The present tense

What is the present tense?
The present tense is used to talk about what is true at the moment, what happens regularly, and what is happening now – for example: *He is a cook, He works in the kitchen, He is preparing peacock for dinner*.

In English, there is more than one way to express the present tense. For example, you can say *I drink*, *I am drinking*, or, occasionally, *I do drink*. In Latin, you use the same form (**bibō**) for all of these.

In English, you can also use the present tense to talk about something that is going to happen in the near future (for example, *I am going to Pompeii next year*). You cannot do the same in Latin.

In English, writers sometimes use the present tense as a lively or vivid way of describing something that has happened in the past – for example: *Everyone was asleep and all was quiet. Suddenly they hear a noise*.) This is called the ***historic present***. You can use the present tense in Latin in this way, too.

✔ **TIP**
Although in English we sometimes use parts of the verb *to be* to form the present tense of other verbs (for example: *I am working*, *She is drinking*), in Latin you can **NEVER** use the verb **esse** in this way.

The present tense: regular *-āre* (first conjugation) verbs

If an infinitive in Latin ends in **-āre**, it means the verb belongs to the ***first conjugation*** (for example, **amāre**, **labōrāre**, **portāre**).

To know which form of the verb to use in Latin in the present tense, you need to work out what the root of the verb is and then add the correct ending. The root of **-āre** verbs is formed by taking the ***infinitive*** and chopping off the **-āre** ending.

Infinitive	Root (without -āre)
amāre (meaning *to love*)	**am-**
labōrāre (meaning *to work*)	**labōr-**
portāre (meaning *to carry*)	**port-**

Now you know how to find the root of the verb, you can add the correct ending. Which one you choose will depend on whether you are referring to *I*, *you* (singular), *he*, *she*, *it*, *we*, *you* (plural), or *they*; this is called the ***person***.

Here are the present tense endings for **-āre** verbs:

Person	Ending	Add to root, e.g. am-	Meanings
1st singular	**-ō**	**amō**	I love I am loving
2nd singular	**-ās**	**amās**	You love You are loving
3rd singular	**-at**	**amat**	He/she/it loves He/she/it is loving
1st plural	**-āmus**	**amāmus**	We love We are loving
2nd plural	**-ātis**	**amātis**	You love You are loving
3rd plural	**-ant**	**amant**	They love They are loving

poēta ancillam amat. *The poet loves the slave-girl.*
coquus nōn labōrat. *The cook is not working.*
cibum nostrum portāmus. *We are carrying our own food.*

Key points

- Verbs ending in **-āre** belong to the first conjugation and form their root by losing the **-āre** from the infinitive.
- The present tense endings for **-āre** verbs are: **-ō**, **-ās**, **-at**, **-āmus**, **-ātis**, **-ant**.

The present tense: regular *-ēre* (second conjugation) verbs

If an infinitive in Latin ends in **-ēre**, it means the verb belongs to the ***second conjugation*** (for example, **habēre**, **docēre**, **terrēre**).

The root of **-ēre** verbs in the present tense is formed by taking the ***infinitive*** and chopping off the **-ēre** ending.

Infinitive	Root (without -ēre)
habēre (meaning *to have*)	**hab-**
docēre (meaning *to teach*)	**doc-**
terrēre (meaning *to frighten*)	**terr-**

Now add the correct ending, depending on whether you are referring to *I*, *you* (singular), *he*, *she*, *it*, *we*, *you* (plural), or *they*.

Here are the present tense endings for **-ēre** verbs:

Person	Ending	Add to root, e.g. hab-	Meanings
1st singular	**-eō**	**hab<u>eō</u>**	I have I am having
2nd singular	**-ēs**	**hab<u>ēs</u>**	You have You are having
3rd singular	**-et**	**hab<u>et</u>**	He/she/it has He/she/it is having
1st plural	**-ēmus**	**hab<u>ēmus</u>**	We have We are having
2nd plural	**-ētis**	**hab<u>ētis</u>**	You have You are having
3rd plural	**-ent**	**hab<u>ent</u>**	They have They are having

librum <u>habeō</u>. *I have a book.*
magister puerōs <u>docet</u>. *The master is teaching the boys.*
animālia mē <u>terrent</u> *Animals frighten me.*

Key points

- Verbs ending in **-ēre** belong to the second conjugation and form their root by losing the **-ēre** from the infinitive.
- The present tense endings for **-ēre** verbs are: **-eō**, **-ēs**, **-et**, **-ēmus**, **-ētis**, **-ent**.

The present tense: regular *-ere* (third conjugation) verbs

If an infinitive in Latin ends in **-ere**, it most often means the verb belongs to the ***third conjugation*** (for example, **mittere**, **reddere**, **quaerere**).

The root of **-ere** verbs in the present tense is formed by taking the ***infinitive*** and chopping off the **-ere** ending.

Infinitive	Root (without -ere)
mittere (meaning *to send*)	**mitt-**
reddere (meaning *to give back*)	**redd-**
quaerere (meaning *to look for, search*)	**quaer-**

Now add the correct ending, depending on whether you are referring to *I*, *you* (singular), *he*, *she*, *it*, *we*, *you* (plural), or *they*.

Here are the present tense endings for **-ere** verbs:

Person	Ending	Add to root, e.g. mitt-	Meanings
1st singular	**-ō**	**mittō**	I send I am sending
2nd singular	**-is**	**mittis**	You send You are sending
3rd singular	**-it**	**mittit**	He/she/it sends He/she/it is sending
1st plural	**-imus**	**mittimus**	We send We are sending
2nd plural	**-itis**	**mittitis**	You send You are sending
3rd plural	**-unt**	**mittunt**	They send They are sending

servum tibi mittō. — *I am sending the slave to you.*
librum nōn reddit. — *He is not giving back the book.*
ancilla ānulum quaerit. — *The slave-girl looks for the ring.*

Key points
- Verbs ending in **-ere** mainly belong to the third conjugation and form their root by losing the **-ere** from the infinitive.
- The present tense endings for **-ere** verbs are: **-ō**, **-is**, **-it**, **-imus**, **-itis**, **-unt**.

The present tense: regular *-īre* (fourth conjugation) verbs

If an infinitive in Latin ends in **-īre**, it means the verb belongs to the ***fourth conjugation*** (for example, **audīre**, **venīre**, **invenīre**).

The root of **-īre** verbs in the present tense is formed by taking the ***infinitive*** and chopping off the **-īre** ending.

Infinitive	Root (without -īre)
audīre (meaning *to hear*)	**aud-**
venīre (meaning *to come*)	**ven-**
invenīre (meaning *to find*)	**inven-**

Now add the correct ending, depending on whether you are referring to *I*, *you* (singular), *he*, *she*, *it*, *we*, *you* (plural), or *they*.

Here are the present tense endings for **-īre** verbs:

Person	Ending	Add to root, e.g. aud-	Meanings
1st singular	**-iō**	**aud<u>iō</u>**	I hear I am hearing
2nd singular	**-īs**	**aud<u>īs</u>**	You hear You are hearing
3rd singular	**-it**	**aud<u>it</u>**	He/she/it hears He/she/it is hearing
1st plural	**-īmus**	**aud<u>īmus</u>**	We hear We are hearing
2nd plural	**-ītis**	**aud<u>ītis</u>**	You hear You are hearing
3rd plural	**-iunt**	**aud<u>iunt</u>**	They hear They are hearing

columbam <u>audītis</u>. *You hear a dove.*
ancillae pulchrae <u>veniunt</u>. *The pretty slave-girls are coming.*
ānulum meum nōn <u>inveniō</u>. *I am not finding my ring.*

Key points
- Verbs ending in **-īre** belong to the fourth conjugation and form their root by losing the **-īre** from the infinitive.
- The present tense endings for **-īre** verbs are: **-iō**, **-īs**, **-it**, **-īmus**, **-ītis**, **-iunt**.

The present tense: irregular verbs

Some verbs in Latin do not follow the normal rules. These verbs include some very common and important verbs like **esse** (meaning *to be*), **posse** (meaning *to be able*), **ferre** (meaning *to carry*), **fierī** (meaning *to become, to be made*), **īre** (meaning *to go*), **velle** (meaning *to be willing, to want*), **nōlle** (meaning *to be unwilling, to not want*) and **mālle** (meaning *to prefer*). The present tense of these eight verbs is given in full below.

The present tense of *esse*

Person	Form	Meanings
1st singular	**sum**	I am
2nd singular	**es**	You are
3rd singular	**est**	He/she/it is
1st plural	**sumus**	We are
2nd plural	**estis**	You are
3rd plural	**sunt**	They are

rēgīna <u>es</u>. — *You are queen.*
laetī <u>sumus</u>. — *We are happy.*

The present tense of *posse*

Person	Form	Meanings
1st singular	**possum**	I am able
2nd singular	**potes**	You are able
3rd singular	**potest**	He/she/it is able
1st plural	**possumus**	We are able
2nd plural	**potestis**	You are able
3rd plural	**possunt**	They are able

dominus servōs audīre <u>potest</u>. — *The master is able to (or can) hear the slaves.*
aliam amāre nōn <u>possum</u>. — *I cannot love another.*

The present tense of *ferre*

Person	Form	Meanings
1st singular	**ferō**	I carry I am carrying
2nd singular	**fers**	You carry You are carrying
3rd singular	**fert**	He/she/it carries He/she/it is carrying
1st plural	**ferimus**	We carry We are carrying
2nd plural	**fertis**	You carry You are carrying
3rd plural	**ferunt**	They carry They are carrying

cibum <u>ferimus</u>. *We are carrying the food.*
vīnum <u>ferunt</u>. *They are carrying the wine.*

The present tense of *fierī*

Person	Form	Meanings
1st singular	**fīō**	I become I am made
2nd singular	**fīs**	You become You are made
3rd singular	**fit**	He/she/it becomes He/she/it is made
1st plural	-	-
2nd plural	-	-
3rd plural	**fīunt**	They become They are made

cōnsul <u>fit</u>. *He becomes consul.*
miserī <u>fīunt</u>. *They are made unhappy.*

The present tense of *īre*

Person	Form	Meanings
1st singular	**eō**	I go I am going
2nd singular	**īs**	You go You are going
3rd singular	**it**	He/she/it goes He/she/it is going
1st plural	**īmus**	We go We are going
2nd plural	**ītis**	You go You are going
3rd plural	**eunt**	They go They are going

pater ad theātrum <u>it</u>. *My father is going to the theatre.*
māter et ancilla nōn <u>eunt</u>. *My mother and her slave-girl are not going.*

The present tense of *velle*

Person	Form	Meanings
1st singular	**volō**	I am willing I want
2nd singular	**vīs**	You are willing You want
3rd singular	**vult**	He/she/it is willing He/she/it wants
1st plural	**volumus**	We are willing We want
2nd plural	**vultis**	You are willing You want
3rd plural	**volunt**	They are willing They want

tū sōlus poētam audīre <u>vīs</u>. *You alone want to listen to the poet.*
librōs mittere <u>volumus</u>. *We are willing to send the books.*

The present tense of *nōlle*

Person	Form	Meanings
1st singular	**nōlō**	I am not willing I do not want
2nd singular	**nōn vīs**	You are unwilling You do not want
3rd singular	**nōn vult**	He/she/it is unwilling He/she/it does not want
1st plural	**nōlumus**	We are unwilling We do not want
2nd plural	**nōn vultis**	You are unwilling You do not want
3rd plural	**nōlunt**	They are unwilling They do not want

vōs sōlī poētam audīre nōn vultis. *You alone do not want to listen to the poet.*
librōs mittere nōlunt. *They are not willing to send the books.*

The present tense of *mālle*

Person	Form	Meanings
1st singular	**mālō**	I prefer
2nd singular	**māvīs**	You prefer
3rd singular	**māvult**	He/she/it prefers
1st plural	**mālumus**	We prefer
2nd plural	**māvultis**	You prefer
3rd plural	**mālunt**	They prefer

alterum vīnum mālumus. *We prefer the other wine.*
nautam amāre māvult. *She would rather love a sailor.*

Irregular *-ere* verbs

Some verbs have an infinitive that ends in **-ere**, like the third conjugation, but form some of their endings like the fourth conjugation – for example, **capere** (meaning *to take*), **facere** (meaning *to make*), and **iacere** (meaning *to throw*). They belong to what is known as the ***mixed conjugation***.

Here are the present tense endings for mixed conjugation **-ere** verbs:

Person	Form	Form	Form
1st singular	**capiō**	**faciō**	**iaciō**
2nd singular	**capis**	**facis**	**iacis**
3rd singular	**capit**	**facit**	**iacit**
1st plural	**capimus**	**facimus**	**iacimus**
2nd plural	**capitis**	**facitis**	**iacitis**
3rd plural	**capiunt**	**faciunt**	**iaciunt**

canēs celerrimī cervam <u>capiunt</u>. *The fastest dogs take the hind.*
cervus canem minimum <u>iacit</u>. *The stag throws the smallest dog.*

Key points

- Some very important Latin verbs are irregular, including **esse**, **posse**, **īre**, and **velle**. They are worth learning in full.
- Some verbs ending in **-ere** form some of their endings like **-īre** verbs.

Exercise 5

Use all the information on the present tense so far, and the examples of verbs used, to find the Latin for:

a They love. ....

b She is sending. ....

c I have...

d You (plural) are listening. ....

e We are able. ....

f You (singular) make. ....

The imperative

What is the imperative?
An imperative is a form of the verb used when giving orders and instructions – for example: *Sit down!*; *Listen to me!*; *Don't go!*

Using the imperative

In Latin, there are two forms of the imperative that are used to give instructions or orders to someone. These correspond to the second person ***singular*** (pronoun **tū**) and the second person ***plural*** (pronoun **vōs**).

For more information on Pronouns, see page 27.

Forming the imperative

For regular verbs, the second person singular imperative is formed by taking the ***infinitive*** and chopping off the **-re** ending. The second person plural imperative is formed by taking the second person plural of the ***present tense*** and changing the **-is** ending to **-e**.

Person	-āre verbs: amāre	Meaning	-ēre verbs: habēre	Meaning	-ere verbs: mittere	Meaning	-īre verbs: audīre	Meaning
2nd singular	**amā**	love!	**habē**	have!	**mitte**	send!	**audī**	hear!
2nd plural	**amāte**	love!	**habēte**	have!	**mittite**	send!	**audīte**	hear!

ancilla, mē amā! — *Slave-girl, love me!*
puerī, columbam audīte! — *Boys, listen to the dove!*

Two verbs of the third conjugation – **dīcere** (meaning *to say*, *to tell*) and **dūcere** (meaning *to lead*) have a short form of the singular imperative: **dīc** and **dūc**.

Most mixed conjugation verbs follow the same pattern as the third conjugation – for example, **cape** and **capite**. However, **facere** also has a short form of the singular imperative: **fac**.

Imperative forms of irregular verbs

esse (meaning *to be*), **ferre** (meaning *to carry*), **fierī** (meaning *to become, to be made*), **īre** (meaning *to go*), **nōlle** (meaning *to be unwilling, to not want*) have the following imperative forms.

Person	Form				
2nd singular	**es**	**fer**	**fī**	**ī**	**nōlī**
2nd plural	**este**	**ferte**	**fīte**	**īte**	**nōlīte**

laetī este! *Be happy!*
serve, ī! *Slave, go!*

If you are telling somebody **NOT TO DO** something, you use the imperative form of **nōlle** followed by the infinitive.

puerī, istum poētam audīre nōlīte!
Boys, do not listen to that scandalous poet!

KEY POINTS

- The imperative has two forms: singular and plural.
- The singular imperative is the same as the infinitive without the **-re** ending, except for **dīcere**, **dūcere**, and **facere**.
- The plural imperative is the same as the second person plural of the present tense, except that the **-is** ending changes to **-e**.
- **esse**, **ferre**, **fierī**, **īre**, and **nōlle** have irregular imperative forms.
- Use **nōlī** or **nōlīte** to express a command **NOT TO DO** something.

Exercise 6

Use all the information on the imperative so far, and the examples of verbs used, to find the Latin for:

a Teach! (singular)..

b Find! (plural) ....

c Work! (plural) ....

d Search! (singular) ....

e Go! (plural)...

f Do not (singular) throw! ....

The imperfect tense

What is the imperfect tense?
The imperfect tense is one of the verb tenses used to talk about the past, especially in descriptions, and to say what used to happen – for example: *He was working in the garden; I used to read books.*

Using the imperfect tense

The imperfect tense is used:

to describe what things were like and how people felt in the past

*It **was** a very big city.*
*She **was** very sad when he left.*

to say what used to happen or what you used to do regularly in the past

*We **used to work** very hard in those days.*
*They never **used to go** to the theatre.*

to indicate things that were happening or something that was true when something else took place

*I **was reading** in the garden when there was a knock at the door.*
*When **they were walking** home, they saw something very strange.*

to indicate something that began to happen in the past

*Gradually we **began to overcome** the enemy.*
*In those days you **began to write** more clearly.*

Note that if you want to talk about an event or action that took place and was completed in the past, you use the ***perfect tense***.

For more information on the Perfect tense, see page 68.

Remember that you **NEVER** use the verb **esse** to translate *was* or *were* in forms like *was reading* or *were walking* and so on. You change the Latin verb ending instead.

> ✔ **TIP**
> As you become familiar with the endings for the imperfect tense of regular verbs in Latin, you will notice that they all follow a pattern like this:
>
> | | |
> |---|---|
> | **-bam** | *I* |
> | **-bās** | *you (in the singular)* |
> | **-bat** | *he, she* or *it* |
> | **-bāmus** | *we* |
> | **-bātis** | *you (in the plural)* |
> | **-bant** | *they* |

Forming the imperfect tense of *-āre* verbs

To form the imperfect tense of **-āre** verbs, you use the same root of the verb as for the present tense. Then you add the correct ending, depending on whether you are referring to *I*, *you* (singular), *he*, *she*, *it*, *we*, *you* (plural), or *they*.

Person	Ending	Add to root, e.g. am-	Meanings
1st singular	**-ābam**	**am<u>ābam</u>**	I was loving I used to love I began to love
2nd singular	**-ābās**	**am<u>ābās</u>**	You were loving You used to love You began to love
3rd singular	**-ābat**	**am<u>ābat</u>**	He/she/it was loving He/she/it used to love He/she/it began to love
1st plural	**-ābāmus**	**am<u>ābāmus</u>**	We were loving We used to love We began to love
2nd plural	**-ābātis**	**am<u>ābātis</u>**	You were loving You used to love You began to love
3rd plural	**-ābant**	**am<u>ābant</u>**	They were loving They used to love They began to love

poēta ancillam <u>amābat</u>.	*The poet used to love the slave-girl.*
coquus nōn <u>labōrābat</u>.	*The cook was not working.*
cibum nostrum <u>portābāmus</u>.	*We were carrying our own food.*

Forming the imperfect tense of *-ēre* verbs

To form the imperfect tense of **-ēre** verbs, you use the same root of the verb as for the present tense. Then you add the correct ending, depending on whether you are referring to *I*, *you* (singular), *he*, *she*, *it*, *we*, *you* (plural), or *they*.

Person	Ending	Add to root, e.g. hab-	Meanings
1st singular	**-ēbam**	**habēbam**	I was having I used to have I began to have
2nd singular	**-ēbās**	**habēbās**	You were having You used to have You began to have
3rd singular	**-ēbat**	**habēbat**	He/she/it was having He/she/it used to have He/she/it began to have
1st plural	**-ēbāmus**	**habēbāmus**	We were having We used to have We began to have
2nd plural	**-ēbātis**	**habēbātis**	You were having You used to have You began to have
3rd plural	**-ēbant**	**habēbant**	They were having They used to have They began to have

librum habēbam. *I used to have a book.*
magister puerōs docēbat. *The master was teaching the boys.*
animālia mē terrēbant. *Animals began to frighten me.*

Forming the imperfect tense of *-ere* verbs

To form the imperfect tense of **-ere** verbs, you use the same root of the verb as for the present tense. Then you add the correct ending, depending on whether you are referring to *I*, *you* (singular), *he*, *she*, *it*, *we*, *you* (plural), or *they*.

Person	Ending	Add to root, e.g. mitt-	Meanings
1st singular	**-ēbam**	**mittēbam**	I was sending I used to send I began to send
2nd singular	**-ēbās**	**mittēbās**	You were sending You used to send You began to send

3rd singular	**-ēbat**	**mitt<u>ēbat</u>**	He/she/it was sending He/she/it used to send He/she/it began to send
1st plural	**-ēbāmus**	**mitt<u>ēbāmus</u>**	We were sending We used to send We began to send
2nd plural	**-ēbātis**	**mitt<u>ēbātis</u>**	You were sending You used to send You began to send
3rd plural	**-ēbant**	**mitt<u>ēbant</u>**	They were sending They used to send They began to send

servum tibi <u>mittēbam</u>. *I used to send the slave to you.*
librum nōn <u>reddēbat</u>. *He was not giving back the book.*
ancilla ānulum <u>quaerēbat</u>. *The slave-girl began to look for the ring.*

Forming the imperfect tense of *-īre* verbs

To form the imperfect tense of **-īre** verbs, you use the same root of the verb as for the present tense. Then you add the correct ending, depending on whether you are referring to *I*, *you* (singular), *he*, *she*, *it*, *we*, *you* (plural), or *they*.

Person	Ending	Add to root, e.g. aud-	Meanings
1st singular	**-iēbam**	**audi<u>ēbam</u>**	I was hearing I used to hear I began to hear
2nd singular	**-iēbās**	**audi<u>ēbās</u>**	You were hearing You used to hear You began to hear
3rd singular	**-iēbat**	**audi<u>ēbat</u>**	He/she/it was hearing He/she/it used to hear He/she/it began to hear
1st plural	**-iēbāmus**	**audi<u>ēbāmus</u>**	We were hearing We used to hear We began to hear
2nd plural	**-iēbātis**	**audi<u>ēbātis</u>**	You were hearing You used to hear You began to hear
3rd plural	**-iēbant**	**audi<u>ēbant</u>**	They were hearing They used to hear They began to hear

columbam <u>audiēbātis</u>. *You used to hear a dove.*
ancillae pulchrae <u>veniēbant</u>. *The pretty slave-girls were coming.*
ānulum meum nōn <u>inveniēbam</u>. *I did not begin to find my ring.*

Mixed conjugation verbs also follow the same pattern in the imperfect tense as **-īre** verbs.

canēs cibum eius <u>capiēbant</u>. *The dogs used to take his food.*

Irregular verbs in the imperfect tense

The only verbs that are irregular in the imperfect tense are **esse** and **posse**.

Person	Form	Meaning	Form	Meaning
1st singular	**eram**	I was I used to be I began to be	**poteram**	I was able I used to be able I began to be able
2nd singular	**erās**	You were You used to be You began to be	**poterās**	You were able You used to be able You began to be able
3rd singular	**erat**	He/she/it was He/she/it used to be He/she/it began to be	**poterat**	He/she/it was able He/she/it used to be able He/she/it began to be able
1st plural	**erāmus**	We were We used to be We began to be	**poterāmus**	We were able We used to be able We began to be able
2nd plural	**erātis**	You were You used to be You began to be	**poterātis**	You were able You used to be able You began to be able
3rd plural	**erant**	They were They used to be They began to be	**poterant**	They were able They used to be able They began to be able

laetus <u>eram</u>. *I was (or used to be) happy.*
cibum portāre nōn <u>poterat</u>. *He was not able to carry the food.*

To form the imperfect tense of **ferre**, **fierī**, **velle**, **nōlle**, and **mālle**, you take the first person singular of the present tense, chop off the **-ō** ending and add the same endings as for the imperfect of **-ēre** and **-ere** verbs.

laetiōr fīēbam.	*I was becoming happier.*
suum cibum portāre nōlēbat.	*He began not to want to carry his own food.*

To form the imperfect tense of **īre**, you chop off the **-re** ending before adding the regular imperfect endings (**-bam**, **-bās**, **-bat**, **-bāmus**, **-bātis**, **-bant**).

fēminae ad theātrum ībant.	*The women were going* (or *used to go*) *to the theatre.*

Key points

- The imperfect tense endings for **-āre** verbs are: **-ābam**, **-ābās**, **-ābat**, **-ābāmus**, **-ābātis**, **-ābant**.
- The imperfect tense endings for **-ēre** and **-ere** verbs are: **-ēbam**, **-ēbās**, **-ēbat**, **-ēbāmus**, **-ēbātis**, **-ēbant**.
- The imperfect tense endings for **-īre** verbs are: **-iēbam**, **-iēbās**, **-iēbat**, **-iēbāmus**, **-iēbātis**, **-iēbant**.
- **esse** and **posse** are irregular in the imperfect tense.

Exercise 7

Use all the information on the imperfect tense so far, and the examples of verbs used, to find the Latin for:

a He was. ....

b We were carrying..............................

c You (singular) used to come. ....

d They began to give back. ....

e You (plural) used to have. ....

f I was taking. ....

The future tense

What is the future tense?
The future tense is a verb tense used to talk about something that will happen or will be true – for example: *I shall see you tomorrow*; *They will be sorry when they hear the news*.

Using the future tense

In English, the future tense is often shown by *will* or *shall* or their shortened from *'ll*.

*What **will** you do?*
*I'**ll** give you a call.*

In English, you can use the present tense to refer to something that is going to happen in the future (for example: *I am going to take the ten o'clock train later*). In Latin, you **NEVER** use the present tense to refer to the future.

In English, we often use *going to* followed by an infinitive to talk about something that will happen in the immediate future (for example: *He is going to miss that train*). In Latin, you can **NEVER** use the verb **īre** (meaning *to go*) followed by an infinitive in this way.

Remember that Latin has no direct equivalent of the word *will* or *shall* in verb forms like *will be* or *shall see* and so on. You change the Latin verb ending instead to form the future tense.

✔ **TIP**
As you become familiar with the endings for the future tense of regular verbs in Latin, you will notice that **-āre** and **-ēre** verbs follow a pattern like this:

-bō	*I*
-bis	*you (in the singular)*
-bit	*he, she or it*
-bimus	*we*
-bitis	*you (in the plural)*
-bunt	*they*

However, **-ere** and **-īre** verbs follow a pattern like this:

-am	*I*
-ēs	*you (in the singular)*
-et	*he, she or it*
-ēmus	*we*
-ētis	*you (in the plural)*
-ent	*they*

Forming the future tense of -āre verbs

To form the future tense of **-āre** verbs, you use the same root of the verb as for the present and imperfect tenses. Then you add the correct ending, depending on whether you are referring to *I*, *you* (singular), *he*, *she*, *it*, *we*, *you* (plural), or *they*.

Person	Ending	Add to root, e.g. am-	Meanings
1st singular	**-ābō**	**am<u>ābō</u>**	I will love I will be loving
2nd singular	**-ābis**	**am<u>ābis</u>**	You will love You will be loving
3rd singular	**-ābit**	**am<u>ābit</u>**	He/she/it will love He/she/it will be loving
1st plural	**-ābimus**	**am<u>ābimus</u>**	We will love We will be loving
2nd plural	**-ābitis**	**am<u>ābitis</u>**	You will love You will be loving
3rd plural	**-ābunt**	**am<u>ābunt</u>**	They will love They will be loving

poēta ancillam <u>amābit</u>.	*The poet will love the slave-girl.*
coquus nōn <u>labōrābit</u>.	*The cook will not be working.*
cibum nostrum <u>portābimus</u>.	*We will be carrying our own food.*

Forming the future tense of -ēre verbs

To form the future tense of **-ēre** verbs, you use the same root of the verb as for the present and imperfect tenses. Then you add the correct ending, depending on whether you are referring to *I*, *you* (singular), *he*, *she*, *it*, *we*, *you* (plural), or *they*.

Person	Ending	Add to root, e.g. hab-	Meanings
1st singular	**-ēbō**	**hab<u>ēbō</u>**	I will have I will be having
2nd singular	**-ēbis**	**hab<u>ēbis</u>**	You will have You will be having
3rd singular	**-ēbit**	**hab<u>ēbit</u>**	He/she/it will have He/she/it will be having
1st plural	**-ēbimus**	**hab<u>ēbimus</u>**	We will have We will be having
2nd plural	**-ēbitis**	**hab<u>ēbitis</u>**	You will have You will be having
3rd plural	**-ēbunt**	**hab<u>ēbunt</u>**	They will have They will be having

librum <u>habēbō</u>. — *I will have a book.*
magister puerōs <u>docēbit</u>. — *The master will be teaching the boys.*
animālia mē <u>terrēbunt</u>. — *The animals will frighten me.*

Forming the future tense of -ere verbs

To form the future tense of **-ere** verbs, you use the same root of the verb as for the present and imperfect tenses. Then you add the correct ending, depending on whether you are referring to *I*, *you* (singular), *he*, *she*, *it*, *we*, *you* (plural), or *they*.

Person	Ending	Add to root, e.g. mitt-	Meanings
1st singular	**-am**	**mitt<u>am</u>**	I will send I will be sending
2nd singular	**-ēs**	**mitt<u>ēs</u>**	You will send You will be sending
3rd singular	**-et**	**mitt<u>et</u>**	He/she/it will send He/she/it will be sending
1st plural	**-ēmus**	**mitt<u>ēmus</u>**	We will send We will be sending
2nd plural	**-ētis**	**mitt<u>ētis</u>**	You will send You will be sending
3rd plural	**-ent**	**mitt<u>ent</u>**	They will send They will be sending

servum tibi <u>mittam</u>. — *I will be sending the slave to you.*
librum nōn <u>reddet</u>. — *He will not give back the book.*
ancilla ānulum <u>quaeret</u>. — *The slave-girl will look for the ring.*

Forming the future tense of -īre verbs

To form the future tense of **-īre** verbs, you use the same root of the verb as for the present and imperfect tenses. Then you add the correct ending, depending on whether you are referring to *I*, *you* (singular), *he*, *she*, *it*, *we*, *you* (plural), or *they*.

Person	Ending	Add to root, e.g. aud-	Meanings
1st singular	**-iam**	**aud<u>iam</u>**	I will hear I will be hearing
2nd singular	**-iēs**	**aud<u>iēs</u>**	You will hear You will be hearing
3rd singular	**-iet**	**aud<u>iet</u>**	He/she/it will hear He/she/it will be hearing
1st plural	**-iēmus**	**aud<u>iēmus</u>**	We will hear We will be hearing
2nd plural	**-iētis**	**aud<u>iētis</u>**	You will hear You will be hearing
3rd plural	**-ient**	**aud<u>ient</u>**	They will hear They will be hearing

columbam <u>audiētis</u>. — *You will hear a dove.*
ancillae pulchrae <u>venient</u>. — *The pretty slave-girls will be coming.*
ānulum meum nōn <u>inveniam</u>. — *I will not find my ring.*

Mixed conjugation verbs also follow the same pattern in the future tense as **-īre** verbs.

canēs cibum eius <u>capient</u>. — *The dogs will be taking his food.*

Irregular verbs in the future tense

The only verbs that are irregular in the future tense are **esse** and **posse**.

Person	Form	Meaning	Form	Meaning
1st singular	**erō**	I will be I shall be	**poterō**	I will be able I shall be able
2nd singular	**eris**	You will be You shall be	**poteris**	You will be able You shall be able
3rd singular	**erit**	He/she/it will be He/she/it shall be	**poterit**	He/she/it will be able He/she/it shall be able
1st plural	**erimus**	We will be We shall be	**poterimus**	We will be able We shall be able

2nd plural	**eritis**	You will be You shall be	**poteritis**	You will be able You shall be able
3rd plural	**erunt**	They will be They shall be	**poterunt**	They will be able They shall be able

laetus erō. — *I shall be happy.*
suum cibum portāre nōn poterit. — *He will not be able to carry his own food.*

To form the future tense of **ferre**, **fierī**, **velle**, **nōlle**, and **mālle**, you take the first person singular of the present tense, chop off the **-ō** ending and add the same endings as for the future of **-ere** verbs.

laetiōr fīam. — *I shall become happier.*
suum cibum portāre nōlet. — *He will not want to carry his own food.*

To form the future tense of **īre**, you chop off the **-re** ending before adding the regular future endings (**-bō**, **-bis**, **-bit**, **-bimus**, **-bitis**, **-bunt**).

fēminae ad theātrum ībunt. — *The women will be going to the theatre.*

Key points

- The future tense endings for **-āre** verbs are: **ābō**, **-ābis**, **-ābit**, **-ābimus**, **-ābitis**, **-ābunt**.
- The future tense endings for **-ēre** verbs are: **-ēbō**, **-ēbis**, **-ēbit**, **-ēbimus**, **-ēbitis**, **-ēbunt**.
- The future tense endings for **-ere** verbs are: **-am**, **-ēs**, **-et**, **-ēmus**, **-ētis**, **-ent**.
- The future tense endings for **-īre** verbs are: **-iam**, **-iēs**, **-iet**, **-iēmus**, **-iētis**, **-ient**.
- **esse** and **posse** are irregular in the future tense.

Exercise 8

Use all the information on the future tense so far, and the examples of verbs used, to find the Latin for:

a It will frighten. ....

b They will be unwilling. ....

c I shall find. ....

d You (plural) will love. ....

e We shall be able. ....

f You (singular) will be sending. ....

The perfect tenses

What is the perfect tense?
The perfect is one of the verb tenses used to talk about the past, especially about actions that took place and were completed in the past – for example: *I saw her yesterday*; *They wept when they heard the news*.

Using the perfect tense

You can often recognise a perfect tense in English by a form like *I gave* or *I have finished*.

*I **gave** her my phone number.*
*I **have finished** my soup.*

The perfect is the tense you will need most to talk about things that have happened or were true in the past. It is used to talk about actions that took place and **WERE COMPLETED** in the past.

Use the ***imperfect tense*** for regular events and in most descriptions.

For more information on the Imperfect tense, see page 57.

✔ **TIP**
As you become familiar with the endings for the perfect tense of verbs in Latin, you will notice that they all follow a pattern like this:

-ī	*I*
-istī	*you (in the singular)*
-it	*he, she* or *it*
-imus	*we*
-istis	*you (in the plural)*
-ērunt	*they*

Forming the perfect tense of -āre verbs

To form the perfect tense of **-āre** verbs, you need to work out what the ***perfect stem*** of the verb is and then add the correct ending. The perfect stem of **-āre** verbs is most often formed by taking the ***infinitive*** and replacing the **-re** ending with **-v-**.

Infinitive	Perfect stem (replacing -re with -v-)
amāre (meaning *to love*)	**amā<u>v</u>-**
labōrāre (meaning *to work*)	**labōrā<u>v</u>-**
portāre (meaning *to carry*)	**portā<u>v</u>-**

Now you know how to find the perfect stem of the verb, you can add the correct ending. Which one you choose will depend on whether you are referring to *I*, *you* (singular), *he*, *she*, *it*, *we*, *you* (plural), or *they*.

Here are the perfect tense endings for **-āre** verbs:

Person	Ending	Add to perfect stem, e.g. amāv-	Meanings
1st singular	**-ī**	**amāv<u>ī</u>**	I loved I have loved
2nd singular	**-istī**	**amāv<u>istī</u>**	You loved You have loved
3rd singular	**-it**	**amāv<u>it</u>**	He/she/it loved He/she/it has loved
1st plural	**-imus**	**amāv<u>imus</u>**	We loved We have loved
2nd plural	**-istis**	**amāv<u>istis</u>**	You loved You have loved
3rd plural	**-ērunt**	**amāv<u>ērunt</u>**	They loved They have loved

poēta ancillam <u>amāvit</u>. *The poet loved the slave-girl.*
coquus nōn <u>labōrāvit</u>. *The cook did not work.*
cibum nostrum <u>portāvimus</u>. *We have carried our own food.*

Forming the perfect tense of -ēre verbs

The perfect stem of **-ēre** verbs is most often formed by taking the ***infinitive*** and replacing the **-ēre** ending with **-u-**.

Infinitive	Perfect stem (replacing -ēre with -u-)
habēre (meaning *to have*)	**hab<u>u</u>-**
docēre (meaning *to teach*)	**doc<u>u</u>-**
terrēre (meaning *to frighten*)	**terr<u>u</u>-**

Now add the correct ending, depending on whether you are referring to *I*, *you* (singular), *he*, *she*, *it*, *we*, *you* (plural), or *they*.

Here are the perfect tense endings for **-ēre** verbs:

Person	Ending	Add to perfect stem, e.g. habu-	Meanings
1st singular	**-ī**	**habuī**	I had I have had
2nd singular	**-istī**	**habuistī**	You had You have had
3rd singular	**-it**	**habuit**	He/she/it had He/she/it has had
1st plural	**-imus**	**habuimus**	We had We have had
2nd plural	**-istis**	**habuistis**	You had You have had
3rd plural	**-ērunt**	**habuērunt**	They had They have had

librum habuī. — *I had a book.*
magister puerōs docuit. — *The master has taught the boys.*
animālia mē terruērunt. — *The animals frightened me.*

Forming the perfect tense of -ere verbs

Once the **-ere** ending of the ***infinitive*** is chopped off, the perfect stem of **-ere** verbs is not formed in a regular way and you will have to learn them as you come across them.

Infinitive	Perfect stem (after removing -ere)
mittere (meaning *to send*)	**mīs-**
reddere (meaning *to give back*)	**reddid-**
quaerere (meaning *to look for*)	**quaesīv-**

Now add the correct ending, depending on whether you are referring to *I*, *you* (singular), *he*, *she*, *it*, *we*, *you* (plural), or *they*.

Here are the perfect tense endings for **-ere** verbs:

Person	Ending	Add to perfect stem, e.g. mīs-	Meanings
1st singular	-ī	mīs<u>ī</u>	I sent I have sent
2nd singular	-istī	mīs<u>istī</u>	You sent You have sent
3rd singular	-it	mīs<u>it</u>	He/she/it sent He/she/it has sent
1st plural	-imus	mīs<u>imus</u>	We sent We have sent
2nd plural	-istis	mīs<u>istis</u>	You sent You have sent
3rd plural	-ērunt	mīs<u>ērunt</u>	They sent They have sent

servum tibi <u>mīsī</u>. *I have sent the slave to you.*
librum nōn <u>reddidit</u>. *He did not give back the book.*
ancilla ānulum <u>quaesīvit</u>. *The slave-girl looked for the ring.*

Mixed conjugation verbs are like **-ere** verbs in the perfect tense and do not form their perfect stem in a regular way. For example, the perfect stem of **capere** is **cēp-**.

canēs cibum eius <u>cēpērunt</u>. *The dogs have taken his food.*

Forming the perfect tense of -īre verbs

The perfect stem of **-īre** verbs is usually formed by taking the ***infinitive*** and replacing the **-re** ending with **-v-**.

Infinitive	Perfect stem (replacing -re with -v-)
audīre (meaning *to hear*)	**audī<u>v</u>-**

However, the perfect stem of some **-īre** verbs is formed by chopping off the **-īre** ending of the ***infinitive*** and changing in a different way. You will have to learn them as you come across them.

Infinitive	Perfect stem (removing -īre and changing)
venīre (meaning *to come*)	**vēn-**
invenīre (meaning *to find*)	**invēn-**

Now add the correct ending, depending on whether you are referring to *I*, *you* (singular), *he*, *she*, *it*, *we*, *you* (plural), or *they*.

Here are the perfect tense endings for **-īre** verbs:

Person	Ending	Add to perfect stem, e.g. audīv-	Meanings
1st singular	**-ī**	**audīvī**	I heard I have heard
2nd singular	**-istī**	**audīvistī**	You heard You have heard
3rd singular	**-it**	**audīvit**	He/she/it heard He/she/it has heard
1st plural	**-imus**	**audīvimus**	We heard We have heard
2nd plural	**-istis**	**audīvistis**	You heard You have heard
3rd plural	**-ērunt**	**audīvērunt**	They heard They have heard

columbam audīvistis. *You heard a dove.*
ancillae pulchrae vēnērunt. *The pretty slave-girls have come.*
ānulum meum nōn invēnī. *I did not find my ring.*

✔ **TIP**

You can sometimes end the 3rd person plural form of the perfect tense in **-ēre** instead of **-ērunt**, but be careful not to mistake it for the infinitive of a second conjugation verb.

labōrāvēre = labōrāvērunt *they have worked*
vēnēre = vēnērunt *they have come*

Irregular verbs in the perfect tense

Like **-ere** verbs, you will have to learn the perfect stem of irregular verbs in Latin as you come across them. Then you add the correct ending in the usual way.

Infinitive	Perfect stem
esse (meaning *to be*)	**fu-**
posse (meaning *to be able*)	**potu-**
ferre (meaning *to carry*)	**tul-**
īre (meaning *to go*)	**i-**
velle (meaning *to be willing, to want*)	**volu-**
nōlle (meaning *to be unwilling, to not want*)	**nōlu-**
mālle (meaning *to prefer*)	**mālu-**

laetus <u>fuī</u>. — *I was happy.*
suum cibum portāre nōn <u>potuit</u>. — *He was not able to carry his own food.*
suum cibum portāre <u>nōluit</u>. — *He did not want to carry his own food.*
fēminae ad theātrum <u>iērunt</u>. — *The women have gone to the theatre.*

✔ Tip

For the perfect tenses of **fierī**, the passive form of **faciō** is used.
laetiōr <u>factus sum</u>. *I became happier* (literally *I was made happier*).

For more information on the Passive, see page 77.

Key points

- Verbs ending in **-āre** form their perfect stem by replacing the **-re** of the infinitive with **-v-**.
- Verbs ending in **-ēre** mostly form their perfect stem by replacing the **-ēre** of the infinitive with **-u-**.
- Verbs ending in **-ere** do not form their perfect stem in a regular way. It is worth learning them as you come across them.
- Verbs ending in **-īre** usually form their perfect stem by replacing the **-re** of the infinitive with **-v-**.
- Some verbs ending in **-īre** form their perfect stem in an irregular way.

- Mixed conjugation verbs are like **-ere** verbs in the perfect tense.
- It is worth learning the perfect stem of irregular verbs in full.
- The perfect tense endings for all verbs are: **-ī**, **-istī**, **-it**, **-imus**, **-istis**, **-ērunt**.

The pluperfect tense

What is the pluperfect tense?
The pluperfect is a verb tense which describes something that ***had*** happened or ***had been*** true at a point in the past – for example: *He had seen her yesterday; They'd wept when they heard the news.*

To form the pluperfect tense of any Latin verb, you take the ***perfect stem*** of the verb and then add the correct form of the ***imperfect tense*** of **esse**, depending on whether you are referring to *I*, *you* (singular), *he, she, it, we*, *you* (plural), or *they*.

Here are the pluperfect tense endings for all Latin verbs:

Person	Ending	Add to perfect stem, e.g. amāv-	Meanings
1st singular	**-eram**	**amāveram**	I had loved
2nd singular	**-erās**	**amāverās**	You had loved
3rd singular	**-erat**	**amāverat**	He/she/it had loved
1st plural	**-erāmus**	**amāverāmus**	We had loved
2nd plural	**-erātis**	**amāverātis**	You had loved
3rd plural	**-erant**	**amāverant**	They had loved

poēta ancillam amāverat. *The poet had loved the slave-girl.*
librum habueram. *I had had a book.*
servum tibi mīseram. *I had sent the slave to you.*
columbam audīverāmus. *You had heard a dove.*
canēs cibum eius cēperant. *The dogs had taken his food.*
fēminae ad theātrum ierant. *The women had gone to the theatre.*

✔ **TIP**

You can sometimes shorten the endings for the perfect tenses of verbs ending in **-āre**.

nōn amāstī = **nōn amāvistī** *you did not love*
portārat = **portāverat** *he had carried*

KEY POINTS

- The pluperfect tense is made up of the perfect stem of the verb and the imperfect tense of **esse**.
- The pluperfect tense endings for all verbs are: **-eram**, **-erās**, **-erat**, **-erāmus**, **-erātis**, **-erant**.

The future perfect tense

What is the future perfect tense?
The future perfect is a verb tense which describes something that ***will have*** happened or ***will have been*** true by some point in the future – for example: *He will have seen her yesterday; They'll have been sad when they heard the news*. In English, the present or perfect tense can often be used to mean the same thing.

To form the future perfect tense of any Latin verb, you take the ***perfect stem*** of the verb and then add the correct form of the ***future tense*** of **esse**, depending on whether you are referring to *I*, *you* (singular), *he*, *she*, *it*, *we*, *you* (plural), or *they*. The only exception is that the third person plural ends in **-erint** rather than **-erunt**.

Here are the future perfect tense endings for all Latin verbs:

Person	Ending	Add to perfect stem, e.g. amāv-	Meanings
1st singular	**-erō**	**amāverō**	I will have loved
2nd singular	**-eris**	**amāveris**	You will have loved
3rd singular	**-erit**	**amāverit**	He/she/it will have loved
1st plural	**-erimus**	**amāverimus**	We will have loved
2nd plural	**-eritis**	**amāveritis**	You will have loved
3rd plural	**-erint**	**amāverint**	They will have loved

poēta ancillam amāverit.	*The poet will have loved the slave-girl.*
librum habuerō.	*I will have had a book.*
servum tibi mīserō.	*I will have sent the slave to you.*
columbam audīverimus.	*You will have heard a dove.*
canēs cibum eius cēperint.	*The dogs will have taken his food.*
fēminae ad theātrum ierint.	*The women will have gone to the theatre.*

✔ **Tip**

You can sometimes leave out the **-v-** in the perfect tenses of **-īre** verbs.

columbam audiī = columbam audīvī *I've heard a dove.*

Key points

- The future perfect tense is made up of the perfect stem of the verb and the future tense of **esse** (except for the third person plural).
- The future perfect tense endings for all verbs are: **-erō**, **-eris**, **-erit**, **-erimus**, **-eritis**, **-erint**.

Exercise 9

Use all the information on the perfect tenses so far, and the examples of verbs used, to find the Latin for:

a You (singular) looked for. ....

b We have worked. ....

c She listened. ....

d You (plural) preferred. ....

e I have taken. ....

f They taught. ....

g We will have carried. ....

h He had come. ....

i I will have wanted. ....

j You (plural) will have made. ....

k They had given back. ....

l You (singular) had frightened. ....

The passive

What is the passive?
The passive is a form of the verb that is used when the subject of the verb is the person or thing that is affected by the action – for example: *I am told*, *We will be given*, *It has been made*.

Using the passive

In a normal, or *active* sentence, the 'subject' of the verb is the person or thing that carries out the action described by the verb. The 'object' of the verb is the person or thing that the action of the verb 'happens' to.
- Lucia (*subject*) greeted (*active verb*) me (*object*).

In English, as in Latin, you can turn an ***active*** sentence round to make a ***passive*** sentence.
- I (*subject*) was greeted (*passive verb*) by Lucia (*agent*).

Very often, however, you cannot identify who is carrying out the action indicated by the verb.
- I am being taken to the shops.
- The water will be heated.
- She was chosen to sing.

✔ **TIP**
There is a very important difference between Latin and English in sentences containing an ***indirect object***. In English, we can quite easily turn a normal (active) sentence with an indirect object into a passive sentence.

Active:
- Theodorus (*subject*) gave (*active verb*) a book (*direct object*) to me (*indirect object*).

Passive:
- I (*subject*) was given (*passive verb*) a book (*direct object*) by Theodorus (*agent*).

In Latin, an indirect object can **NEVER** become the subject of a passive verb.

Forming the present, imperfect, and future passive tenses

In Latin, the present, imperfect, and future tenses in their passive form use the same root of the verb as the present, future, and imperfect tenses in their active form, but the endings are different.

> ✔ **TIP**
> As you become familiar with the endings for the different tenses of Latin verbs in their passive form, you will notice that they follow a pattern like this:
>
> | | |
> |---|---|
> | **-r** | *I* |
> | **-ris** | *you (in the singular)* |
> | **-tur** | *he, she* or *it* |
> | **-mur** | *we* |
> | **-minī** | *you (in the plural)* |
> | **-ntur** | *they* |

Here are the present, imperfect and future tense endings for **-āre** verbs in their passive form:

Person	Present	Meaning	Imperfect	Meaning	Future	Meaning
1st singular	**amor**	I am loved	**amābar**	I was being loved	**amābor**	I will be loved
2nd singular	**amāris**	You are loved	**amābāris**	You were being loved	**amāberis**	You will be loved
3rd singular	**amātur**	He/she/it is loved	**amābātur**	He/she/it was being loved	**amābitur**	He/she/it will be loved
1st plural	**amāmur**	We are loved	**amābāmur**	We were being loved	**amābimur**	We will be loved
2nd plural	**amāminī**	You are loved	**amābāminī**	You were being loved	**amābiminī**	You will be loved
3rd plural	**amantur**	They are loved	**amābantur**	They were being loved	**amābuntur**	They will be loved

ancilla amātur.	*The slave-girl is loved.*
portābantur.	*They were being carried.*

Key points
- The present tense endings for **-āre** verbs in the passive are: **-or**, **-āris**, **-ātur**, **-āmur**, **-āminī**, **-antur**.
- The imperfect tense endings are: **-ābar**, **-ābāris**, **-ābātur**, **-ābāmur**, **-ābāminī**, **-ābantur**.
- The future tense endings are: **-ābor**, **-āberis**, **-ābitur**, **-ābimur**, **-ābiminī**, **-ābuntur**.

Here are the present, imperfect, and future tense endings for **-ēre** verbs in their passive form:

Person	Present	Meaning	Imperfect	Meaning	Future	Meaning
1st singular	**hab<u>eor</u>**	I am held	**hab<u>ēbar</u>**	I was being held	**hab<u>ēbor</u>**	I will be held
2nd singular	**hab<u>ēris</u>**	You are held	**hab<u>ēbāris</u>**	You were being held	**hab<u>ēberis</u>**	You will be held
3rd singular	**hab<u>ētur</u>**	He/she/it is held	**hab<u>ēbātur</u>**	He/she/it was being held	**hab<u>ēbitur</u>**	He/she/it will be held
1st plural	**hab<u>ēmur</u>**	We are held	**hab<u>ēbāmur</u>**	We were being held	**hab<u>ēbimur</u>**	We will be held
2nd plural	**hab<u>ēminī</u>**	You are held	**hab<u>ēbāminī</u>**	You were being held	**hab<u>ēbiminī</u>**	You will be held
3rd plural	**hab<u>entur</u>**	They are held	**hab<u>ēbantur</u>**	They were being held	**hab<u>ēbuntur</u>**	They will be held

liber <u>habēbātur</u>. — *The book was being held.*
puerī <u>docēbuntur</u>. — *The boys will be taught.*

Key points
- The present tense endings for **-ēre** verbs in the passive are: **-eor**, **-ēris**, **-ētur**, **-ēmur**, **-ēminī**, **-entur**.
- The imperfect tense endings are: **-ēbar**, **-ēbāris**, **-ēbātur**, **-ēbāmur**, **-ēbāminī**, **-ēbantur**.
- The future tense endings are: **-ēbor**, **-ēberis**, **-ēbitur**, **-ēbimur**, **-ēbiminī**, **-ēbuntur**.

Here are the present, imperfect, and future tense endings for **-ere** verbs in their passive form:

Person	Present	Meaning	Imperfect	Meaning	Future	Meaning
1st singular	**mitt<u>or</u>**	I am sent	**mitt<u>ēbar</u>**	I was being sent	**mitt<u>ar</u>**	I will be sent
2nd singular	**mitter<u>is</u>**	You are sent	**mitt<u>ēbāris</u>**	You were being sent	**mitt<u>ēris</u>**	You will be sent
3rd singular	**mitt<u>itur</u>**	He/she/it is sent	**mitt<u>ēbātur</u>**	He/she/it was being sent	**mitt<u>ētur</u>**	He/she/it will be sent
1st plural	**mitt<u>imur</u>**	We are sent	**mitt<u>ēbāmur</u>**	We were being sent	**mitt<u>ēmur</u>**	We will be sent
2nd plural	**mitt<u>iminī</u>**	You are sent	**mitt<u>ēbāminī</u>**	You were being sent	**mitt<u>ēminī</u>**	You will be sent
3rd plural	**mitt<u>untur</u>**	They are sent	**mitt<u>ēbantur</u>**	They were being sent	**mitt<u>entur</u>**	They will be sent

servus tibi <u>mittētur</u>. *The slave will be sent to you.*
<u>quaerimur</u>. *We are being looked for.*

Key points
- The present tense endings for **-ere** verbs in the passive are: **-or**, **-eris**, **-itur**, **-imur**, **-iminī**, **-untur**.
- The imperfect tense endings are: **-ēbar**, **-ēbāris**, **-ēbātur**, **-ēbāmur**, **-ēbāminī**, **-ēbantur**.
- The future tense endings are: **-ar**, **-ēris**, **-ētur**, **-ēmur**, **-ēminī**, **-entur**.

Here are the present, imperfect, and future tense endings for **-īre** verbs in their passive form:

Person	Present	Meaning	Imperfect	Meaning	Future	Meaning
1st singular	**aud<u>ior</u>**	I am heard	**audi<u>ēbar</u>**	I was being heard	**audi<u>ar</u>**	I will be heard
2nd singular	**aud<u>īris</u>**	You are heard	**audi<u>ēbāris</u>**	You were being heard	**audi<u>ēris</u>**	You will be heard
3rd singular	**aud<u>ītur</u>**	He/she/it is heard	**audi<u>ēbātur</u>**	He/she/it was being heard	**audi<u>ētur</u>**	He/she/it will be heard
1st plural	**aud<u>īmur</u>**	We are heard	**audi<u>ēbāmur</u>**	We were being heard	**audi<u>ēmur</u>**	We will be heard
2nd plural	**aud<u>īminī</u>**	You are heard	**audi<u>ēbāminī</u>**	You were heard	**audi<u>ēminī</u>**	You will be heard
3rd plural	**audi<u>untur</u>**	They are heard	**audi<u>ēbantur</u>**	They were being heard	**audi<u>entur</u>**	They will be heard

columba <u>audītur</u>. *A dove is heard.*
<u>inveniēminī</u>. *You will be found.*

Key points

- The present tense endings for **-īre** verbs in the passive are: **-ior**, **-īris**, **-ītur**, **-īmur**, **-īminī**, **-iuntur**.
- The imperfect tense endings are: **-iēbar**, **-iēbāris**, **-iēbātur**, **-iēbāmur**, **-iēbāminī**, **-iēbantur**.
- The future tense endings are: **-iar**, **-iēris**, **-iētur**, **-iēmur**, **-iēminī**, **-ientur**.

✔ Tip

You can sometimes shorten the ending of the second person singular in the imperfect and future tenses of verbs in the passive from **-ris** to **-re**.

mittēr<u>e</u> = **mittēr<u>is</u>** *you will be sent*
audiēbār<u>e</u> = **audiēbār<u>is</u>** *you were being heard*

Here are the present, imperfect, and future tense endings for mixed conjugation **-ere** verbs in their passive form:

Person	Present	Meaning	Imperfect	Meaning	Future	Meaning
1st singular	**capi<u>or</u>**	I am taken	**capi<u>ēbar</u>**	I was being taken	**capi<u>ar</u>**	I will be taken
2nd singular	**cap<u>eris</u>**	You are taken	**capi<u>ēbāris</u>**	You were being taken	**capi<u>ēris</u>**	You will be taken
3rd singular	**capi<u>tur</u>**	He/she/ it is taken	**capi<u>ēbātur</u>**	He/she/it was being taken	**capi<u>ētur</u>**	He/she/it will be taken
1st plural	**capi<u>mur</u>**	We are taken	**capi<u>ēbāmur</u>**	We were being taken	**capi<u>ēmur</u>**	We will be taken
2nd plural	**capi<u>minī</u>**	You are taken	**capi<u>ēbāminī</u>**	You were taken	**capi<u>ēminī</u>**	You will be taken
3rd plural	**capi<u>untur</u>**	They are taken	**capi<u>ēbantur</u>**	They were being taken	**capi<u>entur</u>**	They will be taken

cerva <u>capiētur</u>. *The hind will be taken.*

Key points
- The present tense endings for mixed conjugation **-ere** verbs in the passive are: **-ior**, **-eris**, **-itur**, **-imur**, **-iminī**, **-iuntur**.
- The imperfect and future tense endings are the same as those for **-īre** verbs.

Here are the present, imperfect, and future tense endings for the irregular verb **ferre** in its passive form:

Person	Present	Meaning	Imperfect	Meaning	Future	Meaning
1st singular	**feror**	I am carried	**ferēbar**	I was being carried	**ferar**	I will be carried
2nd singular	**ferris**	You are carried	**ferēbāris**	You were being carried	**ferēris**	You will be carried
3rd singular	**fertur**	He/she/it is carried	**ferēbātur**	He/she/it was being carried	**ferētur**	He/she/it will be carried
1st plural	**ferimur**	We are carried	**ferēbāmur**	We were being carried	**ferēmur**	We will be carried
2nd plural	**feriminī**	You are carried	**ferēbāminī**	You were carried	**ferēminī**	You will be carried
3rd plural	**feruntur**	They are carried	**ferēbantur**	They were being carried	**ferentur**	They will be carried

cibus et vīnum feruntur. *The food and wine are being carried.*

Key points
- The present tense endings for **ferre** in the passive are: **-or**, **-ris**, **-tur**, **-imur**, **-iminī**, **-untur**.
- The imperfect and future tense endings are the same as those for **-ere** verbs.

The past participle

In English, we use the verb *to be* with the ***past participle*** to form the passive – for example, *is carried*, *will be given*, *has been taught*. In Latin, only the perfect tenses of the passive are formed in this way, using the past participle and the verb **esse**.

The past participle acts like a first and second declension adjective such as **bonus**, **bona**, **bonum**, which means it agrees with the subject of the passive verb, or any noun or pronoun that it describes. You must always make sure that its ending is correct, depending on the gender and case of the noun or pronoun that goes with it, and whether it is singular or plural.

For more information on Adjectives, Nouns or Pronouns, see pages 16, 2 and 27.

To form the past participle of any verb in Latin, you take the ***supine*** of the verb and replace the **-um** at the end with **-us**.

Infinitive	Supine	Past participle	Meaning
amāre	**amātum**	**amātus**	having been loved
habēre	**habitum**	**habitus**	having been held
mittere	**missum**	**missus**	having been sent
audīre	**audītum**	**audītus**	having been heard
capere	**captum**	**captus**	having been taken
ferre	**lātum**	**lātus**	having been carried

ancilla amāta poētam audit. — *The beloved slave-girl is listening to the poet.*

servī mihi missī nōn labōrābant. — *The slaves who were sent to me were not working.*

animālia audīta eam terruērunt. — *When she heard the animals they terrified her.*

captus miserrimus erat. — *Having been caught he was very sad.*

In English, we often find that one half of a sentence describes an action that is separate from the main action in the other half of the sentence but helps to explain it in some way – for example: *When the marking had been completed, the teacher had a cup of coffee.*

In Latin, you use a past participle with the noun or pronoun to do this and they must all be in the ablative case. This is what is known as an ***ablative absolute***.

ānulō inventō, ancillam mihi mīsit. *After the ring had been found* literally *(With the ring having been found), he sent me the slave-girl.*

The ablative absolute can also be used with present and future participles.

For more information on Present or Future participles, see pages 87 and 91.

> ✔ **TIP**
> When you look up a verb in a Latin dictionary, you will usually find the supine form is given – for example, **mitto**, **mittere**, **mīsī**, **missum**. It is the fourth of what we call a verb's ***principal parts*** and it is worth learning it whenever you come across a new verb.

For Common principal parts of verbs, see supplement.

Forming the perfect passive tenses

Here is the perfect tense of a Latin verb in its passive form:

Person	Past participle	Present tense of esse	Meaning
1st singular	**amātus**	**sum**	I was loved I have been loved
2nd singular	**amātus**	**es**	You were loved You have been loved
3rd singular	**amātus/amāta/ amātum**	**est**	He/she/it was loved He/she/it has been loved
1st plural	**amātī**	**sumus**	We were loved We have been loved
2nd plural	**amātī**	**estis**	You were loved You have been loved
3rd plural	**amātī**	**sunt**	They were loved They have been loved

cibus portātus est. *The food has been carried.*
puerī doctī sunt. *The boys were taught.*
tibi missī sumus. *We have been sent to you.*
territa sum. *I (a woman/girl) was frightened.*

deae cerva <u>capta est</u>.	*The hind of the goddess was caught.*
vōs rēgī <u>lātī estis</u>.	*You have been brought to the king.*

You can form the other perfect tenses of the passive by changing the tense of the verb **esse**.

Pluperfect: **amāta <u>erat</u>** (***imperfect*** *tense of* **esse**) *She had been loved*
Future perfect: **amātī <u>erunt</u>** (***future*** *tense of* **esse**) *They will have been loved*

For more information on the Pluperfect or Future perfect tenses, see pages 74 and 75.

Imperative forms in the passive

For almost all verbs in Latin, the second person singular imperative in the passive is the same as the ***infinitive***. The second person plural imperative is the same as the second person plural of the ***present tense*** in the passive.

Person	-āre verbs	-ēre verbs	-ere verbs	-īre verbs	Mixed -ere verbs	ferre
2nd singular	**am<u>āre</u>**	**hab<u>ēre</u>**	**mitt<u>ere</u>**	**aud<u>īre</u>**	**cap<u>ere</u>**	**fer<u>re</u>**
2nd plural	**am<u>āminī</u>**	**hab<u>ēminī</u>**	**mitt<u>iminī</u>**	**aud<u>īminī</u>**	**cap<u>iminī</u>**	**fer<u>iminī</u>**

ancilla, <u>amāre</u>!	*Slave-girl, be loved!*
servī, <u>mittiminī</u>!	*Slaves, be sent!*

Key points

- The past participle is formed by changing the **-um** ending of the supine to **-us**.
- The past participle always agrees with the ***subject*** of the passive verb.
- The perfect tense of the passive is formed by using the past participle with the present tense of **esse**.
- The pluperfect tense of the passive is formed by using the past participle with the imperfect tense of **esse**.
- The future perfect tense of the passive is formed by using the past participle with the future tense of **esse**.
- The singular imperative in the passive is the same as the infinitive.
- The plural imperative is the same as the second person plural of the present tense.

Exercise 10

Use all the information on the passive so far, and the examples of verbs used, to find the Latin for:

a You (plural) are being looked for.

....

b We will be loved.

....

c It was being heard.

....

d Having been found. (feminine singular)

....

e Having been brought. (masculine plural)

....

f With them having been sent.

....

g With him having been taught.

....

h You (feminine singular) were brought.

....

i We (feminine) had been loved.

....

j I (masculine) will have been found.

....

k Be terrified! (plural)

....

l Be carried! (singular)

....

The present participle

What is a present participle?
The present participle is a verb form ending in *-ing* which is used in English to form verb tenses, and which may also be used as an adjective or a noun – for example: *What are you doing?*; *the setting sun*; *Teaching is easy!*

Using the present participle

In Latin, the present participle is often used as an adjective to describe an additional action going on at the same time as the main action in the sentence – for example: *Seeing the accident, the slaves rushed forward to help*.

✔ **TIP**
The Latin present participle is **NEVER** used to translate English verb forms like *I am leaving*, *They were walking*.

For more information on the Present or Imperfect tenses, see pages 45 and 57.

Forming the present participle

The present participle follows the same pattern of case endings as third declension adjectives like **prūdēns**. However, the ablative singular case ending is always **-e** when a present participle acts as a verb rather than an adjective – for example: *With the baby finally sleeping, the nurse left the room.*

For more information on Adjectives, see page 16.

To form the present participle of a regular Latin verb, you take the ***root*** of the verb and add the correct ending (**-āns**, **-ēns** or **-iēns**), depending on which conjugation the verb belongs to.

Infinitive	Root	Ending	Present Participle	Meaning
amāre	am-	-āns	amāns	loving
habēre	hab-	-ēns	habēns	having, holding
mittere	mitt-	-ēns	mittēns	sending
audīre	aud-	-iēns	audiēns	hearing

poēta amāns	*the loving poet*
coquum labōrantem audiunt.	*They are listening to the cook working.*
puerōs docēns	*teaching the boys*
tibi ānulum quaerentī ancillām mittam.	*I shall send a slave-girl to you as you look for your ring.*
animālia audientēs	*when they heard the animals*

Mixed conjugation verbs form their present participles like verbs ending in **-īre** – for example, **capere** becomes **capiēns**. The irregular verb **ferre** becomes **ferēns**.

Only compounds of the verb **esse** have a present participle – for example, **absēns** from the verb **abesse** (meaning *to be absent*), **dēsēns** from **dēesse** (meaning *to be missing*), and **praesēns** from **praeesse** (meaning *to be in charge*).

The present participle of **posse** is always used as an adjective: **potēns** (meaning *powerful*).

Present participles of the verb **īre** include **exiēns** from **exīre** (meaning *to go out*), **periēns** from **perīre** (meaning *to perish*), and **rediēns** from **redīre** (meaning *to return*).

The present participle of the irregular verbs **velle**, **nōlle**, and **mālle** is formed by chopping off the **-ō** from the first person singular of the present tense and adding **-ēns**: **volēns**, **nōlēns**, and **mālēns**.

In Latin, the present participle can be used in the same way as a past participle in an ***ablative absolute***.

ancillā poētam amante, coquus miser est. *With the slave-girl loving the poet, the cook is sad.*

For more information on Past participles, see page 83.

The gerund

In English, the present participle can be used as a noun – for example: *Teaching is an art; Do you enjoy teaching?; The art of teaching is difficult.* In Latin, the present participle is **NEVER** used in this way. Instead, you use a form of the verb known as the ***gerund***.

Gerunds are neuter nouns but they do not have a nominative form or any plural forms. Otherwise they follow the same pattern of case endings as second declension nouns like **bellum**.

For more information on Nouns, see page 2.

To form the gerund of most verbs in Latin, you take the ***root*** of the verb and add the correct ending (**-andum**, **-endum** or **-iendum**), depending on which conjugation the verb belongs to.

Infinitive	Root	Ending	Gerund	Meaning
amāre	**am-**	**-andum**	**amandum**	loving
habēre	**hab-**	**-endum**	**habendum**	having, holding
mittere	**mitt-**	**-endum**	**mittendum**	sending
audīre	**aud-**	**-iendum**	**audiendum**	hearing
capere	**cap-**	**-iendum**	**capiendum**	taking
ferre	**fer-**	**-endum**	**ferendum**	carrying

poēta amandō amat. *A poet loves by loving.*
ars docendī difficilis est. *The art of teaching is difficult.*

The irregular verb **īre** becomes **eundum**, **velle** becomes **volendum**, **nōlle** becomes **nōlendum**, and **mālle mālendum**.

You mainly use the gerund in its accusative form after the preposition **ad** (meaning *to*) in order to express a purpose or intention.
coquus ad labōrandum it. *The cook goes to work.*

For more information on Prepositions, see page 132.

✔ **Tip**
When you need a verb to act as the subject or direct object in a sentence, you use the ***infinitive*** rather than the gerund.
docēre est difficilis. *Teaching is difficult.*
servī labōrāre nōn amant. *Slaves do not love working.*

For more information on Infinitives, see page 110.

Key points

- Present participles are **never** used to form tenses in Latin, but they can be used as verbs or adjectives.
- Present participles always agree with the noun or pronoun they describe.
- They are usually formed by adding **-āns**, **-ēns**, or **-iēns** to the root of the verb. Some verbs are irregular in how they form their present participles.
- Gerunds are usually formed by adding **-andum**, **-endum**, or **-iendum** to the root of the verb. A few verbs are irregular in how they form their gerunds.
- Gerunds follow the same case endings as second declension neuter nouns but with no nominative or plural forms.

Exercise 11

Use all the information on the present participle so far, and the examples of verbs used, to find the Latin for:

a Giving back. (accusative plural masculine/feminine)

....

b Having. (genitive plural)..

c Being in charge. (dative singular)..

d Going out. (accusative singular neuter)

....

e Of carrying..

f By listening..

Future participles

What is a future participle?
A future participle is not a verb form that is used in English. However, there are two types of sentence in English that require you to use a future participle in Latin – for example: *I am about to read my book*. (This has an active meaning); and *There is wine to be drunk*. (This has a passive meaning and a sense of something needing to happen or be done).

Forming the future participle

To form the future participle of any verb in Latin when you want an active meaning, you take the ***supine*** of the verb and replace the **-um** at the end with **-ūrus**.

Infinitive	Supine	Past participle	Meaning
amāre	**amātum**	**amātūrus**	about to love
habēre	**habitum**	**habitūrus**	about to have
mittere	**missum**	**missūrus**	about to send
audīre	**audītum**	**audītūrus**	about to hear
capere	**captum**	**captūrus**	about to take
ferre	**lātum**	**lātūrus**	about to carry
īre	**itum**	**itūrus**	about to go

coquum labōrātūrum audiunt. — *They are listening to the cook who is about to work.*

tibi ānulum quaesītūro ancillam mittam. — *I shall send a slave-girl to you as you are about to look for your ring.*

The future participle of the irregular verb **esse** is **futūrus** (meaning *about to be*).

meus dominus cōnsul futūrus est. — *My master is about to be consul.*

In Latin, the future participle can be used in the same way as a past participle in an ***ablative absolute***.

ancillā poētam amātūrā, coquus miser erit. — *With the slave-girl about to love the poet, the cook will be sad.*

For more information on Past participles, see page 83.

The gerundive

To form the future participle of any verb in Latin when you want a passive meaning, you take the ***root*** of the verb and add the correct ending (**-andus**, **-endus**, or **-iendus**), depending on which conjugation the verb belongs to. This form of the verb is called the ***gerundive***.

Infinitive	Root	Ending	Gerundive	Meaning
amāre	**am-**	**-andus**	**am<u>andus</u>**	needing to be loved
habēre	**hab-**	**-endus**	**hab<u>endus</u>**	needing to be held
mittere	**mitt-**	**-endus**	**mitt<u>endus</u>**	needing to be sent
audīre	**aud-**	**-iendus**	**aud<u>iendus</u>**	needing to be heard

ancilla <u>amanda</u> est. — *She is a slave-girl who should be loved.*
tibi puerōs <u>docendōs</u> mittam. — *I shall send to you boys needing to be taught.*

Mixed conjugation verbs form their gerundives like verbs ending in **-īre** – for example, **capere** becomes **cap<u>iendus</u>**. The irregular verb **ferre** becomes **fer<u>endus</u>**.

cervus <u>capiendus</u> est. — *The stag needs to be caught.*
vīnum <u>ferendum</u> est. — *There is wine to be brought.*

If you want to show that someone specific has to do something, you use a noun or pronoun in the dative case.

vīnum <u>servīs</u> portandum est. — *The slaves must carry the wine.*
ānulus <u>mihi</u> quaerendus erit. — *I will have to find the ring.*

For more information on Nouns or Pronouns, see pages 2 and 27.

The future participles follow the same pattern of case endings as first and second declension adjectives like **bonus**, **bona**, **bonum**.

For more information on Adjectives, see page 16.

Key points

- Future participles always agree with the noun or pronoun they describe.
- Future participles with an active meaning are formed by changing the **-um** ending of the supine to **-ūrus**.
- Gerundives are formed by adding **-andus**, **-endus**, or **-iendus** to the root of the verb.

Exercise 12

Use all the information on the future participle so far, and the examples of verbs used, to find the Latin for:

a Being about to work. (ablative plural feminine)

....

b Being about to come. (genitive singular neuter)

....

c Being about to be. (nominative plural feminine)

....

d Needing to be brought. (dative singular masculine)

....

e Needing to be sent. (accusative plural neuter)

....

f Needing to be found. (ablative singular masculine)

....

Impersonal verbs

What is an impersonal verb?
An impersonal verb is one that does not refer to a real person or thing and where the subject is represented by *it* – for example: *It's raining*; *It's time to go*.

Impersonal verbs are usually only used in the third person singular, or sometimes the infinitive. The noun or pronoun affected appears in either the accusative or the dative case.

Infinitive	Meaning	Expression	Meaning
miserēre	to move to pity	**mē miseret**	I am sorry for
paenitēre	to repent	**mē paenitet**	I repent of
pigēre	to vex	**mē piget**	I am cross that
pudēre	to shame	**mē pudet**	I am ashamed that
taedēre	to weary	**mē taedet**	I am tired of

decēre	to be fitting	**mē decet**	It suits me to
dēdecēre	to not be fitting	**mē dēdecet**	It does not suit me
oportēre	to behove	**mē oportet**	I ought to, I must
libēre	to please	**mihi libet**	I like to, I am glad to
licēre	to be lawful	**mihi licet**	I am allowed to, I may
placēre	to be pleasing	**mihi placet**	I decide to

A number of the common expressions that can be used in this way are followed by an infinitive.

ancillam <u>amāre</u> mē nōn pudet. *I am not ashamed to love a slave-girl.*
vīnum <u>bibere</u> tē taedēbat. *You began to get tired of drinking wine.*
tibi servum <u>mittere</u> nōs oportet. *We must send you a slave.*
puerōs <u>docēre</u> magistrō nōn licuit. *The teacher was not allowed to instruct the boys.*

For more information on the Infinitive, see page 110.

Several impersonal verbs relate to the weather or the time of day, without any noun or pronoun.

Infinitive	Meaning	Expression	Meaning
pluere	to rain	**pluit**	it's raining
ningere	to snow	**ningit**	it's snowing
tonāre	to thunder	**tonat**	it thunders
fulgurāre	to flash with lightning	**fulgurat**	it's flashing with lightning
lūcēscere	to dawn	**lūcēscit**	it dawns
vesperāscere	to get late	**vesperāscit**	it's getting late

There is another group of useful expressions that start with an impersonal verb. There are followed by the word **ut** (meaning *that*) and a form of the verb called the ***subjunctive***.

accidit ut *it happens that*
appāret ut *it is evident that*
cōnstat ut *it is agreed that*
convenit ut *it suits that*
ēvenit ut *it turns out that*
sequitur ut *it follows that*

For more information on the subjunctive, see opposite.

Exercise 13

Use all the information on impersonal verbs so far, and the examples used, to find the Latin for:

a The master is cross that... ....

b The teacher decided that... ....

c We were glad to... ....

d My mother is ashamed that... ....

e The slave-girls are not allowed to... ....

f It flashed with lightning. ....

The subjunctive

What is the subjunctive?
The subjunctive is a verb form that is used in certain circumstances to express some sort of feeling, or to show there is doubt about whether something will happen or whether something is true. It is only used occasionally in modern English – for example: *If I were you, I wouldn't do that; So be it; Wish you were here!*

Using the subjunctive

So far all the Latin verb forms we have looked at have dealt with facts and things we know to be real or true – for example: *I am coming*; *We shall see*; *She did not like it*. This is called the ***indicative***.

The subjunctive deals with ideas, and things that are possible or necessary.

A subjunctive verb in Latin is often translated into English with words like *may*, *might*, *could*, *would*, *should* or *must* – for example: *I might come*; *We could see*; *She should like it*.

Coming across the subjunctive

In Latin, you will often come across the subjunctive. It can be used in the part of a sentence where the main action is taking place:

asking a question when you are wondering what to do: *Where am I to hide this ring?*

giving an order in the first person plural, the third person, and sometimes the second person: *Let's listen!*; *Let them eat cake*; *You are to apologize*.

expressing a wish about the present, past, or future: *May you win!*; *If only it hadn't happened!*; *Long live the queen!*

where English uses *would* or *should* after a sentence starting with *if*: *If she hadn't found it, I would have cried*.

The subjunctive can also be used in the part of the sentence where an action separate from the main action is taking place but closely linked to it:

expressing purpose: *I shall send someone to help you. I was waiting for you to come*.

showing the result or consequence of something happening: *He ate so much food that he felt sick*.

showing the cause or reason for something happening: *Since you are my friend, I will trust you*.

showing the time that something happened: *When he was cooking, a fire broke out*.

where English uses the word *although*: *Although they had been taught, they had learnt nothing*.

making a comparison with an imaginary event: *She looked as if she'd seen a ghost*.

expressing a fear that something might happen, is happening, or has happened: *We were afraid that we'd lost you*.

in a sentence starting with *if* and where English then uses *would* or *should*: *If I'd tried, I would have won*.

when a question is reported indirectly: *We'd like to find out where you've hidden the money*.

when a command is reported indirectly: *His brother told him to try it*.

expressing an action separate from the main action of a reported event: *You said they would come quickly after they'd finished*.

In Latin, there are four tenses of the subjunctive: present, imperfect, perfect, and pluperfect. Which one you use depends on the way the verb in the subjunctive is being used in the sentence.

> ✔ **Tip**
> There is no future or future perfect tense in the subjunctive.
> If you need to refer to the future, you use the ***future participle*** followed by the present or imperfect subjunctive of **esse**.

For more information on Future participles, see page 91.

Forming the subjunctive

In Latin, the present tense of the subjunctive is formed from the same ***root*** of the verb as the present indicative, but the endings are different.

To form the imperfect tense, you take the ***infinitive*** of the verb, chop off the **-e** and add the same endings as for the present tense of **-āre** verbs in the subjunctive.

To form both the perfect and pluperfect tenses, you take the ***perfect stem*** of the verb, but add different endings.

Here are the present, imperfect, perfect, and pluperfect tense endings for **-āre** verbs in the subjunctive:

Person	Root of the verb	Present tense	Infinitive without -e	Imperfect tense	Perfect stem	Perfect tense	Pluperfect tense
1st sing	**am-**	**amem**	**amār-**	**amārem**	**amāv-**	**amāverim**	**amāvissem**
2nd sing	**am-**	**amēs**	**amār-**	**amārēs**	**amāv-**	**amāverīs**	**amāvissēs**
3rd sing	**am-**	**amet**	**amār-**	**amāret**	**amāv-**	**amāverit**	**amāvisset**
1st plural	**am-**	**amēmus**	**amār-**	**amārēmus**	**amāv-**	**amāverīmus**	**amāvissēmus**
2nd plural	**am-**	**amētis**	**amār-**	**amārētis**	**amāv-**	**amāverītis**	**amāvissētis**
3rd plural	**am-**	**ament**	**amār-**	**amārent**	**amāv-**	**amāverint**	**amāvissent**

Key points

- The present tense endings for **-āre** verbs in the subjunctive are added to the root of the verb: **-em**, **-ēs**, **-et**, **-ēmus**, **-ētis**, **-ent**.
- The imperfect tense endings are the same but added to the infinitive without the **-e**.
- The perfect tense endings are added to the perfect stem: **-erim**, **-erīs**, **-erit**, **-erīmus**, **-erītis**, **-erint**.
- The pluperfect tense endings are: **-issem**, **-issēs**, **-isset**, **-issēmus**, **-issētis**, **-issent**.

Here are the present, imperfect, perfect, and pluperfect tense endings for **-ēre** verbs in the subjunctive:

Person	Root of the verb	Present tense	Infinitive without -e	Imperfect tense	Perfect stem	Perfect tense	Pluperfect tense
1st sing	**hab-**	**habeam**	**habēr-**	**habērem**	**habu-**	**habuerim**	**habuissem**
2nd sing	**hab-**	**habeās**	**habēr-**	**habērēs**	**habu-**	**habuerīs**	**habuissēs**
3rd sing	**hab-**	**habeat**	**habēr-**	**habēret**	**habu-**	**habuerit**	**habuisset**
1st plural	**hab-**	**habeāmus**	**habēr-**	**habērēmus**	**habu-**	**habuerīmus**	**habuissēmus**
2nd plural	**hab-**	**habeātis**	**habēr-**	**habērētis**	**habu-**	**habuerītis**	**habuissētis**
3rd plural	**hab-**	**habeant**	**habēr-**	**habērent**	**habu-**	**habuerint**	**habuissent**

Key points

- The present tense endings for **-ēre** verbs in the subjunctive are added to the root of the verb: **-eam**, **-eās**, **-eat**, **-eāmus**, **-eātis**, **-eant**.
- The imperfect tense endings are the same as for **-āre** verbs in the present and added to the infinitive without the **-e**.
- The perfect tense endings are added to the perfect stem: **-erim**, **-erīs**, **-erit**, **-erīmus**, **-erītis**, **-erint**.
- The pluperfect tense endings are: **-issem**, **-issēs**, **-isset**, **-issēmus**, **-issētis**, **-issent**.

Here are the present, imperfect, perfect, and pluperfect tense endings for **-ere** verbs in the subjunctive:

Person	Root of the verb	Present tense	Infinitive without -e	Imperfect tense	Perfect stem	Perfect tense	Pluperfect tense
1st sing	**mitt-**	**mittam**	**mitter-**	**mitterem**	**mīs-**	**mīserim**	**mīsissem**
2nd sing	**mitt-**	**mittās**	**mitter-**	**mitterēs**	**mīs-**	**mīserīs**	**mīsissēs**
3rd sing	**mitt-**	**mittat**	**mitter-**	**mitteret**	**mīs-**	**mīserit**	**mīsisset**
1st plural	**mitt-**	**mittāmus**	**mitter-**	**mitterēmus**	**mīs-**	**mīserīmus**	**mīsissēmus**
2nd plural	**mitt-**	**mittātis**	**mitter-**	**mitterētis**	**mīs-**	**mīserītis**	**mīsissētis**
3rd plural	**mitt-**	**mittant**	**mitter-**	**mitterent**	**mīs-**	**mīserint**	**mīsissent**

Key points

- The present tense endings for **-ere** verbs in the subjunctive are added to the root of the verb: **-am**, **-ās**, **-at**, **-āmus**, **-ātis**, **-ant**.
- The imperfect tense endings are the same as for **-āre** verbs in the present and added to the infinitive without the **-e**.
- The perfect tense endings are added to the perfect stem: **-erim**, **-erīs**, **-erit**, **-erīmus**, **-erītis**, **-erint**.
- The pluperfect tense endings are: **-issem**, **-issēs**, **-isset**, **-issēmus**, **-issētis**, **-issent**.

Here are the present, imperfect, perfect, and pluperfect tense endings for **-īre** and mixed conjugation **-ere** verbs in the subjunctive:

Person	Root of the verb	Present tense	Infinitive without -e	Imperfect tense	Perfect stem	Perfect tense	Pluperfect tense
1st sing	**aud-**	**aud<u>iam</u>**	**audīr-**	**audī<u>rem</u>**	**audīv-**	**audīv<u>erim</u>**	**audīv<u>issem</u>**
2nd sing	**aud-**	**aud<u>iās</u>**	**audīr-**	**audīr<u>ēs</u>**	**audīv-**	**audīv<u>erīs</u>**	**audīv<u>issēs</u>**
3rd sing	**aud-**	**aud<u>iat</u>**	**audīr-**	**audīr<u>et</u>**	**audīv-**	**audīv<u>erit</u>**	**audīv<u>isset</u>**
1st plural	**aud-**	**aud<u>iāmus</u>**	**audīr-**	**audīr<u>ēmus</u>**	**audīv-**	**audīv<u>erīmus</u>**	**audīv<u>issēmus</u>**
2nd plural	**aud-**	**aud<u>iātis</u>**	**audīr-**	**audīr<u>ētis</u>**	**audīv-**	**audīv<u>erītis</u>**	**audīv<u>issētis</u>**
3rd plural	**aud-**	**aud<u>iant</u>**	**audīr-**	**audīr<u>ent</u>**	**audīv-**	**audīv<u>erint</u>**	**audīv<u>issent</u>**

Key points

- The present tense endings for **-īre** verbs in the subjunctive are added to the root of the verb: **-iam**, **-iās**, **-iat**, **-iāmus**, **-iātis**, **-iant**.
- The imperfect tense endings are the same as for **-āre** verbs in the present and added to the infinitive without the **-e**.
- The perfect tense endings are added to the perfect stem: **-erim**, **-erīs**, **-erit**, **-erīmus**, **-erītis**, **-erint**.
- The pluperfect tense endings are: **-issem**, **-issēs**, **-isset**, **-issēmus**, **-issētis**, **-issent**.
- Mixed conjugation **-ere** verbs follow **-īre** verbs in all forms of the subjunctive.

✔ **TIP**

You will sometimes come across shortened endings of the perfect and pluperfect tenses of verbs in the subjunctive.

amāssem = amā<u>vi</u>ssem

audierit = audī<u>v</u>erit

Forming the subjunctive of irregular verbs

Here is the present subjunctive of those very common Latin verbs that do not follow the normal rules:

Person	Form	Form	Form	Form	Form	Form	Form	Form
1st sing	**sim**	**possim**	**feram**	**fīam**	**eam**	**velim**	**nōlim**	**mālim**
2nd sing	**sīs**	**possīs**	**ferās**	**fīās**	**eās**	**velīs**	**nōlīs**	**mālīs**
3rd sing	**sit**	**possit**	**ferat**	**fīat**	**eat**	**velit**	**nōlit**	**mālit**
1st plural	**sīmus**	**possīmus**	**ferāmus**	**fīāmus**	**eāmus**	**velīmus**	**nōlīmus**	**mālīmus**
2nd plural	**sītis**	**possītis**	**ferātis**	**fīātis**	**eātis**	**velītis**	**nōlītis**	**mālītis**
3rd plural	**sint**	**possint**	**ferant**	**fīant**	**eant**	**velint**	**nōlint**	**mālint**

However, to form the imperfect, perfect, and pluperfect tenses of these irregular verbs in the subjunctive, you do follow the normal rules. Remember that you express the perfect and pluperfect of **fierī** by using the passive forms of **facere**.

essem *first person singular imperfect subjunctive of* **esse**
potuerīs *second person singular perfect subjunctive of* **posse**
tulisset *third person singular pluperfect subjunctive of* **ferre**
factī sīmus *first person plural pluperfect subjunctive of* **fierī**
ierītis *second person plural perfect subjunctive of* **īre**
vellent *third person plural imperfect subjunctive of* **velle**

KEY POINTS

- Irregular verbs do not always follow the normal rules when forming the present tense of the subjunctive.
- They do follow the normal rules when forming the imperfect, perfect, and pluperfect tenses.

Forming the subjunctive in the passive

The present tense of the subjunctive in the passive is formed from the same ***root*** of the verb as the present tense in the active, but the endings are different.

To form the imperfect tense, you take the ***infinitive*** of the verb, chop off the **-e** and add the same endings as for the present tense of **-āre** verbs in the subjunctive passive.

To form both the perfect and pluperfect tenses, you take the ***past participle*** of the verb and add the correct form of the verb **esse**.

Here are the present, imperfect, perfect, and pluperfect tense endings for **-āre** verbs in the subjunctive passive:

Person	Root of the verb	Present tense	Infinitive without -e	Imperfect tense	Past participle	Perfect tense	Pluperfect tense
1st sing	**am-**	**amer**	**amār-**	**amārer**	**amātus**	**amātus sim**	**amātus essem**
2nd sing	**am-**	**amēris**	**amār-**	**amārēris**	**amātus**	**amātus sīs**	**amātus essēs**
3rd sing	**am-**	**amētur**	**amār-**	**amārētur**	**amātus**	**amātus sit**	**amātus esset**
1st plural	**am-**	**amēmur**	**amār-**	**amārēmur**	**amātī**	**amātī sīmus**	**amātī essēmus**
2nd plural	**am-**	**amēminī**	**amār-**	**amārēminī**	**amātī**	**amātī sītis**	**amātī essētis**
3rd plural	**am-**	**amentur**	**amār-**	**amārentur**	**amātī**	**amātī sint**	**amātī essent**

Key points

- The present tense endings for **-āre** verbs in the subjunctive passive are added to the root of the verb: **-er**, **-ēris**, **-ētur**, **-ēmur**, **-ēminī**, **-entur**.
- The imperfect tense endings are the same but added to the infinitive without the **-e**.
- The perfect tense is formed by adding the present tense of **esse** to the past participle.
- The pluperfect tense is formed by adding the imperfect tense of **esse** to the past participle.

Here are the present, imperfect, perfect, and pluperfect tense endings for **-ēre** verbs in the subjunctive passive:

Person	Root of the verb	Present tense	Infinitive without -e	Imperfect tense	Past participle	Perfect tense	Pluperfect tense
1st sing	**hab-**	**habear**	**habēr-**	**habērer**	**habitus**	**habitus sim**	**habitus essem**
2nd sing	**hab-**	**habeāris**	**habēr-**	**habērēris**	**habitus**	**habitus sīs**	**habitus essēs**
3rd sing	**hab-**	**habeātur**	**habēr-**	**habērētur**	**habitus**	**habitus sit**	**habitus esset**
1st plural	**hab-**	**habeāmur**	**habēr-**	**habērēmur**	**habitī**	**habitī sīmus**	**habitī essēmus**
2nd plural	**hab-**	**habeāminī**	**habēr-**	**habērēminī**	**habitī**	**habitī sītis**	**habitī essētis**
3rd plural	**hab-**	**habeantur**	**habēr-**	**habērentur**	**habitī**	**habitī sint**	**habitī essent**

Key points

- The present tense endings for **-ēre** verbs in the subjunctive passive are added to the root of the verb: **-ear**, **-eāris**, **-eātur**, **-eāmur**, **-eāminī**, **-eantur**.
- The imperfect tense endings are the same as for **-āre** verbs in the present and added to the infinitive without the **-e**.
- The perfect tense is formed by adding the present tense of **esse** to the past participle.
- The pluperfect tense is formed by adding the imperfect tense of **esse** to the past participle.

Here are the present, imperfect, perfect, and pluperfect tense endings for **-ere** verbs in the subjunctive passive:

Person	Root of the verb	Present tense	Infinitive without -e	Imperfect tense	Past participle	Perfect tense	Pluperfect tense
1st sing	**mitt-**	**mittar**	**mitter-**	**mitterer**	**missus**	**missus sim**	**missus essem**
2nd sing	**mitt-**	**mittāris**	**mitter-**	**mitterēris**	**missus**	**missus sīs**	**missus essēs**
3rd sing	**mitt-**	**mittātur**	**mitter-**	**mitterētur**	**missus**	**missus sit**	**missus esset**

1st plural	**mitt-**	**mitt<u>āmur</u>**	**mitter-**	**mitter<u>ēmur</u>**	**missī**	**missī <u>sīmus</u>**	**missī <u>essēmus</u>**
2nd plural	**mitt-**	**mitt<u>āminī</u>**	**mitter-**	**mitter<u>ēminī</u>**	**missī**	**missī <u>sītis</u>**	**missī <u>essētis</u>**
3rd plural	**mitt-**	**mitt<u>antur</u>**	**mitter-**	**mitter<u>entur</u>**	**missī**	**missī <u>sint</u>**	**missī <u>essent</u>**

Key points

- The present tense endings for **-ere** verbs in the subjunctive passive are added to the root of the verb: **-ar**, **-āris**, **-ātur**, **-āmur**, **-āminī**, **-antur**.
- The imperfect tense endings are the same as for **-āre** verbs in the present and added to the infinitive without the **-e**.
- The perfect tense is formed by adding the present tense of **esse** to the past participle.
- The pluperfect tense is formed by adding the imperfect tense of **esse** to the past participle.

Here are the present, imperfect, perfect, and pluperfect tense endings for **-īre** and mixed conjugation **-ere** verbs in the subjunctive passive:

Person	Root of the verb	Present tense	Infinitive without -e	Imperfect tense	Past participle	Perfect tense	Pluperfect tense
1st sing	**aud-**	**audi<u>ar</u>**	**audīr-**	**audīr<u>er</u>**	**audītus**	**audītus <u>sim</u>**	**audītus <u>essem</u>**
2nd sing	**aud-**	**audi<u>āris</u>**	**audīr-**	**audīr<u>ēris</u>**	**audītus**	**audītus <u>sīs</u>**	**audītus <u>essēs</u>**
3rd sing	**aud-**	**audi<u>ātur</u>**	**audīr-**	**audīr<u>ētur</u>**	**audītus**	**audītus <u>sit</u>**	**audītus <u>esset</u>**
1st plural	**aud-**	**audi<u>āmur</u>**	**audīr-**	**audīr<u>ēmur</u>**	**audītī**	**audītī <u>sīmus</u>**	**audītī <u>essēmus</u>**
2nd plural	**aud-**	**audi<u>āminī</u>**	**audīr-**	**audīr<u>ēminī</u>**	**audītī**	**audītī <u>sītis</u>**	**audītī <u>essētis</u>**
3rd plural	**aud-**	**audi<u>antur</u>**	**audīr-**	**audīr<u>entur</u>**	**audītī**	**audītī <u>sint</u>**	**audītī <u>essent</u>**

KEY POINTS

- The present tense endings for **-īre** verbs in the subjunctive passive are added to the root of the verb: **-iar**, **-iāris**, **-iātur**, **-iāmur**, **-iāminī**, **-iantur**.
- The imperfect tense endings are the same as for **-āre** verbs in the present and added to the infinitive without the **-e**.
- The perfect tense is formed by adding the present tense of **esse** to the past participle.
- The pluperfect tense is formed by adding the imperfect tense of **esse** to the past participle.
- Mixed conjugation **-ere** verbs follow **-īre** verbs in all forms of the subjunctive.

✔ TIP

You will sometimes come across endings of the second person singular in the present and imperfect tenses of verbs in the subjunctive passive shortened from **-ris** to **-re**.
mittāre = **mittāris**
habērēre = **habērēris**

When to use the subjunctive

In Latin, you will find the subjunctive in many different types of sentence.

The present tense of the subjunctive is used when you want to ask a ***question*** which involves wondering what to do.

quid faciāmus?	*What are we to do?*
maneam an eam?	*Should I stay or should I go?*

For more information on Questions, see page 127.

You also use the present tense for giving an ***order*** in the first person plural, the third person, and sometimes the second person. If the command is for someone not to do something, you use **nē** in front of the verb.

audiāmus!	*Let's listen!*
servī vīnum portent.	*Let the slaves carry the wine.*
hunc librum nē legās.	*You are not to read this book.*

For other types of command, use the imperative.

For more information on the Imperative, see page 55.

When you want to express a ***wish*** about something in the future you use the present tense of the subjunctive. If it is about something in the present you use **utinam** followed by the imperfect subjunctive, and if it's in the past, then the pluperfect subjunctive. You add **nē** if the sense is negative.

vīvat rēgīna!	*Long live the queen!*
utinam Lūcia adesset!	*If only Lucia were here!*
utinam exercitus nē victus esset.	*If only the army had not been defeated.*

Where English uses *would* ***or*** *should* after a sentence starting with *if*, you also use the present tense of the subjunctive when you are referring to the future, the imperfect subjunctive when you are referring to the present, and the pluperfect subjunctive when you are referring to the past.

sī iste cōnsul exercitum dūcat, Rōma vincātur.
If that consul were to lead the army, Rome would be defeated.
sī rēx Rōmānus vōs regeret, miserrimī essētis.
If a king of Rome were ruling you, you would be very sad.
sī domina cibum gustāvisset, mē laudāvisset.
If my mistress had tasted the food, she would have praised me.

✔ **TIP**
Remember not to use the subjunctive if you are not using *would* or *should* in English.
sī tū in Graeciā manēbis, omnēs laetissimī erimus.
If *you* stay in Greece, we'll all be very happy.

You use the subjunctive when you want to express a ***purpose***; **ut**, **nē** (for the negative), or the relative pronoun **quī** is followed by the present subjunctive if you are talking about something happening in the present, and the imperfect subjunctive if it is in the past.

puellae currunt ut fūrēs effugiant.
The girls are running to escape the thieves.
fēlēs arborem ascendit nē canibus caperētur.
The cat climbed the tree not to be caught by the dogs.
amīcus servum mīsit quī mē adiuvāret.
My friend sent a slave to help me.

For more information on Relative pronouns, see page 36.

You also use the subjunctive when you want to express a ***purpose*** with an idea of time using the conjunctions **priusquam** (meaning *before*) and **dum** or **dōnec** (meaning *while, until*).

fugiendum est vōbīs priusquam vōs cōnspiciant.
You must flee before they catch sight of you.
exspectābant dum centuriō signum daret.
They were waiting until the centurion should give the signal.

For more information on Conjunctions, see page 139.

You use the subjunctive, usually in the present or imperfect tense following **ut**, if you want to show the ***result*** or consequence of something happening. You use **ut nōn** if the sense is negative.

tam perītus erat poēta ut ab omnibus laudārētur.
The poet was so skilful that he was praised by everyone.

✔ Tip

Here are some of the adjectives and adverbs that will show you the result or consequence of something is about to be described.

tam	*so*
tālis, tāle	*such*
tantus, tanta, tantum	*so big, so great*
tot	*so many*
adeō	*so (= to such an extent)*
ita, sīc	*so (= in such a way)*

For more information on Adjectives or Adverbs, see pages 16 and 127.

You can also use **quī** (meaning *of the sort who*) to show a result or consequence.

illae fēminae erant quī animālibus terrērentur.
Those women were the sort who were terrified by animals.

When you use the conjunction **cum** (meaning *since* or *because*) to show the ***cause or reason*** for something happening, then you use the subjunctive.

cum candidātō mercātōrum favērētis, vōbīs pecūniam dābō.
Since you were supporting the merchants' candidate, I shall give you some money.

> ✔ **TIP**
> If you are using the conjunction **quia** or **quod** (meaning *because*) you do not use the subjunctive unless you are quoting a reason put forward by somebody else that you might or might not agree with.
> **candidātō fabrum nōn favēmus quod mendāx est.**
> *We do not support the craftsmen's candidate because he is* (in fact) *a liar.*
> **candidātō fabrum nōn favēmus quod mendāx sit.**
> *We do not support the craftsmen's candidate because he is* (according to some people) *a liar.*

For more information on Conjunctions, see page 139.

When you use the conjunction **cum** (meaning *when*) to show the ***time*** that something happened, then you use the imperfect or pluperfect subjunctive.

cum Herculēs leōnem interfēcisset, pāstōrēs gāvīsī sunt.
When Hercules had killed the lion, the shepherds rejoiced.

When you use the conjunction **quamvīs** or **cum** (meaning *although*) to express some sort of ***concession***, then you use the subjunctive. But you don't use the subjunctive if you use **quamquam**.

quamvīs vēnātiō perīculōsa sit, paucī bēstiāriī interficiuntur.
Although the animal hunt is dangerous, few trained animal-hunters are killed.
quamquam gladiātor callidissimus erat, is interfectus est.
Although the gladiator was very cunning, he was killed.

If you are making a ***comparison*** with an imaginary event, you use **quasi** or **tamquam** (meaning *as if, as though*) followed by the subjunctive. But you don't use the subjunctive when you use **sīcut** or **ut** with **ita** and are making a comparison with a real event.

servus valdē timēbat, quasi umbram cōnspexisset.
The slave was very afraid, as if he'd seen a ghost.
coquus pāvōnem parat, sīcut domina iusserat.
The cook is preparing peacock, just as his mistress had ordered.
ita Herculēs leōnem petīvit, ut canis fēlem agitāvit.
Just as Hercules attacked the lion, so the dog chased the cat.

When you want to express a ***fear*** that something might happen, is happening or has happened you use the subjunctive after the word **nē**. If you are afraid it might not happen, you use **nē nōn** (or sometimes **ut**). The tense of the verb in the second half of the sentence is the same as the verb in the first half.

ancilla verēbātur nē pōculum frangeret.
The slave-girl was afraid she might break the wine-cup.

perīculum est nē vīcīnī cognōscant.
There is a risk that the neighbours may find out.
puella timēbat nē amīcae nōn venīrent.
The girl was afraid her friends would not come.

When a ***question*** is reported indirectly, you use the subjunctive after the question word. The tense will be the same as it would be in English.

medicus scīre vult quandō puella in morbum gravem incíderit.
The doctor wants to know when the girl fell seriously ill.
spectātōrēs nesciēbant quī āthlēta vīcisset.
The spectators did not know which athlete had won.
agricolae nōs rogant num lupum captūrī sīmus.
The farmers are asking us whether we will catch the wolf.

When a ***command*** is reported indirectly, you use the present or imperfect tense of the subjunctive after **ut** or **nē**.

argentārius agricolam hortātur ut fundum vendat et tabernam emat.
The moneylender is encouraging the farmer to sell his farm and buy a shop.
domina coquō imperāvit ut pāvōnem parāret.
The mistress ordered the cook to prepare peacock.
haruspex imperātōrem monuit nē ex domō exīret.
The soothsayer advised the general not to leave the house.

✔ **TIP**

If you use the verbs **iubēre** (meaning *to command*) or **vetāre** (meaning *to forbid*), you use the infinitive to report the command not the subjunctive.

domina coquum iussit pāvōnem parāre.
The mistress ordered the cook to prepare peacock.
haruspex imperātōrem vetuit ex domō exīre.
The soothsayer forbade the general to leave the house.

For more information on Infinitives, see page 110.

Finally, when you are talking about an action separate from the main action of a ***reported event***, you usually use the subjunctive.

argentārius dīxit agricolās quī fundum venderent multam pecūniam acceptūrōs esse.
The moneylender said that farmers who sold their farms would receive a lot of money.

For more information on Reported speech, see page 113.

Key points

You ***must*** use the subjunctive in Latin when:

- asking a question if you are wondering what to do
- giving an order in the first person plural, the third person, and sometimes the second person
- expressing a wish about the present, past, or future
- where English uses *would* or *should* after a sentence starting with *if*
- expressing purpose
- showing the result or consequence of something happening
- showing the cause or reason for something happening with the word **cum**
- showing the time that something happened with the word **cum**
- where English uses the word *although* and Latin uses **quamvīs** or **cum**
- expressing a fear that something might happen, is happening, or has happened
- when a question is reported indirectly
- when a command is reported indirectly
- expressing an action separate from the main action of a reported event
- sometimes you can avoid using the subjunctive by using a different conjunction or verb.

Exercise 14

Use all the information on the subjunctive so far, and the examples of verbs used, to find the Latin for:

a I may work. (present)..

b You (singular) might come. (present) ....

c She would listen. (imperfect)..

d We might have searched. (perfect).....................................

e You (plural) would have gone. (pluperfect)

....

f They would be. (imperfect) ....

g I may be carried. (present)..

h You (singular) could be taught. (present)

....

i He might be terrified. (imperfect)

....

j We (feminine) might have been found. (perfect)

....

k You (masculine plural) would have been taken. (pluperfect)

....

l They (neuter) would have been made. (pluperfect)

....

The infinitives

What is an infinitive?
An infinitive is a verb form that gives the basic meaning of the verb – for example, *to walk* and *to have walked*.

Using the infinitives

In English, we have two forms of the infinitive. The ***present infinitive*** is made up of the word *to* and the base form of the verb that you will find in a dictionary – for example, *to be*, *to drink*, *to read*.

The ***perfect infinitive*** is made up of the words *to have* and the past participle – for example, *to have been*, *to have drunk*, *to have read*.

For more information on the Past participle, see page 83.

In Latin, however, you will come across three forms of the infinitive: present, perfect, and future. We have already met the present infinitive and it is always listed in Latin dictionaries as the second of a verb's ***principal parts***.

For Common principal parts of verbs, see supplement.

The infinitives have three main functions in a Latin sentence:
- to complete the meaning of the main action: *We wanted to find the ring at all costs.*
- as a noun when it is the subject of the sentence: *To have won was not easy.*
- as the verb in a statement that is being reported: *He said that a slave-girl would come soon.*

Forming the infinitives

To form the present infinitive of a regular verb in Latin you take the ***root*** of the verb and add the correct ending (**-āre**, **-ēre**, **-ere**, **-īre**), which depends on the conjugation the verb belongs to.

To form the perfect infinitive you add the ending **-isse** to the ***perfect stem*** of the verb.

You form the future infinitive by adding the verb **esse** after the ***future participle*** of the verb.

For more information on the Future participle, see page 91.

Here are the present, perfect, and future infinitives of regular verbs and mixed conjugation **-ere** verbs:

Conjugation	Root of the verb	Present infinitive	Perfect stem	Perfect infinitive	Future participle	Future infinitive
-āre verbs	**am-**	**amāre**	**amāv-**	**amāvisse**	**amātūrus**	**amātūrus esse**
-ēre verbs	**hab-**	**habēre**	**habu-**	**habuisse**	**habitūrus**	**habitūrus esse**
-ere verbs	**mitt-**	**mittere**	**mīs-**	**mīsisse**	**mīsurus**	**mīsurus esse**
-īre verbs	**aud-**	**audīre**	**audīv-**	**audīvisse**	**audītūrus**	**audītūrus esse**
mixed **-ere** verbs	**cap-**	**capere**	**cēp-**	**cēpisse**	**captūrus**	**captūrus esse**

You form the perfect and some future infinitives of irregular verbs in exactly the same way as for regular verbs:

Present infinitive	Perfect stem	Perfect infinitive	Future participle	Future infinitive
esse	**fu-**	**fuisse**	**fūtūrus**	**fūtūrus esse**
posse	**potu-**	**potuisse**	-	-
ferre	**tul-**	**tulisse**	**lāturus**	**lāturus esse**
īre	**i-**	**iisse**	**itūrus**	**itūrus esse**
velle	**volu-**	**voluisse**	-	-
nōlle	**nolu-**	**noluisse**	-	-
mālle	**malu-**	**maluisse**	-	-

You will also sometimes come across the word **fore** as the future infinitive of **esse**.

The verb **fierī** uses the passive of **facere** to form its perfect and future infinitives: **factus esse** and **factūrus esse**.

Forming the infinitives in the passive

To form the present infinitive of a regular verb in the passive you take the ***root*** of the verb and add the correct ending (**-ārī**, **-ērī**, **-ī**, **-īrī**), which depends on the conjugation the verb belongs to. Mixed conjugation **-ere** verbs follow the third conjugation.

You form the perfect infinitive of any verb in the passive by adding the verb **esse** after the ***past participle*** of the verb.

For more information on the Past participle, see page 83.

You form the future infinitive of any verb in the passive by adding the word **īrī** after the ***supine*** of the verb. Remember that the supine of a verb is usually listed in a Latin dictionary as the fourth ***principal part*** and its ending here does not change.

For Common principal parts of verbs, see supplement.

Here are the present, perfect, and future infinitives of all verbs in the passive:

Conjugation	Root of the verb	Present infinitive	Past participle	Perfect infinitive	Supine	Future infinitive
-āre verbs	**am-**	**amārī**	**amātus**	**amātus esse**	**amātum**	**amātum īrī**
-ēre verbs	**hab-**	**habērī**	**habitus**	**habitus esse**	**habitum**	**habitum īrī**
-ere verbs	**mitt-**	**mittī**	**missus**	**missus esse**	**missum**	**missum īrī**
-īre verbs	**aud-**	**audīrī**	**audītus**	**audītus esse**	**audītum**	**audītum īrī**
mixed **-ere** verbs	**cap-**	**capī**	**captus**	**captus esse**	**captum**	**captum īrī**

The present infinitive of the irregular verb **ferre** becomes **ferrī** in the passive. The perfect and future infinitives are formed in exactly the same way as for all other verbs: **lātus esse** and **lātum īrī**.

> **KEY POINTS**
> - To form the present infinitive you add **-āre**, **-ēre**, **-ere** or **-īre** to the root of the verb.
> - Some present infinitives are irregular.
> - To form the perfect infinitive you add **-isse** to the perfect stem of the verb.
> - To form the future infinitive you take the future participle and add **esse**.
> - To form the present infinitive in the passive you add **-ārī**, **-ērī**, **-ī** or **-īrī** to the root of the verb.
> - To form the perfect infinitive in the passive you take the past participle and add **esse**.
> - To form the future infinitive in the passive you take the supine and add **īrī**.

Reported speech

In English, when we report something that has been said, what has been said is often introduced by the word *that*, any pronouns and verb tenses change, and we do not use any speech marks. For example, the saying of Descartes, '*I think therefore I am*' would be reported as *Descartes said that he thought therefore he was.*

In Latin, when you want to report something that has been said, known, thought, or felt, you have to use the ***accusative*** case for the noun or pronoun that is the subject of the verb which must be in the ***infinitive***.

the statement made by Descartes: **cogitō ergō sum.**

Descartes' statement reported by someone else: **Cartesius dīxit sē** (accusative) **cogitāre** (infinitive) **ergō sē** (accusative) **esse** (infinitive)**.**

For more information on Nouns or Pronouns, see pages 2 and 27.

Remember that there are three tenses of the infinitive in Latin and you have to use the correct tense depending on when the action of the reported statement took place in relation to the main action of the sentence.

the present infinitive must be used in **BOTH** of these sentences: *The master will say that the slaves are not working.* AND *The master said that the slaves were not working.*

the perfect infinitive passive must be used in **BOTH** of these sentences: *The consuls will have known that the army has been defeated.* AND *The consuls knew that the army had been defeated.*

the future infinitive must be used in **BOTH** of these sentences: *The slave-girl thinks that she will find the ring.* AND *The slave-girl had thought that she would find the ring.*

dominus negābit servōs labōrāre.
The master will say the slaves are not working.
dominus negāvit servōs labōrāre.
The master said the slaves were not working.

cōnsulēs scīverint exercitum victum esse.
The consuls will have known the army has been defeated.
cōnsulēs sciēbant exercitum victum esse.
The consuls knew the army had been defeated.

ancilla putat sē ānulum inventūram esse.
The slave-girl thinks she will find the ring.
ancilla putāverat sē ānulum inventūram esse.
The slave-girl had thought she would find the ring.

✔ Tip
When you talk about hoping, promising, or threatening to do something in the future, you always use the accusative with the future infinitive.

spērāvī mē ventūrum esse. *I hoped to come.*
puellae pollicitae sunt sē doctum īrī. *The girls promised to be taught.*

Key points
- In reported statements, use the accusative case for the subject and the infinitive form of the verb.
- Special care must be taken to use the correct tense of the infinitive.

Exercise 15
Use all the information on the infinitive so far, and the examples of verbs used, to find the Latin for:

a To throw. ....

a To have sent. ....

b To be about to come. (masculine singular)

....

c To be about to be taught. ....

d To be carried. ....

e To have been given back. (feminine plural)

....

Deponent verbs

> **What is a deponent verb?**
> A deponent verb is one that has passive forms but active meanings. Deponent verbs are only found in Latin, not in English.

Like other verbs, ***deponent*** verbs are grouped into four main conjugations:

- **-ārī** verbs (first conjugation) – for example, **cōnārī** (meaning *to try*)
- **-ērī** verbs (second conjugation) – for example, **verērī** (meaning *to fear*)
- **-ī** verbs (third conjugation) – for example, **sequī** (meaning *to follow*)
- **-īrī** verbs (fourth conjugation) – for example, **mentīrī** (meaning *to lie*)

There is also a group of mixed conjugation **-ī** verbs which follow the third conjugation in some forms and the fourth in others – for example, **patī** (meaning *to suffer*), **gradī** (meaning *to walk*), and **morī** (meaning *to die*).

To find the correct form of any deponent verb, you check the conjugation that it belongs to and then use the endings of the tense you want in its ***passive*** form. But remember that the meaning in English can only be active.

suum cibum portāre cōnātur.	*He is trying to carry his own food.*
canēs verēbar.	*I used to be afraid of dogs.*
servī dominum secūtī sunt.	*The slaves followed the master.*
puellae nōn mentītae erant.	*The girls had not lied.*
nōs cīvēs patimur.	*We citizens are suffering.*

To form the singular imperative of deponent verbs, you take the second person singular of the ***present tense*** and change the **-is** ending to **-e**. The plural imperative is the same as the second person plural.

Person	-ārī verbs	Meaning	-ērī verbs	Meaning	-ī verbs	Meaning	-īrī verbs	Meaning
2nd sing	**cōnāre**	try!	**verēre**	fear!	**sequere**	follow!	**mentīre**	lie!
2nd plural	**cōnaminī**	try!	**verēminī**	fear!	**sequiminī**	follow!	**mentīminī**	lie!

ancilla, poētam verēre!	*Slave-girl, be afraid of the poet!*
servī, mē sequiminī!	*Slaves, follow me!*

Mixed conjugation **-ī** verbs follow the same pattern of endings in the imperative as third conjugation **-ī** verbs.

For more information on the Imperative, see page 55.

Past participles of deponent verbs are very useful because they are among the few past participles that are active in meaning. It is worth learning them when you comes across them. You can translate them into English in a number of ways.

suum cibum portāre <u>cōnātus</u>	*Having tried to carry his own food*
canēs <u>verita</u>	*Having been afraid of dogs*
servī dominum <u>secūtī</u>	*When the slaves followed the master*
puellae nōn <u>mentītae</u>	*Since the girls had not lied*
nōs cīvēs <u>passī</u>	*We citizens who have suffered*

For more information on Past participles, see page 83.

You form the present participle of a deponent verb like regular Latin verbs, by taking the ***root*** of the verb and adding the correct ending (**-āns**, **-ēns** or **-iēns**), which depends on the conjugation the verb belongs to.

Infinitive	Root	Ending	Present Participle	Meaning
cōnārī	**cōn-**	**-āns**	**cōn<u>āns</u>**	trying
verērī	**ver-**	**-ēns**	**ver<u>ēns</u>**	fearing
sequī	**sequ-**	**-ēns**	**sequ<u>ēns</u>**	following
mentīrī	**ment-**	**-iēns**	**ment<u>iēns</u>**	lying

The gerunds of deponent verbs are formed in the same way as other Latin verbs.

For more information on Present participles, see page 87.

You form the future participles of deponent verbs in exactly the same way as you do all other Latin verbs. However, be careful with the ***gerundive*** because its meaning is always passive and not active.

animālia <u>verenda</u>	*animals needing to be feared*

For more information on Future participles, see page 91.

You also form the perfect and future infinitives of deponent verbs in exactly the same way as you do all other Latin verbs in the passive.

cōnātus esse	*to have tried*
mentītūrus esse	*to be about to lie*

For more information on Infinitives, see page 110.

A few verbs are known as ***semi-deponent*** verbs because they form some of their tenses in the ordinary way. **audēre** (meaning *to dare*), **cōnfīdere** (meaning *to trust*), **gaudēre** (meaning *to be glad, to rejoice*), and **solēre** (meaning *to be accustomed*) have active forms in the present, future, and imperfect tenses, but passive forms in the perfect tenses.

coquus vīnum bibere nōn audēbit.
The cook will not dare to drink the wine.
servī labōrāre solitī sunt.
The slaves were accustomed to work.

KEY POINTS
- Deponent verbs have passive forms but active meanings.
- A few verbs are semi-deponent and have both active and passive forms.

Defective verbs

What is a defective verb?
A defective verb is one that is found in only a few forms.

Four verbs in Latin only have three tenses – the perfect, pluperfect, and future perfect forms based on the perfect stem – but they are translated as if they were present, past, and future: **coepisse** (meaning *to begin*), **nōvisse** (meaning *to know*), **meminisse** (meaning *to remember*), and **ōdisse** (meaning *to hate*). They are also found in the perfect and pluperfect subjunctive.

coquus vīnum bibere coepit.
The cook begins to drink the wine.
illās puellās nōvī.
I know those girls.
dominus suōs servōs nōn meminerit.
A master will not remember his own slaves.
cīvēs istum cōnsulem ōdērant.
The citizens hated that wretched consul.

It is worth learning these special forms of defective verbs to do with speech and greetings because you are likely come across them:

ait he/she says; **aiunt** they say

inquit he/she says

fātus having spoken

mementō! remember!

avē! and **salvē!** hello! (to one person); **salvēte!** hello! (to more than one person)

valē! goodbye! (to one person); **valēte!** goodbye! (to more than one person)

Key points

- Some Latin verbs known as defective verbs have only a few forms.
- It is worth learning the commonest forms which are used in speech and greetings.

Exercise 16

Use all the information on deponent and defective verbs so far, and the examples used, to find the Latin for:

a They were trying. ....

b Follow! (singular) ....

c We will be glad. ....

d You (masculine plural) have lied. ....

e She had been afraid. ....

f I will have suffered. (masculine) ....

g You (feminine singular) dared. ....

h They are about to follow. (masculine)

....

i I begin. ....

j She knew. ....

k You (plural) remembered. ....

l We hate. ....

Negatives

What is a negative?
A negative statement is one which contains a word such as *not*, *never*, or *nothing* and is used to say that something is not happening, is not true, or is absent.

Using negatives

In English, we use words like *not*, *no*, *never*, and *nothing* to show a negative.
- I'm ***not*** pleased.
- There's ***no*** food left.
- ***Nothing*** ever happens.
- She ***never*** contacted me.

Not is often combined with certain English verbs – for example, *can't*, *won't*, *didn't*, *hasn't*.
- I ***can't*** wait.
- They ***didn't*** say.

In Latin, if you want to make something negative, you use an adverb like **nōn** (meaning *not*) before the verb, a noun like **nēmō** (meaning *no one, nobody*), or an adjective like **nūllus**, **nūlla**, **nūllum** (meaning *not any, no*).

Adverbs

nōn	*not*
nōndum	*not yet*
numquam	*never, not … ever*
nūsquam	*nowhere*

Nouns

nēmō	*no one, nobody*
nihil	*nothing*

Adjectives

nūllus, nūlla, nūllum	*not any, no*

hospitēs mihi <u>nōn</u> grātiās ēgērunt.	*My guests did not thank me.*
cibus <u>nōndum</u> parātus est.	*The food is not yet ready.*
ōrnātrīx <u>numquam</u> sērius advenit.	*The hairdresser never arrives too late.*

<u>nēmō</u> crūdēlem amat.	*No one loves a cruel person.*
<u>nūlla</u> ancilla crūdēlem dominum amat.	*No slave-girl loves a cruel master.*

> ✔ **Tip**
>
> Remember that **nēmō** is a noun which only has other forms in the accusative and dative: **nēminem** and **nēminī**. For the genitive and ablative cases, you use **nūllīus** and **nūllō**. The neuter noun **nihil** only has a nominative and accusative form.
>
> **rēx nēminī crēdit.** *The king believes no one.*
>
> **pauper hodiē nihil ēdit.** *The poor man ate nothing today.*

For more information on Nouns, Adjectives or Adverbs, see pages 2, 16, and 127.

You use the word **haud** (meaning *not*) if you are talking about other adverbs, adjectives, or some verbs of knowing and thinking (followed by **an** + the subjunctive).

haud procul	*not far away*
haud facilis	*not easy*
haud scio an īre mihi liceat.	*I don't know whether I'm allowed to go.*
haudquāquam dubitō.	*I have absolutely no doubt.*

In English, *do* or *did* is often added when you make a statement negative.

I like him. → *I* ***do*** *not like him.*

We saw them at the weekend. → *We* ***did*** *not see them at the weekend.*

Note that the Latin verb **facere** is **NEVER** used in this way.

As in English, you can use two negatives in Latin to make an affirmative statement.

<u>nūllī</u> comitēs <u>nōn</u> vēnērunt.

All his comrades came (without exception).

The conjunction **nec** or **neque** (meaning *nor*) is used instead of **et nōn**.

ille iuvenis est probus nec mendāx.

That young man is honest and not a liar.

nec is also used to connect other words in a negative statement.

nec quisquam	*and no one*
nec ūllus	*and no one*
nec quidquam	*and nothing*
nec umquam	*and never*

For more information on Conjunctions, see page 139.

neque ... **neque** is the equivalent of the English *neither* ... *nor*.

neque anus neque virgō sum.
Neither an old woman nor a maid am I.

> ✔ **TIP**
> If you are using a verb in the subjunctive, you should use the word **nē** to make the sentence negative.
> **nē videam!** *Let me not see!*

For more information on the Subjunctive, see page 95.

minimē (meaning *no, not at all*) is the usual negative answer to a question.

mēne fugis? minimē!
Are you running away from me? No!

> **KEY POINTS**
> - Negatives indicate when something is not happening or is not true. Latin uses adverbs like **nōn** (or **haud**) to indicate this, as well as certain nouns and adjectives.
> - Two negatives used in the same sentence make it affirmative.
> - Latin does not use **et nōn** but **nec**.
> - Latin does not generally use **nōn** with the subjunctive but **nē**.

Exercise 17

Use all the information on negatives so far, and the examples used, to work out the Latin for *the words in italics* in the following sentences.

a The woman did *not* walk to the theatre.

....

b A merchant saw *no* slaves in the street.

....

c Did the teacher find a book for the boy? *No*.

....

d *Neither* the Senate *nor* the people were deceived by the consuls.

....

e 'I have *never* done my best, master,' replied the cook.

....

f *None of* the nations of the East are *not* in revolt.

....

g *No one* ran away from the bridge before it collapsed.

....

h May they *not* give food to the animals.

....

i Hannibal *and not* Caesar led his army over the Alps into Italy.

....

j I do *not* doubt she left at the final hour of the day.

....

Questions

What is a question?
A question is a sentence which is used to ask someone about something. A question word such as *who?*, *what?*, *why?*, *where?*, *how?* is used to ask a question.

How to ask a question in Latin

The basic rules

There are three main ways of asking questions in Latin:
- by making your voice go up at the end of the sentence
- by adding **-ne** to the end of the first word in the sentence
- by using a question word at the start of the sentence

Asking a question by making your voice go up

If you are expecting the answer to be either *yes* or *no*, there is a very straightforward way of asking a question. You can keep the word order just as it would be in a normal sentence (subject then verb), but turn it into a question by making your voice go up at the end of the sentence. So to turn the sentence **pecūniam habēs** (meaning: *You have some money*) into a question, all you need to do is to add a question mark and make your voice go up at the end.

pecūniam habēs?	*Do you have some money?*
statim discēdimus.	*We're leaving right away.*
statim discēdimus?	*Are we leaving right away?*
pater est in tablīnō.	*My father is in his study.*
pater est in tablīnō?	*Is my father in his study?*

Asking a question by using -ne

The ending **-ne** is used in asking questions. The verb often appears first in a question using **-ne** since it is the word being stressed. **-ne** is added to the first word in the sentence. So to turn the sentence **Corinnam nōvistī** (meaning: *You know Corinna*) into a question, all you need to do is put the verb first and add **-ne** on the end of it.

nōvistī<u>ne</u> Corinnam?	*Do you know Corinna?*
ītis<u>ne</u> ad forum?	*Are you going to the market?*
est<u>ne</u> tua soror laeta?	*Is your sister happy?*

Asking a question by using a question word

A question word is a word like *when?* or *how?* that is used to ask for information. Many question words in Latin are adverbs, and they are sometimes words that we do not have an equivalent for in English. The most common Latin question words are listed below.

For more information on Adverbs, see page 127.

an? when you want to show that you are surprised or annoyed.

<u>an</u> nescīs quae sit illa puella?	*Do you really not know who that girl is?*

cūr? Why?

<u>cūr</u> nōbīscum nōn venit?	*Why isn't he coming with us?*

Instead of **cūr?** you could use **quārē?**, **quam ob rem?**, or **quid?**

nōnne? when you want to suggest that the answer will be *yes*.

<u>nōnne</u> istam cēnam meministī?	*You remember that terrible dinner, don't you?*

num? when you want to suggest that the answer will be *no*.

<u>num</u> lībertus es?	*You're not a freedman, are you?*

quandō? When?

<u>quandō</u> advēnit amīcus?	*When did your friend arrive?*

quō? Where to?

<u>quō</u> vādis?	*Where are you going (to)?*

quam? How? (used with an adjective or adverb)

<u>quam</u> urbānī sunt illī iuvenēs?	*How trendy are those young men?*
<u>quam</u> celeriter cucurrit nūntius?	*How quickly did the messenger run?*

quamdiū? How long?

<u>quamdiū</u> manēbimus, domine?	*How long shall we wait, master?*

quōmodō? In what way?

<u>quōmodō</u> hoc verbum dīcitur?	*How do you say this word?*

Instead of **quōmodō?** you could use **quemadmodum?**

quot? How many?

quot āctōrēs erant in scaenā?	*How many actors were there on the stage?*

quotiēns? How often?

quotiēns illa lacrimābat?	*How often did she cry?*

ubi? Where?

ubi habitant?	*Where do they live?*

Instead of **ubi?** you could use **quā?**

utrum ... an? when you want to ask whether one thing happened or another. You can sometimes leave out the word **utrum**. The negative form of **an** is **annōn**.

utrum rīsit an lacrimāvit?	*Did he laugh or did he cry?*
fēlem an canem ēmistī?	*Did you buy a cat or a dog?*
eōs vīdistis annōn?	*Did you see them or not?*

In questions, **quī**, **quae**, **quod?** (meaning *which? what?*) and **quis**, **quid?** (meaning *who? what?*) are both pronouns.

quī captīvī sunt in carcere?	*Which prisoners are in jail?*
quis est in carcere?	*Who is in jail?*
quid accidit?	*What happened?*

For more information on Pronouns, see page 27.

quālis, **quāle?** (meaning *what sort of?*), **quantus**, **quanta**, **quantum?** (meaning *how large?*), and **uter**, **utra**, **utrum?** (meaning *which (out of two)?*) are all adjectives.

quāle cōnsilium cēpit?	*What kind of plan did she make?*
quantum est amphitheātrum Rōmae?	*How large is the amphitheatre in Rome?*
uter gladiātor erat victor?	*Which gladiator was the winner?*

For more information on Adjectives, see page 16.

Key points

- You can ask a question by keeping the same word order as a normal statement but making your voice go up at the end.
- You can ask a question by changing the word order and adding **-ne** to the first word in the question.
- You can ask a question by starting off with a question word.
- Question words can be adverbs, pronouns or adjectives.

Exercise 18

Use all the information on questions so far, and the examples used, to work out the Latin for *the words in italics* in the following sentences.

a *Where* did the woman walk *to*?

....

b *How many* slaves did the merchant see in the street?

....

c *What* did the teacher find for the boy?

....

d *Where* is the size of the temples legendary?

....

e *Why* was the Senate deceived by the consuls?

....

f Have I done well *or* badly, master?' asked the cook.

....

g *How often* were the nations of the East in revolt?

....

h *Surely* they ran away from the bridge before it collapsed?

....

i 'Citizens!' shouted the king, 'will you stand and fight *or not*?'

....

j *Who* gave food to the animals?

....

k *When* did Hannibal lead his army over the Alps into Italy?

....

l *Did she leave* at the final hour of the day?

....

Adverbs

What is an adverb?
Like an adjective, an adverb is a 'describing' word, but it is used to give more information about when, where, how or in what circumstances something happens (for example, *now*, *there*, *easily*, *quickly*).

Using adverbs

Adverbs can tell you more about a verb (what someone or something does or is, or what happens to them). They can also tell you more about an adjective or another adverb. Generally adverbs are used right next to the word they are describing:
- verbs (speak ***soon***, act ***cruelly***)
- adjectives (***a little*** late, ***extremely*** happy)
- adverbs (***too*** slowly, ***very*** easily)

Adverbs can also relate to a whole sentence, often telling you more about what the speaker is thinking or feeling.
- ***Perhaps*** it was the best thing to do.
- They did not see us, ***fortunately***.

✔ **Tip**
In Latin, the adverb comes before the verb, adjective, or adverb it describes; but if it refers to time, then it often comes at the beginning of the sentence.

For more information on Verbs or Adjectives, see pages 42 and 16.

Adverbs in Latin **NEVER** change their form, no matter what they refer to.

Many English adverbs end in *-ly*, which is added to the end of the adjective (*easy – easily*; *quick – quickly*). In Latin, adjectives that follow the pattern of nouns in the first and second declension change the ending of the genitive singular case to **-ē**.

Adjective	Genitive singular masculine	Adverb	Meaning
laetus	**laetī**	**laetē**	happily
miser	**miserī**	**miserē**	unhappily
pulcher	**pulchrī**	**pulchrē**	beautifully

A few, however, can form adverbs from their ablative singular masculine (ending in **-ō**). For example, **subitus** (meaning *sudden*) changes to **subitō**; **certus** (meaning *certain*) can change to **certē** or **certō**; and **vērus** (meaning *true*) to **vērē** or **vērō**.

Adjectives of the third declension usually change the ending of the genitive singular to **-ter** or **-iter**.

Adjective	Genitive singular	Adverb	Meaning
prūdēns	**prūdentis**	**prūdenter**	shrewdly
fēlīx	**fēlīcis**	**fēlīciter**	luckily
fortis	**fortis**	**fortiter**	bravely
ācer	**ācris**	**ācriter**	keenly
celer	**celeris**	**celeriter**	fast, quickly

A few third declension adjectives, however, form adverbs from their accusative singular neuter (ending in **-e**). For example, **facilis** changes to **facile** (meaning *easily*) and **difficilis** to **difficile** (meaning *with difficulty*).

✔ **Tip**

There are many adverbs that are not formed from an adjective and it is worth learning some of the commonest ones.

diū	*for a long time*	**mox**	*soon*
fortē	*by chance*	**quoque**	*also*
iam	*now, already*	**saepe**	*often*
ibi	*there*	**semper**	*always*
inde	*from there*	**sīc**	*in this way*
iterum	*again*	**statim**	*immediately*

Key points

- Adverbs in Latin do not change their form.
- Most adjectives that follow the pattern of first and second declension nouns form adverbs ending in **-e**.
- Most adjectives that follow the pattern of third declension nouns form adverbs ending in **-ter** or **-iter**.
- Some very common adverbs are not formed from an adjective. They are worth learning.

Comparison of adverbs

In English, we can add *-er* or *-est* to the end of an adverb. For example, *sooner* is what we call the ***comparative*** form of the adverb *soon*, and *soonest* is the ***superlative*** form. We can also add words like *more* or *most* and *quite* or *very* in front of an adverb (for example, *easily – more easily*, *quickly – very quickly*).

Forming comparatives and superlatives

The comparative form of an adverb in Latin is the same as the nominative singular neuter of the comparative adjective; the superlative form of an adverb takes the nominative singular masculine of the superlative adjective and changes the **-us** ending to **-ē**.

Comparative adjective	Comparative adverb	Meaning	Superlative adjective	Superlative adverb	Meaning
laetior	**laetius**	more happily	**laetissimus**	**laetissimē**	most happily, very happily
prūdentior	**prūdentius**	more shrewdly	**prūdentissimus**	**prūdentissimē**	most shrewdly, very shrewdly
ācrior	**ācrius**	more keenly	**ācerrimus**	**ācerrimē**	most keenly, very keenly
facilior	**facilius**	more easily	**facillimus**	**facillimē**	most easily, very easily

Irregular comparatives and superlatives

Just as English has some irregular comparative and superlative forms – *better* instead of 'more well', and *worst* instead of 'most badly' – several common adverbs in Latin also have irregular forms.

Adjective	Meaning	Comparative	Meaning	Superlative	Meaning
bene	well	**melius**	better	**optimē**	best, very well
male	badly	**peius**	worse	**pessimē**	worst, very badly
paulum	little	**minus**	less	**minimē**	least, very little
multum	much	**plūs**	more	**plūrimum**	most, very much

magnopere	greatly	**magis**	more	**maximē**	most, very greatly
diū	for a long time	**diūtius**	longer	**diūtissimē**	longest, for a very long time
prope	near	**propius**	nearer	**proximē**	nearest, very near
saepe	often	**saepius**	more often	**saepissimē**	most often, very often

Special uses of comparatives and superlatives

In the same way that you can sometimes use the superlative form in Latin to mean *very*, you can sometimes use the comparative form to mean *quite* or *too*.

fēlīcissimē *very luckily*
celerius *too fast, too quickly*

Adverbs can be used to make comparisons in Latin just as they can in English. As with adjectives, use the comparative followed by the conjunction **quam** (meaning *than*) and the ablative, or simply use the ablative case.

prūdentius quam mercātōre *more shrewdly than the merchant*
prūdentius mercātōre *more shrewdly than the merchant*

For more information on Conjunctions, see page 139.

Like adjectives, adverbs can be included in the phrase *as ... as possible*, using **quam** followed by the superlative.

quam minimē *as little as possible*
quam celerrimē *as fast as possible*

Key points

- The ending of the comparative form of an adverb in Latin is usually **-ius**.
- The ending of the superlative form is usually **-issimē**, but sometimes **-errimē** or **-illimē**.
- Some common adverbs like **bene**, **male**, **paulum** and **multum** have irregular comparative and superlative forms.
- Unlike adjectives, adverbs do not change their form to agree with the verb, adjective or other adverb they relate to.

Exercise 19

Use all the information on adverbs so far, and the examples used, to work out the Latin for *the words in italics* in the following sentences.

a The woman walked *happily* to the theatre.

....

b A merchant *also* saw the slaves in the street.

....

c The teacher found a book for the boy *as quickly as possible*.

....

d The size of the temples in Rome is *already* legendary.

....

e The Senate was *more easily* deceived by the consuls.

....

f 'I have *always* done my best, master,' replied the cook.

....

g The nations of the East are *often* in revolt.

....

h They *immediately* ran away from the bridge before it collapsed.

....

i 'Citizens!' shouted the king, 'stand and fight *more keenly*!'

....

j *For a very long time* no one gave any food to the animals.

....

k Hannibal *bravely* led his army over the Alps into Italy.

....

l She left *suddenly* at the final hour of the day.

....

Prepositions

What is a preposition?
A preposition is a word such as *at*, *for*, *with*, *into*, or *from* which is usually followed by a noun, pronoun or, in English, a word ending in *-ing*. Prepositions show how people and things relate to the rest of the sentence – for example: *She's at home*; *I've got a tool for cutting the wire*; *This letter is from David*.

Using prepositions

Prepositions are used in front of nouns and pronouns (such as *me*, *her*, *the man*, and so on), and show the relationship between the noun or pronoun and the rest of the sentence. Some prepositions can be used before verb forms ending in *-ing* in English.

I showed my receipt ***to*** *the assistant.*
Come ***with*** *us.*
This cloth is really good ***at*** *cleaning windows.*

For more information on Nouns or Pronouns, see pages 2 and 27.

In English, it is possible to finish a sentence with a preposition such as *for*, *about*, *to*, or *on*, even though some people think this is not good grammar – for example: *Who is this for?*; *That's not what I am talking about*. You can **NEVER** end a Latin sentence with a preposition.

✔ TIP
The Latin preposition is not always the direct equivalent of the preposition that is used in English. It is often difficult to give just one English equivalent for Latin prepositions, as the way they are used varies so much between the two languages.

As in English, prepositions in Latin never change their form. However, the noun or pronoun that follows the preposition will change its ending to either the ***accusative case*** or the ***ablative case***, depending on the meaning of the preposition.

The most common prepositions in Latin are listed below.

Prepositions followed by the ablative case

ā (meaning *from* a person, place or time, or *by* a person) or **ab** if the noun or pronoun following it begins with a vowel:

ā nōbīs abesse	*to be distant **from** us*
hostēs ab arce dēiectī sunt.	*The enemy was driven **from** the citadel.*
ā dextrā	***from** the right*
ā tertiā hōrā	***from** the third hour*
comitibus desertus	*deserted **by** his comrades*

However, if you are talking about going ***away from*** a town or an island that has just one town on it, you do not use the preposition **ā** or **ab**. This is also the case for the nouns **domus** (meaning *a house*), **humus** (meaning *the ground*), and **rūs** (meaning *the country*).

Rōmā	***from** Rome*
Pompēiīs	***from** Pompeii*
rūre	***from** the country*

> ✔ **TIP**
> When you use the word *by* with things, you do not use the preposition **ā** or **ab**. When you use it with animals, you can choose whether to use the preposition or not.
>
> | | |
> |---|---|
> | **clāmōribus excitātī sumus.** | *We were awakened **by** shouts.* |
> | **canibus excitātī =** | |
> | **ā canibus excitātī** | *awakened **by** dogs* |

cum (meaning *with*):

cum cūrā loquī	*to speak **with** care*
summā cum laude	***with** distinction*

> ✔ **TIP**
> If you are using **cum** with a pronoun like *me*, you join the preposition to the end of it.
>
> | | |
> |---|---|
> | **vāde mēcum.** | *Go **with** me.* |

For more information on Pronouns, see page 27.

dē (meaning *down from* or *about*):

dē caelō dēmittere	*to send* ***down from*** *heaven*
dē hāc rē cogitābam.	*I was thinking* ***about*** *this issue.*
quid dē nōbīs fīet?	*What will become* ***of*** *us?*
dē industriā	***on*** *purpose*

ē (meaning *out of* or *from*) or **ex** if the noun or pronoun following it begins with a vowel:

ē carcere effugērunt.	*They escaped* ***from*** *prison.*
ē fenestrā dēsiluit.	*He jumped* ***out of*** *the window.*
quidam ex Hispaniā	*someone* ***from*** *Spain*
ex illō diē	***from*** *that day*

Like with **ā** or **ab**, if you are talking about going ***away from*** a town or an island that has just one town on it, you do not use the preposition **ē** or **ex**. This is also the case for the nouns **domus**, **humus**, and **rūs**.

in (meaning *in*, *on*, or *within*):

puella in illā vīllā laete vīvēbat.	*The girl lived happily* ***in*** *that house.*
in capite corōnam gerēbat.	*He used to wear a crown* ***on*** *his head.*
in animō habēre	*to have* ***in*** *one's mind*
in omnī aetāte	***in*** *every age*

However, if you are talking about something happening ***in*** a town or on an island that has just one town on it, you use what is known as the ***locative case*** instead of the preposition **in**. This is also the case for the nouns **domus**, **humus**, and **rūs**.

Londiniī	***in*** *London*
Athēnīs	***in*** *Athens*
domī	***at*** *home*
humī	***on*** *the ground*

prō (meaning *in front of* or *on behalf of*):

prō iūdice	***in front of*** *the judge*
prō patriā morī	*to die* ***for*** *your country*
prō sē quisque	*everyone* ***for*** *themselves*

sine (meaning *without*):

sine spē	***without*** *hope or hope****less***
sine pecūniā	*penni****less***

sub (meaning positioned *under* a place or power):

sub saxō	***under*** *a rock*
sub principe Rōmānō	***under*** (the authority of) *the Roman emperor*

super (meaning positioned *over* or *above*):

super terrā marīque	***over*** *land and sea*
super montibus	***above*** *the mountains*

Prepositions followed by the accusative case

ad (meaning *to*, *towards*, or *at*):

ad theātrum contendēbant.	*They were hurrying* ***to*** *the theatre.*
oculōs ad caelum sustulit.	*He raised his eyes* ***towards*** *heaven.*
ad portās	***at*** *the gates*
nīl ad mē attinet.	*It means nothing* ***to*** *me.*

However, if you are talking about going ***to*** a town or an island that has just one town on it, you do not use the preposition **ad**. This is also the case for the nouns **domus** (meaning *a house*), **humus** (meaning *the ground*), and **rūs** (meaning *the country*).

Londinium	***to*** *London*
Athēnās	***to*** *Athens*
domum	*home, home**wards***

Like with **in** when it is followed by the ablative case, if you are talking about something happening ***at*** a town or an island that has just one town on it, you use the ***locative case*** instead of the preposition **ad**. This is also the case for the nouns **domus**, **humus**, and **rūs**.

adversum or **adversus** (meaning *opposite*, *facing*, or *against*):

sedēns adversum tē	*sitting* ***opposite*** *you*
adversus Ītaliam	***facing*** *Italy*
adversum flūmen	***against*** *the river,* ***up****stream*

ante (meaning *before*):

ante merīdiem	***before*** *midday*
ante iānuam	***before*** *the door*

apud (meaning *at the house of* or *among*):

apud eum	***at** his house*
apud Graecōs	***among** the Greeks*
apud Platōnem	***in** (the works of) Plato*

circum or **circā** (meaning *around* or *about*):

circum senātum	***around** the senate*
circā decem mīlia Gallōrum	***about** 10,000 Gauls*

contrā (meaning *against* or *facing*):

contrā hostēs	***against** the enemy*
contrā Britanniam	***facing** Britain*

extrā (meaning *outside* or *beyond*):

extrā mūrōs oppidī	***outside** the walls of the town*
extrā iocum	***beyond** a joke, joking **apart***

in (meaning *into*, *against*, or *until*):

in urbem venīre	*to come **into** the city*
in rem publicam aggredī	*to attack the state*
in prīmam lūcem dormīvit.	*He slept **until** dawn.*

Like with **ad**, if you are talking about going into a town or an island that has just one town on it, you do not use the preposition **in**. This is also the case for the nouns **domus**, **humus**, and **rūs**.

inter (meaning *among*, *between*, or *during*):

inter sauciōs	***among** the wounded*
inter oppositās factiōnēs	***between** opposing political parties*
inter manūs	***within** reach*
inter hōs annōs	***during** these years*

intrā (meaning *inside* or *within*):

intrā hōs quattuor pariētēs	***within** these four walls*
intrā quinque annōs	***within** five years*

ob (meaning *because of*):

ob stultitiam	***because of** your foolishness*
quam ob rem	***therefore** (literally **because of** which thing)*

per (meaning *through* or *by means of*):

per noctem	***through*** *the night*
per aetātem periit.	*He died* ***of*** *old age.*
per deōs iūrō.	*I swear* ***by*** *the gods.*

post (meaning *after* or *behind*):

post urbem conditam	***after*** *the foundation of the city*
post tergum	***behind*** *your back*

praeter (meaning *beyond*, *beside*, or *except*):

praeter natūram	***beyond*** *nature*
praeter sē trēs aliōs addūxit.	*He brought three others* ***besides*** *himself.*
praeter paucōs	***except for*** *a few*

prope (meaning *near*):

prope thermās habitāvit.	*He lived* ***near*** *the baths.*

propter (meaning *because of*):

propter metum mortis	***because of*** *the fear of death*

secundum (meaning *along* or *according to*):

secundum lītus	***along*** *the shore*
secundum natūram	***according to*** *nature*

sub (meaning to move *under* or *beneath*):

sub iugum mittere	*to send* ***into*** *slavery* (literally ***under*** *the yoke*)
sub ipsum mūrum	*just* ***beneath*** *the wall*

super (meaning to move *over*):

super capita hostium	***over*** *the heads of the enemy*
aliī super aliōs advēnērunt.	*They arrived one* ***on top of*** *another.*

trāns (meaning *across*):

trāns Rubicōnem	***across*** *the Rubicon*

ultrā (meaning *beyond*):

ultrā vīrēs	***beyond*** *our power*

Key points

- Prepositions in Latin are followed by the ablative or the accusative case.
- Many of them have several possible meanings, which depend upon the context they are used in.
- Some place-names and the nouns **domus**, **humus**, and **rūs** do not use prepositions to show the meaning *to*, *from*, or *in*.

Exercise 20

Use all the information on prepositions so far, and the examples used, to work out the Latin for *the words in italics* in the following sentences.

a The woman walked *to the theatre*.

....

b A merchant saw the slaves *in the street*.

....

c The size of the temples *in Rome* is legendary.

....

d They ran *away from the bridge* before it collapsed.

....

e 'Citizens!' shouted the king *in Athens*, 'stand and fight!'

....

f Hannibal led his army *over the mountains into Italy*.

....

Conjunctions

What is a conjunction?
A conjunction is a word such as *and*, *but*, *so*, *if*, and *because* that links two words or phrases of a similar type, or two parts of a sentence – for example: *Alice <u>and</u> I went to the cinema yesterday*; *We left <u>because</u> we were bored.*

Using conjunctions

In English, the same word can sometimes be used as a conjunction and as a preposition.

- Augustus was emperor some years ***before*** (conjunction) Claudius was born.
- Augustus was emperor some years ***before*** (preposition) Claudius.
- Domitian became emperor ***after*** (conjunction) Titus had died.
- Domitian became emperor ***after*** (preposition) Titus.

In Latin, a different word is used to distinguish between the two. For example, you use **prō** or **ante** to mean *before* when it is a preposition, and **antequam** when it is a conjunction; you use **post** to mean *after* when it is a preposition, and **postquam** when it is a conjunction.

For more information on Prepositions, see page 132.

As in English, conjunctions in Latin never change their form. Sometimes, however, when you use a conjunction to link two parts of a sentence, you have to use a form of the verb in the ***subjunctive***. When you come across a new conjunction that is used to link two parts of a sentence, it is a good idea to learn what form of the verb it is followed by.

For more information on the Subjunctive, see page 95.

The most common conjunctions in Latin are listed below.

and, but, or, however, and **therefore**

and, *but*, *or*, *however*, and *therefore* can be said in a number of different ways in Latin. They are some of the most common conjunctions that you need to know.

ac, **atque**, **et**, **-que** and

in Germāniā ac in Britanniā	*in Germany **and** in Britain*
Marcus Antōnius atque Cleopatra	*Mark Antony **and** Cleopatra*
leō et pūlex	*The Lion **and** the Flea*
Athēnās Alexandrīamque vīsitant.	*They are visiting Athens **and** Alexandria.*

Note that **-que** is added to the end of the second word in the pair that is being joined together.

et ... **et**, **vel** ... **vel** both ... and

et leōnēs et tigrēs	***both** lions **and** tigers*
vel Platōnem vel Aristotelem lēgī.	*I have read **both** Plato **and** Aristotle.*

> ✔ **Tip**
>
> The negative of **et** is **nec** or **neque** (meaning *nor* or *and not*) and the negative of **et** ... **et** is **nec** ... **nec** or **neque** ... **neque** (meaning *neither ... nor*).
>
> | | |
> |---|---|
> | **in Graeciā nec in Ītaliā** | *in Greece **and not** in Italy* |
> | **neque pāstor neque leō** | ***neither** the shepherd **nor** the lion* |

For more information on the Negative, see page 119.

at, **sed** but

at spectātōrēs 'ēheu!' clāmāvērunt.	***But** the spectators cried, 'Oh no!'*
omnēs aurum cupiunt sed paucī argentum.	*Everyone wants gold **but** few people want silver.*

aut or

canis aut fēlēs	*a dog **or** a cat*

aut ... **aut** either ... or

canis aut muscā aut pūlice morsus est.	*The dog was bitten **either** by a fly **or** by a flea.*

autem, **tamen**, **vērum** however

rēgīna autem nōn īrāta est.	*The queen, **however**, was not angry.*
Herculēs tamen mōnstrum interfēcit.	*Hercules, **however**, killed the ogre.*
semper pluit, vērum in Britanniā habitāre volunt.	*It always rains, **however** they want to live in Britain.*

ergō, **igitur**, **itaque** therefore, and so

fortissimus sum, ergō tē nōn timeō.	*I am very brave, **therefore** I am not afraid of you.*
mīlitēs igitur imperātōrī crēdēbant.	***Therefore** the soldiers trusted their general.*
mendāx est, itaque fīdus nōn erit.	*He's a liar, and so he won't be trustworthy.*

enim, **nam** for

quam crūdēlis est! virgō enim mē nōn amat.	*How cruel she is! **For** the girl doesn't love me.*
hospitēs ancillam laudant, nam ea suāviter cantat.	*The guests praise the slave-girl, **for** she sings sweetly.*

Note that **autem**, **tamen**, **igitur**, and **enim** come second in the sentence.

Some other common conjunctions

Here are some other common Latin conjunctions:

antequam, **priusquam** before

Marcus discessit antequam sōl ortus est.	*Marcus left **before** the sun rose.*

Note that **antequam** and **priusquam** are sometimes split into two words.

Marcus ante discessit quam sōl ortus est.	*Marcus left **before** the sun rose.*

Note that if you are using **priusquam** with an additional sense of purpose or uncertainty, then the verb form will be the ***subjunctive***.

For more information on When to use the Subjunctive, see page 104.

cum when, whenever
if you are talking about the present or future:

<u>cum</u> sorōrem tuam vīderis, eam nōlī vituperāre.	***When*** *you see your sister, do not be rude to her.*

if it involves the main action of the sentence:

pāstor dormiēbat, <u>cum</u> ursus eum petīvit.	*The shepherd was asleep* ***when*** *the bear attacked him.*

if you are putting a big emphasis on what was happening:

<u>cum</u> tū in hortō sedēbās, ego in culīnā labōrābam.	***When*** *you were sitting in the garden, I was working in the kitchen.*

cum means *whenever*, and you use the perfect if the main action is in the present and the pluperfect if the main action is in the past:

cum canis fēlem <u>vīdit</u>, ferōciter lātrat.	*Whenever the dog sees the cat, it barks fiercely.*
cum <u>errāveram</u>, dominus mē pūniēbat.	*Whenever I made a mistake, my master used to punish me.*

Note that if you are using **cum** (meaning *when*) to show the time something happened, then the verb form will be the ***subjunctive***.

For more information on When to use the Subjunctive, see page 104.

dōnec, **dum** until, while, as long as

canis in mēnsā stābat <u>dōnec</u> coquus eum cōnspexit.	*The dog stood on the table* ***until*** *the cook caught sight of it.*
coquus dormiēbat dum canis lātrāvit.	*The cook was asleep* ***until*** *the dog barked.*

Note that the tense of the verb used in Latin is not always the same as the tense that we naturally use in English. Where in English we use the imperfect tense in a sentence beginning with *while*, Latin will use the present tense.

<u>dum</u> bellum in Germāniā <u>geritur</u>, multī interfectī sunt.	*While the war* ***was being waged*** *in Germany, many were killed.*

For more information on the Present tense, see page 42.

Note that if you are using **dōnec** or **dum** with an additional sense of purpose or uncertainty, then the verb form will be the ***subjunctive***.

For more information on When to use the subjunctive, see page 104.

quamquam although

<u>quamquam</u> gladiātor callidissimus erat, is interfectus est. — ***Although*** *the gladiator was very cunning, he was killed.*

Note that if you are using **quamvīs** or **cum** (meaning *although*), then the verb form will be the ***subjunctive***.

For more information on When to use the subjunctive, see page 104.

postquam after

dominus ad vīllam rediit <u>postquam</u> fundum īnspexit. — *The master returned to his villa* ***after*** *he had inspected the farm.*

quia, **quod**, **quoniam** because, since

quia fessus erat, mox dormiēbat. — *Because he was tired, he was soon asleep.*

quod valēs, gaudeō. — *Since you are well, I am pleased.*

Note that if you are using **quia** or **quod** (meaning *because*) and you are quoting a reason put forward by somebody else that you might or might not agree with, or **cum** (meaning *since*), then the verb form will be the ***subjunctive***.

For more information on When to use the subjunctive, see page 104.

sī if

<u>sī</u> servus pecūniam nōn habet, miser est. — ***If*** *the slave has no money, he is sad.*

<u>sī</u> servus pecūniam cēpit, scelus grave commīsit. — ***If*** *the slave took the money, he's committed a serious crime.*

Note that where we use the present tense in English in a sentence beginning with *if*, Latin will use the future or future perfect tense.

<u>sī</u> servus pecūniam <u>cēperit</u>, dominus eum pūniat. — ***If*** *the slave* ***takes*** (literally *will have taken) the money, his master will punish him.*

For more information on the Future and Future perfect tenses, see pages 63 and 75.

> ✔ **TIP**
> The negative of **sī** is **nisi** (meaning *unless* or *if ... not*).
> **<u>nisi</u> novae cōpiae missae erint, oppidum capiētur.**
> ***Unless** reinforcements are sent, the town will be captured.*
> **nēmō <u>nisi</u> cōmis hūc admittitur.**
> *No one is admitted here **unless** well-dressed.*

To give more emphasis, you can use **etsī** or **tametsī** (meaning *even if*).

<u>etsī</u> ea mox adveniat, sērius erit.	***Even if** she arrives soon, she will be too late.*

Note that if you are using **sī**, **etsī**, or **tametsī** to talk about things that might happen or would have happened, then the verb form will be the ***subjunctive***.

For more information on When to use the subjunctive, see page 104.

simulac, **simulatque** as soon as

<u>simulac</u> iānuam pulsāvī, canis lātrāvit.	***As soon as** I knocked on the door, the dog barked.*

ubi when

<u>ubi</u> senātōrēs cōnsilium audīverant, libenter cōnsēnsērunt.	***When** the senators had heard the plan, they willingly agreed.*

ut when, as

<u>ut</u> valētūdō Germānicī nuntiāta est, magna īra erat.	***When** Germanicus' state of health was reported, there was great anger.*
Herculēs leōnem petīvit <u>ut</u> canis fēlem agitat.	*Hercules attacked the lion **as** a dog chases a cat.*

Note that if you are using **ut** to mean *in order that* or *so that*, then the verb form will be the ***subjunctive***.

For more information on When to use the subjunctive, see page 104.

> **KEY POINTS**
> - Many conjunctions in Latin have several possible meanings, which depend upon the context they are used in.
> - **cum**, **sī** and **ut** are the commonest conjunctions that are sometimes followed by the subjunctive form of the verb.

Exercise 21

Use all the information on conjunctions so far, and the examples used, to work out the Latin for *the words in italics* in the following sentences.

a *When* the woman walked to the theatre, it was still early.

....

b *While* the merchant was in the street, he saw the slaves.

....

c *As soon as* the teacher found the book, he gave it to the boy.

....

d *For* the size of the temples in Rome is legendary.

....

e The Senate, *therefore*, was deceived by the consuls.

....

f '*And so* I have done my best, master,' replied the cook.

....

g The nations of *both* the East *and* the West are in revolt.

....

h They ran away from the bridge *before* it collapsed.

....

i 'Citizens!' shouted the king, '*either* flee *or* fight!'

....

j *But* no one gave any food to the animals.

....

k Hannibal, *however*, led his army over the Alps into Italy.

....

l She left *as* the final hour of the day approached.

....

Numbers

Cardinal numbers

What is a cardinal number?
In Latin, a cardinal number tells you how many there are of something, or how many people there are (for example, *one*, *sixteen*, *twenty-one*).

1	I	**ūnus, ūna, ūnum**
2	II	**duo, duae, duo**
3	III	**trēs, tria**
4	IV	**quattuor**
5	V	**quīnque**
6	VI	**sex**
7	VII	**septem**
8	VIII	**octō**
9	IX	**novem**
10	X	**decem**
11	XI	**ūndecim**
12	XII	**duodecim**
13	XIII	**trēdecim**
14	XIV	**quattuordecim**
15	XV	**quīndecim**
16	XVI	**sēdecim**
17	XVII	**septendecim**
18	XVIII	**duodēvīgintī**
19	XIX	**ūndēvīgintī**
20	XX	**vīgintī**
21	XXI	**ūnus et vīgintī** (or **vīgintī ūnus**)
30	XXX	**trīgintā**
40	XL	**quadrāgintā**
50	L	**quīnquāgintā**
60	LX	**sexāgintā**
70	LXX	**septuāgintā**
80	LXXX	**octōgintā**
90	XC	**nōnāgintā**
100	C	**centum**
200	CC	**ducentī, ducentae, ducenta**
300	CCC	**trecentī, trecentae, trecenta**
400	CCCC	**quadringentī, quadringentae, quadringenta**

500	D	**quīngentī, quīngentae, quīngenta**
600	DC	**sescentī, sescentae, sescenta**
700	DCC	**septingentī, septingentae, septingenta**
800	DCCC	**octingentī, octingentae, octingenta**
900	DCCCC	**nōngentī, nōngentae, nōngenta**
1,000	M	**mīlle**
2,000	MM	**duo mīlia**

✔ **TIP**

Sometimes you will find that the figure 500 is written as IↃ instead of D; 1,000 is then CIↃ and 2,000 is CIↃCIↃ.

Only a few cardinal numbers change their endings like adjectives: **ūnus**, **ūna**, **ūnum** (meaning *one*) follows the pattern of first and second declension adjectives like **bonus**, except that the genitive singular ends in **-īus** and the dative in **-ī**.

ūnīus puerī	*of one boy*
ūnī ancillae	*for one slave-girl*

duo, **duae**, **duo** (meaning *two*) changes its endings like this, as does **ambō** (meaning *both*):

Case	Masculine	Feminine	Neuter
Nominative	**duo**	**duae**	**duo**
Accusative	**duōs / duo**	**duās**	**duo**
Genitive	**duōrum**	**duārum**	**duōrum**
Dative	**duōbus**	**duābus**	**duōbus**
Ablative	**duōbus**	**duābus**	**duōbus**

trēs, **tria** (meaning *three*) changes its endings like this:

Case	Masculine	Feminine	Neuter
Nominative	**trēs**	**trēs**	**tria**
Accusative	**trēs**	**trēs**	**tria**
Genitive	**trium**	**trium**	**trium**
Dative	**tribus**	**tribus**	**tribus**
Ablative	**tribus**	**tribus**	**tribus**

centum (meaning *one hundred*) does not change its endings, but **ducentī, ducentae**, **ducenta** (meaning *two hundred*), and other multiples of a hundred change their endings in the same way as the plural of **bonus**, except that the genitive ends in **-um**.

<u>centum</u> mīlitibus	*for one hundred soldiers*
<u>trecentīs</u> mīlitibus	*for three hundred soldiers*

mīlle (meaning *one thousand*) does not change its endings, but **mīlia** (meaning *thousands*) changes its endings in the same way as the plural of **animal** and is always followed by a noun in the genitive case.

<u>mīlle</u> passūs	*one thousand paces* (or *one mile*)
<u>duo mīlia</u> passuum	*two thousand(s)* (of) *paces* (or *two miles*)

Ordinal numbers

> **What is an ordinal number?**
> In Latin, an ordinal number tells you about the order something or someone comes in (for example, *first*, *sixteenth*, *twenty-first*).

1st	**prīmus, prīma, prīmum**
2nd	**secundus, secunda, secundum**
3rd	**tertius, tertia, tertium**
4th	**quārtus, quarta, quartum**
5th	**quīntus, quīnta, quīntum**
6th	**sextus, sexta, sextum**
7th	**septimus, septima, septimum**
8th	**octāvus, octāva, octāvum**
9th	**nōnus, nōna, nōnum**
10th	**decimus, decima, decimum**
11th	**ūndecimus**
12th	**duodecimus**
13th	**tertius decimus**
14th	**quārtus decimus**
15th	**quīntus decimus**
16th	**sextus decimus**
17th	**septimus decimus**
18th	**duodēvicēsimus**
19th	**ūndēvicēsimus**

20th	**vicēsimus, vicēsima, vicēsimum**
100th	**centēsimus, centēsima, centēsimum**

Ordinal numbers follow the pattern of first and second declension adjectives like **bonus**.

secundā mēnsā	*for the second course* (of a meal)
legiōnis nōnae	*of the ninth legion*

You will sometimes find numbers like '20th' and '100th' in Latin written with an extra 'n', for example **vicēnsimus** and **centēnsimus**.

Fractions in Latin are expressed as follows: **dīmidia pars** (meaning *a half*); **tertia pars** (meaning *a third*); and **quārta pars** (meaning *a quarter*).

Distributive numbers

What is a distributive number?
In Latin, a distributive number tells you how many there are each of something or how many people there are each (for example, *one each*, *ten each*).

singulī, singulae, singula	one each
bīnī, bīnae, bīna	two each
ternī, ternae, terna	three each
quaternī, quaternae, quaterna	four each
quīnī, quīnae, quīna	five each
sēnī, sēnae, sēna	six each
septēnī, septēnae, septēna	seven each
octōnī, octōnae, octōna	eight each
novēnī, novēnae, novēna	nine each
dēnī, dēnae, dēna	ten each
vīcēnī, vīcēnae, vīcēna	twenty each
centēnī, centēnae, centēna	one hundred each

Distributive numbers change their endings in the same way as the plural of **bonus**.

bīnī gladiātōrēs	*pairs of gladiators* (literally *two gladiators each*)
quaternī dēnāriī	*four denarii each*

> ✔ **TIP**
> If you want to say how many there are of a noun which is plural in form but singular in meaning, like **castra**, **castrōrum** (meaning *a camp*), use a distributive number rather than a cardinal number.
>
> | | |
> |---|---|
> | **<u>bīna</u> castra** | *two camps* |

Numeral adverbs

> **What is a numeral adverb?**
> In Latin, a numeral adverb tells you how many times something happened or how many times something is multiplied (for example, *once*, *ten times*).

semel	once
bis	twice
ter	three times
quater	four times
quīnquiēs	five times
sexiēs	six times
septiēs	seven times
octiēs	eight times
noviēs	nine times
deciēs	ten times
vīciēs	twenty times
centiēs	one hundred times

Like all adverbs, numeral adverbs do not change their form in Latin.

nōn plūs quam <u>semel</u>	*not more than once*
<u>ter</u> quattuor	*twelve* (literally *three times four*)

For more information on Adverbs, see page 128.

You will sometimes find numbers from 'five times' onwards in Latin written with an extra 'n', for example **quīnquiē<u>n</u>s** and **vīciē<u>n</u>s**.

Exercise 22

Use all the information on numbers so far, and the examples used, to work out the Latin for *the words in italics* in the following sentences.

a The *second* woman walked to the theatre *twice*.

....

b A merchant saw the *three* slaves in the street.

....

c The *first* teacher found *one* book *each* for the *ten* boys.

....

d The size of *four* of the temples in Rome is legendary.

....

e The Senate was deceived by *both* consuls.

....

f 'Citizens!' shouted the king *three times*, 'stand and fight!'

....

g No one gave any food to the *sixty* animals.

....

h Hannibal led his army over the Alps into Italy *once*.

....

i She left at the final hour of the *sixth* day.

....

Time and date

Expressing time

In Latin, if you want to say how long something has been going on, you use the ***accusative case***.

duās hōrās	*for two hours*
quīnque diēs	*for five days*

> ✔ **TIP**
>
> If you want to say how old someone is, you add the word **nātus** (meaning *having been born*) which is the past participle of the deponent verb **nascī** (meaning *to be born*).
>
> **puella duodecim annōs nāta** *a twelve-year-old girl*

For more information on Past participles or Deponent verbs, see pages 83 and 115.

If you want to say when something happens or the time within which something happens, you use the ***ablative case***.

sextō mēnse	*in the sixth month*
quārtō annō	*in the fourth year*
tribus diēbus	*within three days*

The adverb **abhinc** (meaning *ago*) can be used alongside expressions of time in either the accusative or the ablative case.

abhinc trēs annōs	*three years ago*
abhinc novem mēnsibus	*nine months ago*

For more information on Adverbs, see page 127.

You can also use these other ways of expressing time:

sub lūcem	towards daybreak
prīmā lūce	at dawn
sōlis ortū	at sunrise
māne	in the morning, early in the day
merīdiē	at midday
sub vesperum	towards evening
vesperī	in the evening

sōlis occāsū	at sunset
noctū / nocte	at night
mediā nocte	at midnight

> ✔ **TIP**
> The daytime was divided into twelve **hōrae** (meaning *hours*), and the hours of darkness were divided into four **vigiliae** (meaning *watches*) of three hours each, from 6–9pm, 9–12pm, 12–3am, 3–6am.

Calculating dates

A Roman year was usually identified by using the names of the consuls holding office that year in the ***dative case***.

Lentulō Gaetūlicō C. Calvisiō cōnsulibus	*During the consulship of Lentulus Gaetulicius and Gaius Calvisius*

Once 753 BCE was accepted as the year of the foundation of Rome, successive years were calculated from this date.

LV ab urbe conditā	*55 [years] from the foundation of the city or 55 AUC*

Julius Caesar's reforms of 46 BCE first established the year as we now know it. There were seven months of 31 days, four of 30 days, and one of 28 with an extra day each leap year. Each month was identified by the following adjectives:

Iānuārius	January
Februārius	February
Martius	March
Aprīlis	April
Māius	May
Iūnius	June
Iūlius (Quīntīlis)	July
Augustus (Sextīlis)	August
September	September
Octōber	October
November	November
December	December

Months ending in **-us** follow the same pattern as first and second declension adjectives like **bonus**; months ending in **-is** as third declension adjectives like **fortis**; and months ending in **-er** like **ācer**.

If you want to calculate a date in the Roman calendar accurately, you need to remember these three important days in each month:

Kalendae, Kalendārum	*Kalends* or 1st
Nōnae, Nōnārum	*Nones* or 5th
Īdūs, Īduum	*Ides* or 13th

> **✔ TIP**
> These three nouns are all feminine.
> In the months of March, May, July, and October, the Nones are two days later on the 7th, and therefore the Ides are on the 15th.

If you want to refer to these specific dates, you use the ***ablative case***.

Kalendīs Martiīs	*on March 1st*
Īdibus Decembribus	*on December 13th*

If you want to refer to the day before any of these specific dates, you must use the word **prīdiē** (meaning *on the day before*) followed by the ***accusative case***.

prīdiē Nōnās Ianuāriās	*on January 4th*

All other days are reckoned by counting (inclusively) the days before the next main day in the month. Once you have worked out the correct number, you use **ante diem** (meaning *before the day*) followed by the ordinal number you have calculated and the next main date, all in the ***accusative case***.

For example, February 9th is five days before February 13th (counting inclusively); April 17th is fifteen days before May 1st, and July 4th is four days before July 7th.

ante diem quīntum Īdūs Februāriās	*February 9th*
ante diem quīntum decimum Kalendās Maiās	*April 17th*
ante diem quārtum Nōnās Iūliās	*July 4th*

In Latin, as in English, dates are usually abbreviated.

a.d. v Īd. Feb.	*Feb. 9th*
a.d. xv Kal. Mai.	*Apr. 17th*

Exercise 23

Use all the information on time and date so far, and the examples used, to work out the Latin for *the words in italics* in the following sentences.

a They have been married *for twenty years*.

....

b She always gets up *at dawn*.

....

c My wife's birthday is on *February 21st*.

....

d *April 6th* is the first day of the new tax year.

....

e *October 8th* is a date that I will always remember.

....

f Our son was born early on *November 4th*.

....

Part Two

Latin Literature

Introduction

This section offers a selection of original Latin literature to illustrate the work of some of the best-known authors of the Roman world. There are five prose writers; Cicero, Caesar, Livy, Tacitus, and Pliny, and five poets; Catullus, Virgil, Horace, Ovid, and Martial. They are arranged in roughly chronological order. You can download and listen to all the Latin texts being read out at **www.collinslanguage.com/latin-audio**. The relevant track number is shown in headphones beside each extract. A list of sources for the extracts is given at the back of the book.

1 **Introduction**

Cicero

summum bonum – The highest good

The selections from the moving speeches and polished letters of Cicero in this unit will give you a sense of the huge influence that the Romans have had on later times. Hugely successful as a lawyer, but also a brilliant political theorist, philosopher, and literary critic, Cicero rose from humble beginnings to become consul in 63 BCE. However, he lived in turbulent times and was murdered 20 years later after he had fallen foul of the authorities once too often.

The case against Catiline

Right from the very beginning of the prosecution speech, you will hear an impassioned orator at the height of his powers.

2 **quō usque[1] tandem[2] abūtēre[3], Catilīna[6], patientia[5] nostra[4]? quam diū[1] etiam[5] furor[3] iste[2] tuus[4] nōs[7] ēlūdet[6]? quem[2] ad[1] fīnem[3] sēsē[7] effrēnāta[4] iactābit[6] audācia[5]? nihilne[1] tē[26] nocturnum[2] praesidium[3] Palātī[4], nihil[5] urbis[7] vigiliae[6], nihil[8] timor[9] populī[10], nihil[11] concursus[12] bonōrum[14] omnium[13], nihil[15] hic[16] mūnītissimus[17] habendī[19] senātūs[20] locus[18], nihil[21] hōrum[24] ōra[22] vultūsque[23] mōvērunt[25]? patere[4] tua[2] cōnsilia[3] nōn sentīs[1], constrictam[10] iam[8] hōrum[13] omnium[12] scientiā[11] tenērī[9] coniūrātiōnem[7] tuam[6] nōn vidēs[5]? quid[1] proximā[3], quid[4] superiōre[6] nocte[5] ēgerīs[2], ubi[7] fuerīs[8], quōs[9] convocāverīs[10], quid[11] cōnsiliī[12] cēperīs[13], quem[14] nostrum[15] ignorāre[17] arbitrāris[16]?**

How far[1] at last[2] will you abuse[3] our[4] patience[5], Catiline[6]? How long[1] will that[2] rage[3] of yours[4] still[5] mock[6] us[7]? To[1] what[2] limit[3] will your unbridled[4] audacity[5] throw[6] itself[7] [about]? Has not at all[1] the nightly[2] guard[3] on the Palatine Hill[4], not at all[5] the watchfulness[6] of the city[7], not at all[8] the fear[9] of the people[10], not at all[11] the union[12] of all[13] good[14] [men], not at all[15] this[16] most fortified[17] place[18] for the holding[19] of the Senate[20], have not at all[21] the faces[22] and expressions[23] of these[24] [men] moved[25] you[26]? Do you not realise[1] your[2] plans[3] lie exposed[4], do you not see[5] that your[6] conspiracy[7] is now[8] held[9] constrained[10] by the knowledge[11] of all[12] these[13] [men]? What[1] you did[2] last[3] [night], what[4] the night[5] before[6], where[7] you were[8], whom[9] you called together[10], what[11] plan[12] you made[13] – which[14] of us[15] do you think[16] is unaware[17]?

Nota bene

abūtēre is an alternative form of the second person singular of the future tense of the deponent verb **abūtī**. For more information on deponent verbs, see page 115. **nihil** is an adverb here. For more information on adverbs, see page 127. **habendī** is the genitive singular of the gerund of **habēre**. For information on gerunds, see page 88. **tua cōnsilia** and **coniūrātiōnem tuam** are in the accusative case and **patere** and **tenērī** are infinitives because they are part of reported speech following the verbs **sentīs** and **vidēs**. For more information on reported speech, see page 113. **ēgerīs**, **fuerīs**, **convocāverīs** and **cēperīs** are all subjunctives because they follow **quid**, **ubi** or **quōs** which are question words after **ignorāre**. For more information on when to use the subjunctive, see page 104. **quem** is in the accusative case and **ignorāre** is an infinitive because they are part of reported speech following the deponent verb **arbitrāris**. **cōnsiliī** and **nostrum** are both in the genitive case. For more information on use of the cases, see the supplement on page 277.

You will no doubt recognise the famous phrase that the next section of the speech starts with.

ō[1] tempora[2], ō[3] mōrēs[4]! senātus[1] haec[3] intellegit[2]. cōnsul[1] videt[2]; hic[3] tamen[4] vīvit[5]. vīvit[6]? immō vērō[1] etiam[2] in[4] senātum[5] venit[3], fit[6] publicī[8] cōnsiliī[9] particeps[7], notat[10] et[11] dēsignat[12] oculīs[13] ad[16] caedem[17] ūnum quemque[14] nostrum[15]. nōs[1] autem[4] fortēs[2] virī[3] satis[7] facere[6] reī publicae[8] vidēmur[5], sī[9] istius[14] furōrem[11] ac[12] tēla[13] vītēmus[10]. ad[6] mortem[7] tē[1], Catilīna[2], dūcī[5] iussū[8] cōnsulis[9] iam pridem[4] oportēbat[3], in[11] tē[12] cōnferrī[10] pestem[13], quam[14] tū[15] in[18] nōs[19] omnēs[20] iam diū[16] māchināris[17].

O[1] the times[2], O[3] the customs[4]! The Senate[1] understands[2] these things[3]. The consul[1] sees[2] [them]; he[3], however[4], lives[5]. He lives[6]? Yes indeed[1], he even[2] comes[3] into[4] the Senate[5], becomes[6] a partner[7] in state[8] planning[9], distinguishes[10] and[11] marks out[12] with his eyes[13] every one[14] of us[15] for[16] slaughter[17]. We[1] brave[2] men[3] moreover[4] seem[5] to do[6] enough[7] for the Republic[8], if[9] we avoid[10] the rage[11] and[12] darts[13] of that wretch[14]. You[1], Catiline[2], ought[3] long ago[4] to have been lead[5] to[6] death[7] on the order[8] of the consul[9], to have had brought down[10] on[11] you[12] the destruction[13] which[14] you[15] have now long[16] been plotting[17] against[18] us[19] all[20].

Nota bene

nostrum is in the genitive case. For more information on use of the cases, see the supplement on page 277. **vītēmus** is a subjunctive because it follows **sī**. For more information on when to use the subjunctive, see page 104. **oportēbat** is a form of the impersonal verb **oportet**. For more information on impersonal verbs, see page 93. **māchināris** is a form of the deponent verb **māchinārī**. For more information on deponent verbs, see page 115.

Writing to Atticus

Cicero wrote numerous letters to his close friend Atticus. They were also related by marriage, which provided plenty to talk about. Cicero's brother Quintus was the husband of Atticus' sister Pomponia, but you will discover that all was not well in their domestic life.

4

postrīdiē[1] ex[3] Arpīnātī[4] profectī sumus[2]. ut[3] in[6] Arcānō[7] Quīntus[4] manēret[5] diēs[1] fēcit[2], ego[8] Aquīnī[9], sed[10] prandimus[11] in[12] Arcānō[13]. nōstī[1] hunc[2] fundum[3]. quō[3] ut[1] vēnimus[2], hūmānissimē[6] Quīntus[4] 'Pompōnia[7]' inquit[5] 'tū[8] invītā[9] mulierēs[10], ego[11] virōs[13] accīverō[12].' nihil[1] potuit[2], mihi[6] quidem[4] ut[3] vīsum est[5], dulcius[7] idque[8] cum[9] verbīs[10] tum[11] etiam[12] animō[13] ac[14] vultū[15]. at[1] illa[2] audientibus[4] nōbis[3] 'ego[6] ipsa[10] sum[7]' inquit[5] 'hīc[9] hospita[8],' id[2] autem[1] ex[5] eō[6], ut[3] opīnor[4], quod[7] antecesserat[9] Stātius[8] ut[10] prandium[12] nōbis[13] vidēret[11]. tum[1] Quīntus[2] 'ēn[5]' inquit[3] mihi[4] 'haec[8] ego[6] patior[7] cotīdiē[9].'

On the following day[1] we set out[2] from[3] [our house] at Arpinum[4]. A holiday[1] made[2] [it] so that[3] Quintus[4] stayed[5] in[6] Arcanum[7], I[8] in Aquinum[9], but[10] we lunched[11] in[12] Arcanum[13]. You know[1] this[2] estate[3]. When[1] we reached[2] it[3], Quintus[4] said[5] very courteously[6], 'Pomponia[7], you[8] invite[9] in the women[10], I[11] will fetch[12] the men[13].' Nothing[1] could[2] be, so[3] indeed[4] it seemed[5] to me[6], more gentle[7] and [as] it[8] [was] with[9] his words[10] so[11] also[12] [it was] with his attitude[13] and[14] expression[15]. But[1] she[2], with us[3] listening[4], said[5], 'I[6] am[7] a guest[8] here[9] myself[10]', and[1] that[2] [was], so[3] I believe[4], from[5] the fact[6] that[7] Statius[8] had gone ahead[9] in order to[10] see to[11] the lunch[12] for us[13]. Then[1] Quintus[2] said[3] to me[4], 'See[5], I[6] endure[7] these things[8] every day[9].'

Nota bene

profectī sumus is from the deponent verb **proficiscī** and **patior** from **patī**. For more information on deponent verbs, see page 115. **manēret** and **vidēret** are both subjunctives because they both follow **ut**. For more information on when to use the subjunctive, see page 104. **nōstī** is a contracted form of **nōvistī**. For more information on defective verbs, see page 117. **hūmānissimē** is the superlative form of the adverb **hūmānē**. For more information on the comparison of adverbs, see page 129. **dulcius** is a comparative form of the adjective **dulcis**. For more information on the comparison of adjectives, see page 22. **audientibus** is the ablative plural of the present participle of **audīre**. For more information on present participles, see page 87.

The letter continues in much the same vein.

5

dīcēs[1] 'quid[2] quaesō[3] istūc[5] erat[4]?' magnum[6]; itaque[1] mē[4] ipsum[3] commōverat[2]; sīc[2] absurdē[3] et[4] asperē[5] verbīs[6] vultūque[7] responderat[1]. dissimulāvī[1] dolēns[2]. discubuimus[2] omnēs[1] praeter[3] illam[4], cui[5] tamen[6] Quīntus[7] dē[9] mēnsā[10] mīsit[8]. illa[1] rēiēcit[2]. quid[1] multa[2]? nihil[1] meō[5] frātre[6] lēnius[4], nihil[7] asperius[8] tuā[9] sorōre[10] mihi[3] vīsum est[2]; et[1] multa[3] praetereō[2] quae[4] tum[5] mihi[9] maiōrī[7] stomachō[8] quam[10] ipsī[12] Quīntō[11] fuērunt[6]. ego[1] inde[2] Aquīnum[3]. Quīntus[1] in[3] Arcānō[4] remansit[2] et[5] Aquīnum[11] ad[7] mē[8] postrīdiē[10] māne[9] vēnit[6] mihique[2] narrāvit[1] nec sēcum[6] illam[3] dormīre[5] voluisse[4] et[7] cum[8] discessūra esset[9] fuisse[10] eius[11] modī[12] quālem[13] ego[14] vīdissem[15].

You will say[1], 'What[2] do I find[3] there was[4] in that[5]?' A great deal[6] – and in this way[1] she had annoyed[2] even[3] me[4]; she had replied[1] so[2] harshly[3] and[4] roughly[5] by her words[6] and expression[7]. I concealed[1] being in distress[2]. We all[1] reclined to dinner[2] except[3] her[4], for whom[5] however[6] Quintus[7] sent[8] [food] from[9] the table[10]. She[1] rejected[2] [it]. Why[1] [say] a lot[2]? Nothing[1] seemed[2] to me[3] more gentle[4] than my[5] brother[6], nothing[7] more rough[8] than your[9] sister[10]; and[1] I am omitting[2] many things[3] which[4] at the time[5] were[6] of greater[7] vexation[8] to me[9] than[10] to Quintus[11] himself[12]. I[1] then[2] [went] to Aquinum[3]. Quintus[1] stayed behind[2] in[3] Arcanum[4] and[5] came[6] to[7] me[8] early[9] the next day[10] at Aquinum[11] and told[1] me[2] that she[3] had not wanted[4] to sleep[5] with him[6] and[7] when[8] she had been about to leave[9] she had behaved[10] in that[11] manner[12] of the kind[13] I[14] had seen[15].

> **Nota bene**
> **dolēns** is the present participle of **dolēre**. For more information on present participles, see page 87. **lēnius** is a comparative form of the adjective **lēnis**, **asperius** of **asperus** and **maiōrī** of **magnus**. For more information on the comparison of adjectives, see page 22. **illam** is in the accusative case and **voluisse** and **fuisse** are infinitives because they are part of reported speech following the verb **narrāvit**. For more information on reported speech, see page 113. **discessūra esset** is a subjunctive because it follows **cum** (meaning *when*); **vīdissem** is also a subjunctive after **quālem**. For more information on when to use the subjunctive, see page 104.

Writing to his wife

Cicero's genuine concern for his daughter's health is compounded by the fact that he has just returned to Italy from Greece after Julius Caesar's decisive victory that summer over Pompey at Pharsalus. Cicero had been backing Pompey and you will notice that he is now finding his position a little delicate. For more information on Caesar, see page 166.

6

Scr.[1] Brundisī[2] iv K. Dec.[3] a. 706[4]
TULLIUS[1] TERENTIAE[4] SUAE[3] S. D.[2]
in[1] maximīs[3] meīs[2] dolōribus[4] excruciat[8] mē[9] valetūdō[5] Tulliae[7] nostrae[6], dē[1] quā[2] nihil[4] est[3] quod[5] ad[8] tē[9] plūra[7] scrībam[6]; tibi[4] enim[1] aequē[5] magnae[6] cūrae[7] esse[4] certō[3] scio[2]. quod[1] mē[3] propius[5] vultis[2] accēdere[4], videō[6] ita[8] esse faciendum[7]: etiam[1] ante[3] fēcissem[2], sed[4] mē[7] multa[5] impedīvērunt[6], quae[8] nē nunc quidem[9] expedita sunt[10]. sed[1] ā[4] Pompōniō[5] exspectō[2] litterās[3], quās[6] ad[10] mē[11] quam prīmum[12] perferendās[9] cūrēs[8] velim[7]. dā operam[1], ut[2] valeās[3].

Written[1] at Brundisium[2], 27th November[3] 48 BCE[4]
Tullius[1] sends greetings[2] to his[3] Terentia[4]
In[1] my[2] very great[3] sorrows[4] the health[5] of our[6] Tullia[7] torments[8] me[9], about[1] which[2] there is[3] nothing[4] that[5] I will write[6] further[7] to[8] you[9]; for[1]

I know[2] for sure[3] that you have[4] equally[5] great[6] concern[7]. Because[1] you want[2] me[3] to come[4] nearer[5], I see[6] that I must do[7] so[8]: and[1] I would have done[2] before[3], but[4] many things[5] have prevented[6] me[7], which[8] not even now[9] have been sorted out[10]. But[1] I am expecting[2] a letter[3] from[4] Pomponius[5], which[6] I would like[7] you to take care of[8] being delivered[9] to[10] me[11] as soon as possible[12]. Make sure[1] that[2] you stay well[3].

Nota bene

Scr. is an abbreviation from **scrībere**. **Brundisī** is in the locative case. For more information on the locative case, see page 134. **K. Dec. a. 706** is an abbreviation for the Kalends of December in the year 706. For more information on the Roman calendar, see page 154. **S. D.** is an abbreviation of the phrase **salūtem dat**. **esse** is in the infinitive because it is part of reported speech following **scio**. For more information on reported speech, see page 113. **vultis** comes from **velle**. **esse** is in the infinitive because it is part of reported speech following **videō** and the accusative **mē** has been left out; **faciendum** is the accusative singular masculine of the gerundive from **facere** and **perferendās** is the accusative plural feminine of the gerundive from **perferre**. For more information on gerundives, see page 88. **cūrēs** is a subjunctive because it follows **velim** (also a subjunctive) which comes from **velle**, and **valeās** because it follows **ut**. For more information on when to use the subjunctive, see page 104.

The way is clearer for Cicero to return home after a two-year absence now that he has received a pardon from Caesar; but from the abruptness of this letter to Terentia, the last he wrote to her, you might not be surprised to discover that they were divorced a few months later.

7

Scr.[1] dē[2] Venusīnō[3] K. Oct.[4] a. 707[5]
TULLIUS[1] S. D.[2] TERENTIAE[4] SUAE[3]
in Tusculānum[4] nōs[2] ventūrōs[3] putāmus[1] aut[5] Nōnīs[6] aut[7] postrīdiē[8]. ibi[5] ut[1] sint[3] omnia[2] parāta[4] (plūrēs[3] enim[1] fortasse[2] nōbiscum[5] erunt[4] et[6], ut[7] arbitror[8], diūtius[11] ibi [10]commorābimur[9]); labrum[3] sī[1] in[4] balineō[5] nōn est[2], ut[6] sit[7], item[1] cētera[2] quae[3] sunt[4] ad[6] victum[7] et[8] ad[9] valetūdinem[10] necessāria[5]. valē[1]. K. Oct.[1] dē[2] Venusīnō[3].

Written[1] from[2] Venusia[3], 1st October[4] 47 BCE[5]
Tullius[1] sends greetings[2] to his[3] Terentia[4]
We think[1] that we[2] will reach[3] our house at Tusculum[4] either[5] on the 7th[6] or[7] the day after[8]. [See] that[1] everything[2] is[3] ready[4] there[5] (for[1]

perhaps[2] several people[3] will be[4] with us[5] and[6], so[7] I believe[8], we will be lingering[9] there[10] longer[11]); if[1] there is not[2] a basin[3] in[4] the bath[5], [see] that[6] there is[7]; likewise[1] the rest of the things[2] that[3] are[4] necessary[5] for[6] nourishment[7] and[8] for[9] health[10]. Goodbye[1]. 1st October[1], from[2] Venusia[3].

Nota bene

Scr. is an abbreviation from **scrībere**. **K. Oct. a. 707** is an abbreviation for the Kalends of October in the year 707. For more information on the Roman calendar, see page 154. **S. D.** is an abbreviation of the phrase **salūtem dat**. **nōs** and **ventūrōs** are in the accusative case because they are part of reported speech following the verb **putāmus**; the infinitive **esse** has been left out. For more information on reported speech, see page 113. **sint** and **sit** are subjunctives because they both follow **ut**; the verbs before **ut** have been left out. For more information on when to use the subjunctive, see page 104. **diūtius** is the comparative form of the adverb **diū**. For more information on the comparison of adverbs, see page 129. **commorābimur** is a form of the deponent verb **commorārī**. For more information on deponent verbs, see page 115.

Culture vulture

A man in Roman times would usually be in his late teens or early twenties when he got married, while on average his bride would be a girl of about 14*. Although legally she was at liberty to refuse, a daughter would normally marry a husband chosen for her by her father.

The **dōs** (meaning *a dowry*) was agreed and then the **spōnsālia** (meaning *an engagement ceremony*) took place, attended by family and friends. Promises were exchanged between the husband-to-be and the father of the bride, and a ring was placed on the third finger of the wife-to-be's left hand. There were gifts, and afterwards a party.

In Cicero's day, the most common form of marriage was known as **cum manū** (meaning literally *with the hand*). The wife ceases to be a member of her parents' family, passes completely under 'the hand' or control of her new husband, and gives up any right to property of her own. He is able to divorce her, but she cannot divorce him.

Later, it became more usual for marriage to be **sine manū** (meaning literally *without the hand*). No special ceremonial arrangements were required for this type of marriage and the woman was still regarded under Roman law as a member of her parents' family. She could possess property and was permitted to divorce her husband.

A Roman wedding was usually celebrated with traditional customs. The bride's hair would be carefully arranged and a veil would be worn; there would be a symbolic joining of hands by the bride and bridegroom; a marriage contract would be signed and witnessed by the guests, who would then be invited to the bride's house for a wedding feast; the bride might pretend to be pulled away from her mother by force and carried across the threshold of her new home by the bridegroom.

The Romans regarded having children as the most important function of marriage. The Emperor Augustus even passed a law that penalised those who didn't get married and gave special privileges to those who had three children or more.

A Roman husband expected his wife to bring up their young children and to be an efficient organiser of their domestic life, including the supervision of the household slaves. He had more legal rights than her (for example, the right to vote or to sit on a jury), but she was not restricted only to the home as was the case in many other countries at the time.

*The age gap could be much greater, however. Pliny was in his early forties when he got married for the third time, to Calpurnia; she was probably 15. (For more information on Pliny, see page 229.)

Caesar

vēnī, vīdī, vīcī – I came, I saw, I conquered

Julius Caesar was not only a great soldier, who landed in Britain, crossed the Rubicon, and loved Cleopatra, before his infamous assassination at the hands of Brutus and co. in 44 BCE. In this unit you will discover that he also has a deserved reputation as a first-class military historian through his own accounts of his conquest of Gaul between 58 and 50 BCE and the ensuing civil war with his great rival Pompey in 49-48 BCE.

Preface

You might recognise the famous opening words of Caesar's account of his military campaigns in Gaul – although there is no mention of that 'one small village'.

8

Gallia[1] est[2] omnis[3] divīsa[4] in[5] partēs[7] trēs[6], quārum[8] ūnam[11] incolunt[10] Belgae[9], aliam[2] Aquītānī[1], tertiam[3] quī[4] ipsōrum[8] linguā[7] Celtae[6], nostrā[10] Gallī[9] appellantur[5].

Gaul[1] is[2] all[3] divided[4] into[5] three[6] parts[7], of which[8] the Belgians[9] inhabit[10] one[11], the Aquitanians[1] another[2], the third[3] [those] who[4] are called[5] Celts[6] in the tongue[7] of them themselves[8], Gauls[9] in ours[10].

Nota bene

The **Belgae** lived in what is now Belgium and northern France, the **Aquītānī** south-west France, and the **Celtae** or **Gallī** much of the rest of France stretching through Switzerland to northern Italy.

Roman bravery

You will see here how Caesar celebrates the kind of soldiers who served under him. The year is 54 BCE but the Romans are no longer in Kent; instead they are under siege from the Nervii in Gaul.

9

erant[1] in[2] eā[3] legiōne[4] fortissimī[5] virī[6], centuriōnēs[7], quī[8] prīmīs[10] ordinibus[11] appropinquārent[9], Titus[12] Pullo[13] et[14] Lūcius[15] Vorēnus[16]. hī[1] perpetuās[3] inter[5] sē[6] controversiās[4] habēbant[2], quīnam[7] anteferrētur[8], omnibusque[9] annīs[10] dē[13] locīs[15] summīs[14] simultātibus[11] contendēbant[12]. ex[1] hīs[2] Pullo[3], cum[4] ācerrimē[5] ad[7]

mūnītiōnēs[8] pugnārētur[6], 'quid[10] dubitās[11],' inquit[9], 'Vorēne[12]? aut[1] quem[2] locum[3] tuae[5] probandae[4] virtūtis[6] exspectās[7]? hic[1] diēs[2] dē[4] nostrīs[5] contrōversiīs[6] iūdicābit[3].' haec[3] cum[1] dīxisset[2], prōcēdit[4] extrā[5] mūnītiōnēs[6] quāque[8] pars[9] hostium[10] confertissima[12] est vīsa[11] irrumpit[7]. nē Vorēnus[1] quidem[2] tum[3] sēsē[5] vallō[6] continet[4], sed[7] omnium[9] veritus[8] existimātiōnem[10] subsequitur[11]. mediocrī[1] spatiō[2] relictō[3] Pullo[4] pīlum[6] in[7] hostēs[8] immittit[5] atque[9] ūnum[11] ex[13] multitūdine[14] prōcurrentem[12] trāicit[10]; quō[1] percussō[2] et[3] exanimātō[4] hunc[6] scūtīs[7] prōtegunt[5], in[11] hostem[12] tēla[9] ūniversī[10] coniciunt[8] neque dant[13] regrediendī[15] facultātem[14].

There were[1] in[2] that[3] legion[4] very brave[5] men[6], centurions[7], who[8] were approaching[9] the first[10] ranks[11], Titus[12] Pullo[13] and[14] Lucius[15] Vorenus[16]. These[1] [men] used to have[2] continual[3] arguments[4] among[5] themselves[6], as to which[7] should be preferred[8], and every[9] year[10] with quarrels[11] they used to fight[12] over[13] the highest[14] positions[15]. Out of[1] these[2] [men], Pullo[3], when[4] there was very fierce[5] fighting[6] at[7] the fortifications[8], said[9], 'Why[10] do you hesitate[11], Vorenus[12]? Or[1] what[2] place[3] for demonstrating[4] your[5] courage[6] are you waiting for[7]? This[1] day[2] will be judge[3] over[4] our[5] arguments[6].' When[1] he had said[2] these things[3], he advances[4] outside[5] the fortifications[6] and rushes in[7] where[8] a section[9] of the enemy[10] seemed[11] most closely pressed together[12]. Vorenus[1] indeed does not[2] then[3] hold[4] himself[5] back on the rampart[6], but[7] fearing[8] everyone's[9] opinion[10] follows after[11]. With a moderate[1] distance[2] left[3] Pullo[4] launches[5] a javelin[6] against[7] the enemy[8] and[9] pierces[10] one[11] [man] running forward[12] out of[13] the crowd[14]; with him[1] hit[2] and[3] winded[4] they protect[5] this[6] [man] with shields[7], hurl[8] spears[9] all together[10] against[11] their enemy[12] and do not give[13] [him] an opportunity[14] of retreating[15].

Nota bene

fortissimī is a superlative form of the adjective **fortis** and **confertissima** of **confertus**. For more information on the comparison of adjectives, see page 22. **appropinquārent**, **anteferrētur** and **pugnārētur** are all subjunctives, because one follows the relative pronoun **quī**, one the question word **quīnam**, and one the conjunction **cum** (meaning *when*). For more information on when to use the subjunctive, see page 104. **ācerrimē** is the superlative form of the adverb **ācriter**. For more information on the comparison of adverbs, see page 129. **probandae** is the genitive singular feminine of the gerundive from **probāre** and **regrediendī** is the genitive singular of the gerund from the deponent verb **regredī**. For more information on gerundives or gerunds, see pages 92 and 88.

dīxisset is a subjunctive because it follows **cum** (meaning *when*). **veritus** is the past participle of the deponent verb **verērī** and **subsequitur** is a form of the deponent verb **subsequī**. For more information on past participles or deponent verbs, see pages 83 and 115; **relictō**, **percussō** and **exanimātō** are all ablative singular forms of past participles. **prōcurrentem** is a form of the present participle of **prōcurrere**. For more information on present participles, see page 87.

The dramatic show of fierce rivalry and heroic comradeship between Pullo and Vorenus continues.

10

trānsfīgitur[3] scūtum[2] Pullōnī[1] et[4] verūtum[5] in[7] balteō[8] dēfīgitur[6]. āvertit[3] hic[1] cāsus[2] vāgīnam[4] et[5] gladium[11] ēdūcere[10] cōnantī[9] dextram[7] morātur[6] manum[8], impeditumque[14] hostēs[12] circumsistunt[13]. succurrit[4] inimīcus[2] illī[1] Vorēnus[3] et[5] labōrantī [7]subvenit[6]. ad[7] hunc[8] sē[4] cōnfestim[3] ā[5] Pullōne[6] omnis[1] multitūdō[2] convertit[4]: illum[10] verūtō[12] arbitrantur[9] occīsum[11]. gladiō[1] comminus[4] rem gerit[3] Vorēnus[2] atque[5] ūnō[6] interfectō[7] reliquōs[9] paulum[10] prōpellit[8]; dum[1] cupidius[3] instat[2], in[6] locum[8] dēiectus[4] īnferiōrem[7] concidit[5]. huic[4] rursus[6] circumventō[5] fert[2] subsidium[3] Pullo[1], atque[7] ambo[8] incolumēs[9] complūribus[10] interfectīs[11] summā[16] cum[15] laude[17] sēsē[12] intrā[13] mūnītiōnēs[14] recipiunt[12]. sīc[1] fortūna[2] in[5] contentiōne[6] et[7] certāmine[8] ūtrumque[4] versāvit[3], ut[9] alter[10] alterī[13] inimīcus[12] auxiliō[14] salūtīque[15] esset[11], neque[1] dīiūdicārī[3] posset[2], ūter[4] ūtrī[7] virtūte[8] anteferendus[6] vidērētur[5].

Pullo's[1] shield[2] is pierced[3] and[4] a spear[5] is fixed[6] in[7] his belt[8]. This[1] accident[2] knocks[3] his scabbard[4] aside and[5] delays[6] his right[7] hand[8] as he tries[9] to draw out[10] his sword[11], and his enemies[12] surround[13] the impeded[14] [man]. His[1] rival[2] Vorenus[3] runs to help[4] and[5] gives support[6] to the struggling[7] [man]. The whole[1] crowd[2] immediately[3] withdraws[4] from[5] Pullo[6] towards[7] this one[8]: they think[9] the other[10] has been killed[11] by the spear[12]. With his sword[1] Vorenus[2] carries on the fight[3] hand to hand[4] and[5] with one[6] killed[7] drives back[8] the rest[9] a little[10]; while[1] he presses on[2] too eagerly[3], thrown down[4] he falls[5] onto[6] a lower[7] spot[8]. Pullo[1] brings[2] relief[3] to this one[4] surrounded[5] again[6], and[7] both[8] unharmed[9] with several[10] killed[11] retreat[12] within[13] the fortifications[14] with[15] the highest[16] honour[17]. Thus[1] destiny[2] dealt with[3] each of them[4] in[5] their rivalry[6] and[7] contest[8], so that[9] one[10] was[11] rival[12] to the other[13] [who was] help[14] and salvation[15], and nor[1] could it[2] be distinguished[3] which of the two[4] seemed[5] that he should be preferred[6] to the other[7] in courage[8].

Nota bene
Pullōnī and **illī** are in the dative case because they are showing possession. For more information on the use of the cases, see the supplement on page 277. **cōnantī** is a form of the present participle of the deponent verb **cōnārī** and **labōrantī** of **labōrāre**; **morātur** is a form of the deponent verb **morārī**. For more information on present participles or deponent verbs, see pages 87 and 115. **impeditum**, **occīsum**, **interfectō**, **dēiectus**, **circumventō**, **interfectīs** are all past participles; **illum** is in the accusative case and **occīsum** is part of an infinitive (with **esse** left out) because they are part of reported speech following the deponent verb **arbitrantur**. For more information on past participles or reported speech, see pages 83 and 113. **esset** and **posset** are both subjunctives because they are expressing a result after **ut** and **viderētur** because it is expressing a question indirectly after **ūter**. For more information on when to use the subjunctive, see page 104. **anteferendus** is the nominative singular masculine of the gerundive from **anteferre**. For more information on gerundives, see page 92.

Gallic savagery

You will find that getting the gods on your side was not a matter for the faint-hearted if you were a Gaul in Caesar's time.

11

nātiō[2] est[4] omnis[1] Gallōrum[3] admodum[5] dēdita[6] religiōnibus[7], atque[1] ob[2] eam[3] causam[4], quī[5] sunt[6] adfectī[7] graviōribus[8] morbīs[9] quīque[10] in[12] proeliīs[13] perīculīsque[14] versantur[11], aut[1] prō[4] victimīs[5] hominēs[3] immolant[2] aut[6] sē[8] immolātūrōs[9] vovent[7] administrīsque[12] ad[13] ea[14] sacrificia[15] druidibus[11] ūtuntur[10], quod[1], prō[6] vītā[7] hominis[8] nisi[2] hominis[4] vīta[3] reddātur[5], nōn posse[13] deōrum[12] immortālium[11] nūmen[10] plācārī[14] arbitrantur[9], pūblicēque[1] eiusdem[5] generis[6] habent[2] īnstitūta[4] sacrificia[3]. aliī[1] immānī[4] magnitūdine[5] simulācra[3] habent[2], quōrum[6] contexta[8] vīminibus[9] membra[7] vīvīs[11] hominibus[12] complent[10]; quibus[1] succēnsīs[2] circumventī[4] flammā[5] exanimantur[6] hominēs[3]. supplicia[2] eōrum[3] quī[4] in[6] fūrtō[7] aut[8] in[9] latrōciniō[10] aut[11] aliquā[12] noxiā[13] sint comprehēnsī[5] grātiōra[15] dīs[17] immortālibus[16] esse[14] arbitrantur[1]; sed[1], cum[2] eius[4] generis[5] cōpia[3] dēfēcit[6], etiam[7] ad[9] innocentium[11] supplicia[10] dēscendunt[8].

The whole[1] nation[2] of the Gauls[3] is[4] completely[5] devoted[6] to superstitions[7], and[1] for[2] this[3] reason[4] [those] who[5] are[6] weakened[7] by more serious[8] illnesses[9] and who[10] take part[11] in[12] battles[13] and dangers[14], either[1] sacrifice[2] men[3] on behalf of[4] the victims[5] or[6] vow[7] that they[8] will sacrifice[9] [them] and use[10] the druids[11] as assistants[12] at[13] these[14] sacrifices[15], because[1], unless[2] the life[3] of a man[4] is given back[5] for[6] the life[7] of a man[8], they think[9] that the power[10] of the immortal[11] gods[12] cannot[13] be appeased[14], and in the name of the state[1] they have[2] sacrifices[3] established[4] of the same[5] kind[6]. Others[1] have[2] figures[3] of enormous[4] size[5], whose[6] limbs[7] woven[8] with branches[9] they fill[10] with living[11] men[12]; with these[1] set alight[2] the men[3] surrounded[4] by fire[5] are asphyxiated[6]. They think[1] that the execution[2] of those[3] who[4] have been caught[5] in[6] theft[7] or[8] in[9] robbery[10] or[11] some[12] offence[13] are[14] more pleasing[15] to the immortal[16] gods[17]; but[1], when[2] the supply[3] of that[4] kind[5] has run out[6], they also[7] stoop[8] to[9] the execution[10] of the innocent[11].

Nota bene

dēdita and **adfectī** are both past participles; **versantur** is a passive form of the verb **versāre** but does not have a passive meaning. For more information on past participles or the passive, see pages 83 and 77. **sē** is in the accusative case and **immolātūrōs** is part of an infinitive (with **esse** left out) because they are part of reported speech following the verb **vovent**. For more information on reported speech, see page 113. **ūtuntur** is a form of the deponent verb **ūtī** and is always followed by the dative case. For more information on deponent verbs, see page 115. **reddātur** is a subjunctive because it follows **nisi**. For more information on when to use the subjunctive, see page 104. **nūmen** is in the accusative case and **posse** is an infinitive because they are part of reported speech after the deponent verb **arbitrantur**. **īnstitūta**, **contexta**, **succēnsīs** and **circumventī** are all past participles. **supplicia** is in the accusative case and **esse** is an infinitive because they are part of reported speech following **arbitrantur**. **sint comprehēnsī** is a subjunctive because it follows the relative pronoun **quī** within reported speech. **grātiōra** is a comparative form of the adjective **grātus**. For more information on the comparison of adjectives, see page 22.

The battle of Pharsalus

It is August 48 BCE and final victory over Pompey is within reach. Just as the best war movies focus on the stories of individual heroes, so here Caesar highlights the courage and devotion of the veteran Crastinus. And you won't be surprised to learn that he will make the ultimate sacrifice.

12

erat[1] C.[6] Crastīnus[7] ēvocātus[2] in[3] exercitū[5] Caesaris[4], quī[1] superiōre[2] annō[3] apud eum[4] prīmum[6] pīlum[7] in[8] legiōne[10] X[9] dūxerat[5], vir[1] singulārī[2] virtūte[3]. hic[3] signō[1] datō[2], 'sequiminī[5] mē[6],' inquit[4], 'manipulārēs[10] meī[9] quī[7] fuistis[8], et[11] vestrō[13] imperātōrī[14] quam[16] cōnstituistis[17] operam[15] date[12]. ūnum[2] hoc[1] proelium[3] superest[4]; quō[1] cōnfectō[2] et[3] ille[4] suam[5] dignitātem[6] et[7] nōs[8] nostram[9] libertātem[10] recuperābimus[11].' simul[1] respiciēns[2] Caesarem[3], 'faciam[5],' inquit[4], 'hodiē[6], imperātor[7], ut[8] aut[11] vīvō[12] mihi[10] aut[13] mortuō[14] grātiās agās[9].' haec[3] cum[1] dīxisset[2], prīmus[5] ex[6] dextrō[7] cornū[8] prōcucurrit[4], atque[9] eum[18] ēlectī[10] mīlitēs[11] circiter[12] CXX[13] voluntāriī[14] eiusdem[15] cohortīs[16] sunt prōsecūtī[17].

There was[1] a recalled veteran[2] in[3] Caesar's[4] army[5], Gaius[6] Crastinus[7], who[1] the previous[2] year[3] in his service[4] had led[5] the first[6] infantry section[7] in[8] the Tenth[9] Legion[10], a man[1] of outstanding[2] courage[3]. With the signal[1] given[2] this[3] [man] said[4], 'Follow[5] me[6], [you] who[7] were[8] my[9] fellow-soldiers[10], and[11] give[12] to your[13] general[14] the service[15] which[16] you have decided on[17]. This[1] one[2] battle[3] remains[4]; with it[1] finished[2] both[3] he[4] his[5] honour[6] and[7] we[8] our[9] liberty[10] will regain[11].'
At the same time[1] looking back at[2] Caesar[3], he said[4], 'I shall serve[5] today[6], general[7], so that[8] you give thanks[9] to me[10] whether[11] alive[12] or[13] dead[14].' When[1] he had said[2] these things[3], he ran forward[4] first[5] from[6] the right[7] wing[8], and[9] select[10] soldiers[11] – about[12] 120[13] volunteers[14] of the same[15] cohort[16] – followed after[17] him[18].

Nota bene

ēvocātus is a past participle used as a noun; **datō** and **cōnfectō** are both past participles. For more information on past participles, see page 83. **sequiminī** is a form of the imperative of the deponent verb **sequī**. For more information on deponent verbs, see page 115. **respiciēns** is a form of the present participle of **respicere**. For more information on present participles, see page 87. **agās** is a subjunctive because it is expressing purpose following **ut**, and **dīxisset** because it follows **cum** (meaning *when*). For more information on when to use the subjunctive, see page 104. **ēlectī** is a past participle. **sunt prōsecūtī** is a form of the deponent verb **prōsequī**.

Culture vulture

The **centuriō** (meaning *a centurion*) was the most important figure in the Roman army. Centurions were highly experienced professional soldiers who had risen from the ranks on merit. They were responsible for the training and discipline of the infantrymen under their command and they provided invaluable advice and expertise to the senior officers in their legion.

A Roman legion was made up of ten cohorts. The first cohort was made up of five centuries of about 160 men each, with a centurion in charge, assisted by an **optiō** (meaning literally *a helper*). The man in command of the first of these five centuries, or the **prīmum pīlum** (meaning literally *the first javelin*), was that legion's top-ranking centurion. Gaius Crastinus at Pharsalus was such a man. There were nine further cohorts, each made up of six centuries of about 80 men.

So there were over 5,000 foot-soldiers in a legion. These legionaries were all Roman citizens who had signed up to serve in the army full-time for 25 years. They were highly trained in infantry warfare, particularly the use of the **gladius** (meaning *a short sword*) and the **pīlum** (meaning *a javelin*). However, they were often tradesmen as well, like blacksmiths, carpenters, or engineers. They made their own weapons and constructed their own forts, dug ditches, and built roads.

This heavily-armed infantry was supported by horsemen and other specialist troops, such as archers and slingers. The cavalry would be positioned on either side of the infantry like wings – and known as a **cornū** (meaning literally *a horn*) – so that it could be deployed either to protect the centre or to attack the opposing forces. On completion of their military service, these auxiliaries were also granted Roman citizenship.

The man overall in charge of the legion was the **lēgātus** (meaning literally *a deputy*). He was a member of the Roman Senate, appointed to lead a legion for only a few years before going back to civilian life. The commander was supported by a **tribūnus mīlitum** (meaning literally *an officer of the soldiers*), usually a young aristocrat at the start of his political career, and five other tribunes of lower rank also aiming to land the more sought-after posts in government and colonial administration.

The legionary fortress not only housed the barracks for the ten cohorts, but also the **prīncipia** (meaning *the camp headquarters*), the **praetōrium** (meaning *the commander's living-quarters*), the **valētūdinārium** (meaning *the hospital*), the **horrea** (meaning *the grain-stores*), and the **thermae** (meaning *the bath-house*). Outside the fortress ramparts was the **amphitheātrum** (meaning *the amphitheatre*) where parades and training took place, and always a large settlement of locals providing goods and services to the soldiers.

The **aquila** (meaning *the eagle*) was the legion's standard and drew intense, almost religious, devotion from the soldiers. This was housed in the **sacellum** (meaning *a chapel*) at the very heart of the fortress.

Catullus

ōdī et amō – I hate and I love

Catullus left his home town of Verona in his early twenties and joined the fashionable literary set in 60s BCE Rome. He soon embarked on a turbulent love affair with the wealthy socialite Clodia, and much of the selection in this unit will show you the effect of their relationship. Barely 40 years old when he died, Catullus had a profound influence on writers as diverse as Virgil and Martial. For more information on Virgil or Martial, see pages 182 and 214.

A lover's pet

You see the young Catullus' playful wit at work in this early poem as he addresses his lover's pet sparrow with the formality that was usually reserved for hymns to a favourite god or goddess.

13

passer[1], dēliciae[2] meae[3] puellae[4],
quīcum[1] lūdere[3], quem[4] in[6] sinū[7] tenēre[5],
cui[8] prīmum digitum[10] dare[9] appetentī[11]
et[12] ācrīs[14] solet[2] incitāre[13] morsūs[15]
cum[1] dēsīderiō[4] meō[4] nitentī[3]
cārum[8] nescio[6] quid[7] lubet[2] iocārī[5],
et[1] sōlāciolum[2] suī[3] dolōris[4],
crēdō[5], ut[6] tum[7] gravis[8] acquiescat[10] ardor[9]:
tēcum[3] lūdere[2] sīcut[4] ipsa[5] possem[1]
et[6] tristīs[8] animī[10] levāre[7] curās[9]!

Sparrow[1], the darling[2] of my[3] girl[4],
Who[1] she likes[2] to play[3] with[1], who[4] to hold[5] in[6] her lap[7],
Who[8] to offer[9] her finger-tip[10] to when pecking[11]
And[12] to excite[13] sharp[14] bites[15] from
When[1] it pleases[2] the radiant[3] object of my desire[4]
To play[5] I know not[6] what[7] dear[8] joke[5]
(And[1] a small consolation[2] for her[3] pain[4],
I believe[5], so that[6] then[7] her heavy[8] passion[9] may be at rest[10]):
Would that I could[1] play[2] with you[3] like[4] her[5]
And[6] lighten[7] the gloomy[8] cares[9] of my heart[10]!

Nota bene

quīcum = **cum quō**. **appetentī** is the dative singular masculine of the present participle of **appetere** and **nitentī** the dative singular feminine of **nitere**. For more information on present participles, see page 87. **ācrīs** is an alternative way to spell the usual accusative plural form **ācrēs**. **lubet** is an impersonal verb that is followed by the dative case and the infinitive (here a deponent verb, **iocārī**). For more information on impersonal or deponent verbs, see pages 93 and 115. **acquiescat** is a subjunctive because it is expressing purpose after **ut** and **possem** because it is expressing a wish. For more information on when to use the subjunctive, see page 104. **tēcum** = **cum tē**. **tristīs** is an alternative form of **tristēs**.

And you can see that he can't resist carrying on the joke when the bird has died. (Ovid also wrote a poem when his girlfriend's pet bird died. For more information on Ovid, see page 206.)

14 **lūgēte[1], ō[2] Venerēs[3] Cupīdinēsque[4],**
et[5] quantum[6] est[9] hominum[8] venustiōrum[7]:
passer[1] mortuus[5] est[4] meae[2] puellae[3],
passer[1], dēliciae[2] meae[3] puellae[4].

Mourn[1], O[2] Venuses[3] and Cupids[4],
And[5] however many[6] more charming[7] people[8] there are[9]:
The sparrow[1] of my[2] girl[3] is[4] dead[5],
The sparrow[1], the darling[2] of my[3] girl[4].

Nota bene

venustiōrum is the genitive plural masculine of the comparative form of the adjective **venustus**. For more information on the comparison of adjectives, see page 22. **hominum venustiōrum** is in the genitive case after **quantum**. For more information on uses of the cases, see the supplement on page 277.

In love with Lesbia

You will search in vain to find out who the real Clodia actually was. As was the custom with poets in those days, Catullus disguises her identity with the pseudonym Lesbia.

15 **vīvāmus[1], mea[2] Lesbia[3], atque[4] amēmus[5],**
rūmōrēsque[6] senum[8] sevēriōrum[7]

omnēs[10] ūnius[11] aestimēmus[9] assis[12]!
solēs[1] occidere[3] et[4] redīre[5] possunt[2];
nōbīs[6] cum[1] semel[2] occidit[5] brevis[3] lūx[4],
nox[9] est[10] perpetua[8] ūna[7] dormienda[11].
dā[1] mī[2] bāsia[4] mille[3], deinde[5] centum[6];
dein[1] mille[2] altera[3], dein[4] secunda[5] centum[6];
deinde[1] usque[2] altera[4] mille[3], deinde[5] centum[6].
dein[1], cum[2] mīlia[5] multa[4] fēcerīmus[3] –
conturbābimus[1] illa[2], nē sciāmus[3],
aut[1] nē quis malus[2] invidēre[4] possit[3],
cum[1] tantum[4] sciat[2] esse[3] bāsiōrum[5].

Let's live[1], my[2] Lesbia[3], and[4] let's love[5],
And the opinions[6] of more austere[7] old men[8]
Let's count[9] them all[10] worth one[11] penny[12]!
Suns[1] can[2] set[3] and[4] return[5];
When[1] once[2] the brief[3] light[4] sets[5] on us[6],
The one[7] eternal[8] night[9] is[10] for sleeping[11].
Give[1] to me[2] a thousand[3] kisses[4], then[5] a hundred[6];
Then[1] a thousand[2] other ones[3], then[4] a second[5] hundred[6];
Then[1] still[2] a thousand[3] other ones[4], then[5] a hundred[6].
Then[1], when[2] we will have done[3] many[4] thousands[5] –
We will muddle[1] them[2] up, so that we do not know[3],
Or[1] so that no evil person[2] can[3] begrudge[4] [us],
When[1] he knows[2] there were[3] so many[4] kisses[5].

Nota bene

vīvāmus, **amēmus** and **aestimēmus** are all subjunctives because they express a command. For more information on when to use the subjunctive, see page 104. **ūnius** ... **assis** is a special use of the genitive case to express price. For more information on the use of cases, see the supplement on page 277. **dormienda** is the nominative singular feminine of the gerundive of **dormīre**. For more information on gerundives, see page 92. **mī** = **mihi**. **sciāmus** and **possit** are subjunctives because they are expressing purpose after the word **nē**. **tantum** is in the accusative and **esse** is the infinitive because they are part of reported speech following the verb **sciat** which is also a subjunctive, here after **cum** (meaning *when*). For more information on reported speech, see page 113. **bāsiōrum** is in the genitive case after **tantum**.

But you are left in no doubt about his own involvement in the affair, especially when things are not going well.

16 **miser[1] Catulle[2], dēsinās[3] ineptīre[4],**
et[1] quod[2] vidēs[3] perisse[4] perditum[6] dūcās[5].

Wretched[1] Catullus[2], will you stop[3] talking like a fool[4],
And[1] what[2] you see[3] has died[4] will you count[5] as lost[6].

Nota bene
dēsinās and **dūcās** are both subjunctives because they express a command. For more information on when to use the subjunctive, see page 104. **perisse** is an infinitive because it is part of reported speech following the verb **vidēs**. For more information on reported speech, see page 113.

On Cicero

You would expect Catullus to pull out all the stops to show gratitude where gratitude is due. This poem to Marcus Tullius Cicero is worthy of the famous orator himself. For more information on Cicero, see page 158.

17 **disertissime[1] Rōmulī[3] nepotum[2],**
quot[1] sunt[2] quotque[3] fuēre[4], Marce[5] Tullī[6],
quotque[7] post[9] aliīs[11] erunt[8] in[10] annīs[12],
grātiās[7] tibi[8] maximās[6] Catullus[1]
agit[5] pessimus[2] omnium[4] poēta[3],
tantō[1] pessimus[2] omnium[4] poēta[3],
quantō[5] tū[6] optimus[7] omnium[9] patrōnus[8].

Most eloquent[1] of the grandsons[2] of Romulus[3],
As many as[1] there are[2] and as many as[3] there were[4], Marcus[5] Tullius[6],
And as many as[7] there will be[8] after[9] in[10] other[11] years[12],
Catullus[1] the worst[2] poet[3] of all[4]
Gives[5] the greatest[6] thanks[7] to you[8] –
By how much[1] [he is] the worst[2] poet[3] of all[4],
By so much[5] you[6] [are] the best[7] patron[8] of all[9].

Nota bene
disertissime is a superlative form of the adjective **disertus**.
For more information on the comparison of adjectives, see page 22.
fuēre is an alternative way to spell **fuērunt**, the usual form of the third person plural of the perfect tense of **esse**.

Conflicting emotions

In his later poems, as the affair with Clodia/Lesbia seems to sour, you can clearly see the struggles going on in Catullus' heart and mind.

18

nūllī[7] sē[4] dīcit[3] mulier[2] mea[1] nūbere[6] mālle[5]
quam[8] mihi[9], nōn[10] sī[11] sē[15] Iuppiter[12] ipse[13] petat[14].
dīcit[1]: sed[2] mulier[4] cupidō[6] quod[3] dīcit[5] amantī[7],
in[10] ventō[11] et[12] rapidā[13] scrībere[9] oportet[8] aquā[14].

My[1] woman[2] says[3] that she[4] prefers[5] to be married[6] to no one[7]
Other than[8] to me[9], not[10] if[11] Jupiter[12] himself[13] asks for[14] her[15].
She says[1] [that]: but[2] what[3] a woman[4] says[5] to her eager[6] lover[7],
She should[8] write[9] in[10] the wind[11] and[12] the fast-flowing[13] water[14].

Nota bene

sē is in the accusative case and **mālle** is an infinitive because they are part of reported speech following the verb **dīcit**. For more information on reported speech, see page 113. **nūbere** is always followed by the dative case. **petat** is a subjunctive because it follows **sī**. For more information on when to use the subjunctive, see page 104. **amantī** is the dative singular masculine of the present participle of **amāre**. For more information on present participles, see page 87. **oportet** is an impersonal verb that is followed by the accusative case (left out here) and an infinitive. For more information on impersonal verbs, see page 93.

19

difficile[2] est[1] longum[5] subitō[3] dēpōnere[4] amōrem[6].
difficile[2] est[1], vērum[3] hoc[5] quālubet[6] efficiās[4].

It is[1] difficult[2] suddenly[3] to lay aside[4] a long-held[5] love[6].
It is[1] difficult[2], but[3] you should achieve[4] this[5] by any means[6].

Nota bene

efficiās is a subjunctive because it expresses a command. For more information on when to use the subjunctive, see page 104.

20

ōdī[1] et[2] amō[3]. quārē[1] id[3] faciam[2], fortasse[4] requīris[5]?
nescio[1], sed[2] fierī[4] sentiō[3] et[5] excrucior[6].

I hate[1] and[2] I love[3]. Why[1] would I do[2] that[3], perhaps[4] you're asking[5]?
I don't know[1], but[2] I feel[3] [it] happening[4] and[5] I am in torment[6].

Nota bene
faciam is a subjunctive because it reports a question indirectly after the word **quārē**. For more information on when to use the subjunctive, see page 104. **fierī** is an infinitive because it is part of reported speech following the verb **sentiō**; the accusative is left out. For more information on reported speech, see page 113.

Love for a brother

But it is not only to his lover that you find Catullus directing his love and his skill. This famous elegy to his dead brother was written when Catullus visited his tomb near Troy – and only a few years before his own death.

multās[3] per[2] gentēs[4] et[5] multa[7] per[6] aequora[8] vectus[1]
adveniō[1] hās[4] miserās[5], frāter[2], ad[3] inferiās[6],
ut[1] tē[3] postrēmō[4] dōnārem[2] mūnere[5] mortis[6]
et[1] mūtam[4] nēquīquam[2] alloquerer[3] cinerem[5].
quandōquidem[1] fortūna[2] mihī[6] tēte[4] abstulit[3] ipsum[5],
heu[1] miser[2] indignē[4] frāter[3] adempte[5] mihī[6],
nunc[1] tamen[2] intereā[3] haec[5], priscō[7] quae[6] mōre[8] parentum[9]
trādita sunt[10] tristī[11] mūnere[12] ad[13] inferiās[14],
accipe[4] frāternō[17] multum[16] mānantia[15] flētū[18],
atque[1] in[2] perpetuum[3], frāter[4], avē[5] atque[6] valē[7].

Having travelled[1] through[2] many[3] nations[4] and[5] through[6] many[7] seas[8]
I arrive[1], brother[2], at[3] these[4] wretched[5] funerary rites[6],
So that[1] I might present[2] you[3] with the last[4] observance[5] of death[6]
And[1] in vain[2] appeal to[3] your dumb[4] ashes[5].
Since[1] fortune[2] has stolen[3] you[4] yourself[5] from me[6],
Alas[1], wretched[2] brother[3] undeservedly[4] taken[5] from me[6],
Now[1] however[2] at any rate[3] receive[4] these things[5], which[6] by ancient[7] custom[8] of our ancestors[9]
Have been handed down[10] for sad[11] observance[12] at[13] funerary rites[14],
Dripping[15] much[16] with a brother's[17] weeping[18],
And[1] for[2] ever[3], brother[4], hail[5] and[6] farewell[7].

Nota bene
vectus is the past participle of the verb **vehere**. For more information on past participles, see page 83. **dōnārem** is a subjunctive and **alloquerer** is a subjunctive from the deponent verb **alloquī** because they are both expressing purpose after **ut**. For more information on when to use the subjunctive or deponent verbs,

see pages 104 and 115. **tēte** is an emphatic form of **tē**. **abstulit** is the third person singular of the perfect active of **auferre** and **adempte** is the vocative singular masculine of the past participle of the verb **adimere**. **mānantia** is the accusative plural neuter of the present participle of **mānāre**. For more information on the present participle, see page 87.

Culture vulture

The official state religion of Rome (before the adoption of Christianity) allowed for a very wide variety of gods and goddesses, and people often kept little models of their favourites in small shrines in their homes. Even foreign gods were tolerated if they shared some characteristic with an equivalent Roman deity and as long as they did not threaten orthodox beliefs and practices.

However, it was the worship of Jupiter (whom the Greeks called Zeus) that took official precedence alongside his immediate 'divine family' – Juno his wife, Ceres his sister, and his children Apollo, Diana, Mars, Minerva, and Venus. The festivals and ceremonies associated with them were strictly organised and meticulously performed by colleges of priests on behalf of the state. During the Principate, the emperor became **pontifex maximus** (meaning *the chief priest*).

Although discouraged at first in Rome, emperor worship itself gradually spread from the East and began to be used as a way of encouraging defeated nations to accept Roman rule. The **genius** (meaning *the guardian spirit*) of the emperor was now promoted as an object of veneration. When an emperor died he was deified and temples in his honour were built throughout the empire.

In order to keep on good terms with the gods, Romans of all backgrounds would sacrifice animals to them and offer them other gifts. They did this in public to secure victory in war or success in a business deal, or to give thanks for safety on a journey or recovery from ill health. And they also made offerings privately to their family and household gods to ensure peace and prosperity.

At the most important sacrifices, a **haruspex** (meaning *a soothsayer*) would examine the entrails of the victim and announce from what they saw whether the gods would be favourable or not. Another type of priest known as an **augur** (meaning *a seer*) observed the flight of birds in order to make predictions about the future.

In Roman times, including when Catullus was alive, the usual way of disposing of the dead was cremation. If the family was wealthy, the ashes of the deceased might be put into an elaborately decorated glass or metal vase and placed on a shelf inside a large tomb alongside other members of the same clan; if poor, a simple clay jar would be used and then buried straight into the earth.

Whatever their status while alive, it was believed that the dead would not be at peace unless they were looked after properly. Useful possessions such as tools, jewellery, clothes, or toys were cremated at the same time as the dead person's body. Food and drink, or flowers, were regularly left at the burial site, and animal sacrifices offered on special occasions. At annual festivals for the dead, deceased relatives were remembered and rites performed to exorcise unhappy ghosts.

Virgil

audentīs fortūna iuvat – Fortune favours the brave

The selection of poetry in this unit will introduce you to Virgil's *Aeneid*, written in the 20s BCE. This epic poem tells the story of Aeneas' hazardous journey from Troy after it had been sacked by the Greeks, and of the bitter war he fought to establish a new home in Italy. Celebrating their spirit and sense of mission in the world, the *Aeneid* was to the Romans what Homer's *Iliad* and *Odyssey* were to the Greeks.

Prologue

In these famous lines that begin the poem, you will find hints of Virgil's great sympathy for the man Aeneas and what he has to endure, as well as real pride in what Aeneas' eventual success achieved.

22

arma[2] virumque[3] canō[1], Troiae[8] quī[4] prīmus[5] ab[6] ōrīs[7]
Ītaliam[4] fātō[2] profugus[1] Lāvīniaque[5] vēnit[3]
lītora[6], multum[2] ille[1] et[4] terrīs[5] iactātus[3] et[6] altō[7]
vī[8] superum[9], saevae[4] memorem[2] Iūnōnis[5] ob[1] īram[3],
multa[4] quoque[2] et[1] bellō[5] passus[3], dum[1] conderet[2] urbem[3]
inferretque[4] deōs[5] Latiō[6]; genus[3] unde[1] Latīnum[2]
Albānīque[4] patrēs[5] atque[6] altae[7] moenia[8] Rōmae[9].

I am singing[1] of arms[2] and a man[3], who[4] first[5] from[6] the shores[7] of Troy[8] –
A fugitive[1] from fate[2] – came[3] to Italy[4] and the Lavinian[5]
Shores[6], a man[1] much[2] harassed[3] both[4] on land[5] and[6] sea[7]
By the power[8] of the gods[9], because of[1] the remembered[2] anger[3] of cruel[4] Juno[5],
And[1] also[2] having suffered[3] many things[4] in war[5], until[1] he could found[2] a city[3]
And bring[4] his gods[5] to Latium[6]; from where[1] [came] the Latin[2] race[3]
And the Alban[4] fathers[5] and[6] the high[7] walls[8] of Rome[9].

Nota bene

The preposition **ad** is left out before **Ītaliam** and **lītora**. For more information on prepositions, see page 132. **iactātus** is a past participle, as is **passus** from the deponent verb **patī**. For more information on past participles or deponent verbs, see pages 83 and 115. **conderet** and **inferret** are subjunctives in order to express a sense of hope after **dum**. For more information on when to use the subjunctive, see page 104. **Latiō** is in the dative case and is used here to indicate a destination. For more information on uses of the cases, see the supplement on page 277.

The fall of Troy

You will know what is meant by a 'Trojan horse'. No one listened to the warnings of the priest Laocoon about the original, but he has given us a proverb that has been in use ever since.

23

prīmus[1] ibi[2] ante[3] omnīs[4] magnā[5] comitante[7] catervā[6]
Lāocoōn[2] ardēns[1] summā[5] dēcurrit[3] ab[4] arce[6],
et[1] procul[2] 'ō[3] miserī[4], quae[6] tanta[7] insānia[8], cīvēs[5]?
crēditis[1] āvectōs[3] hostīs[2]? aut[1] ūlla[3] putātis[2]
dōna[4] carēre[6] dolīs[7] Danaum[5]? sīc[3] nōtus[1] Ulixēs[2]?
aut[1] hōc[3] inclūsī[2] lignō[4] occultantur[6] Achīvī[5],
aut[1] haec[2] in[5] nostrōs[6] fabricāta est[4] māchina[3] mūrōs[7],
inspectūra[1] domōs[2] ventūraque[3] dēsuper[5] urbī[4],
aut[1] aliquis[2] latet[4] error[3]; equō[6] nē crēdite[5], Teucrī[7].
quidquid[1] id[2] est[3], timeō[4] Danaōs[5] et[6] dōna[8] ferentīs[7].'

First[1] there[2] in front of[3] everyone[4] with a great[5] crowd[6] accompanying[7] [him]
Fiery[1] Laocoon[2] runs down[3] from[4] the top of[5] the citadel[6],
And[1] from afar[2] [says]: 'O[3] wretched[4] citizens[5], what[6] so great[7] madness[8] [is this]?
Do you believe[1] your enemies[2] have sailed away[3]? Or[1] do you think[2] any[3]
Gifts[4] of the Greeks[5] are free[6] from tricks[7]? [Is] famous[1] Ulysses[2] so[3]?
Either[1] shut in[2] by this[3] timber[4] the Greeks[5] are hidden[6],
Or[1] this[2] contraption[3] has been built[4] against[5] our[6] walls[7],
About to see into[1] our homes[2] and come upon[3] our city[4] from above[5],
Or[1] some[2] deception[3] lies hidden[4]; do not trust[5] a horse[6], Trojans[7].
Whatever[1] it[2] is[3], I fear[4] the Greeks[5] even[6] bearing[7] gifts[8].'

Nota bene

omnīs, **hostīs** and **ferentīs** are all alternative ways to spell the usual accusative plural forms **omnēs**, **hostēs** and **ferentēs**. **comitante** is a form of the present participle of **comitāre**. For more information on present participles, see page 87. **Danaum** is an alternative way to spell the usual genitive plural form **Danaōrum**. **hostīs** and **āvectōs** (which is the past participle of the verb **āvehere** in its passive form) are in the accusative case because they are part of a reported speech following the verb **crēditis**; the infinitive **esse** has been left out. For more information on past participles or reported speech, see pages 83 and 113. **ūlla dōna** is in the accusative case and **carēre** (which is always followed by the ablative case) is an infinitive because they are part of reported speech following **putātis**. **inclūsī** is a past participle; **inspectūra** and **ventūra** are future participles. For more information on future participles, see page 91. **urbī** is in the dative case and is used here to indicate a destination. For more information on uses of the cases, see the supplement on page 277. **nē crēdite** is an alternative way to express the command **nōlīte crēdere**. For more information on the imperative, see page 55. **crēdere** is always followed by the dative case.

Aeneas and Dido

You won't be surprised that Virgil took care to put these contentious words in the mouth of a god – Mercury, the spokesman for Jupiter, is urging Aeneas to abandon his lover Dido and leave Carthage.

24 **'heīa[1] age[2], rumpe[3] morās[4]. varium[1] et[2] mūtābile[3] semper[4]**
fēmina[5].' sīc[2] fātus[1] noctī[5] sē immiscuit[3] ātrae[4].

'Come[1] act[2], break off[3] your delays[4]. Fickle[1] and[2] changeable[3] always[4] [Is] a woman[5].' Having spoken[1] thus[2] he mixed himself in[3] to the black[4] night[5].

Nota bene

heīa is used in sentences that encourage someone to do something. **fātus** is the past participle of the defective verb **fārī**. For more information on past participles or defective verbs, see pages 83 and 117.

And you won't be surprised that Dido's love turns to hate. As she prepares to die at her own hand, she anticipates the prolonged and bloody rivalry between Rome and Carthage in the Punic Wars.

25 **'tum[1] vōs[2], ō[3] Tyriī[4], stirpem[5] et[6] genus[9] omne[7] futūrum[8]**
exercēte[10] odiīs[11], cinerīque[4] haec[2] mittite[1] nostrō[3]
mūnera[5]. nūllus[2] amor[3] populīs[4] nec[5] foedera[6] suntō[1].
exoriāre[1] aliquis[2] nostrīs[5] ex[4] ossibus[6] ultor[3]
quī[1] face[2] Dardaniōs[5] ferrōque[3] sequāre[4] colōnōs[6],
nunc[1], ōlim[2], quōcumque[3] dabunt[6] sē[7] tempore[4] vīrēs[5].

lītora[1] lītoribus[3] contrāria[2], fluctibus[5] undās[4]
imprecor[6], arma[7] armīs[8]: pugnent[1] ipsīque[2] nepotēsque[3].'

'Then[1] you[2], o[3] Phoenicians[4], his offspring[5] and[6] whole[7] future[8] race[9]
Harass[10] with hatred[11], and send[1] these[2] to our[3] ashes[4]
As funerary gifts[5]. Let there be[1] no[2] love[3] for our peoples[4] nor[5] treaties[6].
May you rise up[1], some[2] avenger[3] from[4] our[5] bones[6]
Who[1] with torch[2] and sword[3] would pursue[4] the Trojan[5] settlers[6],
Now[1], one day[2], at whatever[3] time[4] strength[5] will offer[6] itself[7].
Shores[1] opposed to[2] shores[3], waves[4] to waves[5]
I call down[6], arms[7] to arms[8]: let them fight[1], both they themselves[2] and
their grandchildren[3].'

> **Nota bene**
> **suntō** is a rare form of the imperative of the verb **esse**. For more information on the imperative, see page 55. **exoriāre** is an alternative way to spell the second person singular of the present subjunctive of the deponent verb **exorīrī** and **sequāre** of **sequī**. For more information on deponent verbs, see page 115. **pugnent** is a subjunctive because it is expressing a wish. For more information on when to use the subjunctive, see page 104.

Aeneas in the underworld

You will perhaps recognise this famously quoted line. Virgil has the god Apollo put the original words into the mouth of his priestess when she is offering reassurance that Aeneas would reach his goal – but not without regret.

26

'sed[1] nōn[4] et[2] vēnisse[5] volent[3]. bella[1], horrida[2] bella[3],
et[5] Thȳbrim[6] multō[8] spūmantem[7] sanguine[9] cernō[4].'

'But[1] also[2] they will want[3] not[4] to have come[5]. Wars[1], frightful[2] wars[3],
I see[4] and[5] the Tiber[6] foaming[7] with much[8] blood[9].'

> **Nota bene**
> **spūmantem** is a form of the present participle of **spūmāre**.
> For more information on present participles, see page 87.

You might find something comical about this image of the three-headed guard dog of Hell collapsing after gobbling up food that has been spiked. Hercules fought Cerberus bare-handed and won; but you can tell that Virgil is not modelling Aeneas on Hercules.

27 **Cerberus[2] haec[6] ingēns[1] lātrātū[4] regna[7] trifaucī[3]**
personat[5] adversō[12] recubāns[8] immānis[9] in[10] antrō[11].
cui[3] vātēs[1] horrēre[6] vidēns[2] iam[5] colla[4] colubrīs[7]
melle[4] sopōrātam[3] et[5] medicātīs[6] frūgibus[7] offam[2]
ōbicit[1]. ille[1] famē[6] rabidā[5] tria[3] guttura[4] pandēns[2]
corripit[7] ōbiectam[8], atque[1] immānia[3] terga[4] resolvit[2]
fūsus[5] humī[6] tōtōque[9] ingēns[8] extenditur[7] antrō[10].
occupat[2] Aenēās[1] aditum[3] custōde[4] sepultō[5]
ēvāditque[6] celer[7] rīpam[8] inremeābilis[10] undae[9].

Huge[1] Cerberus[2] with his three-throated[3] barking[4] makes[5] these[6] kingdoms[7]
Resound[5], lying back[8] immense[9] in[10] the cave[11] opposite[12].
The priestess[1], seeing[2] his[3] necks[4] already[5] bristle[6] with snakes[7],
Throws[1] a sop[2] made sleepy[3] with honey[4] and[5] with drugged[6] meal[7]
In front of him[1]. He[1] opening out[2] his three[3] throats[4] with raging[5] hunger[6]
Snatches up[7] what was thrown[8], and[1] relaxes[2] his immense[3] back[4],
Spread out[5] on the ground[6], and is stretched out[7] huge[8] in the whole[9] cave[10].
Aeneas[1] seizes[2] the entrance[3] with its guardian[4] buried[5] [in sleep]
And passes[6] swift[7] over the bank[8] of the river[9] of no return[10].

Nota bene

recubāns, **vidēns** and **pandēns** all present participles. For more information on present participles, see page 87. **cui** is in the dative case to express possession. For more information on uses of the cases, see the supplement on page 277. **colla** is in the accusative case and **horrēre** is an infinitive because they are part of reported speech following **vidēns**. For more information on reported speech, see page 113. **sopōrātam**, **medicātīs**, **ōbiectam**, **fūsus** and **sepultō** are all past participles. For more information on past participles, see page 83.

The ghost of Anchises, Aeneas' father, composes Rome's mission statement in contrast to the achievements of the Greeks and others. You can decide whether they actually lived up to it.

28 **'excūdent[2] aliī[1] spīrantia[4] mollius[3] aera[5]**
(crēdō[2] equidem[1]), vīvōs[2] dūcent[1] dē[4] marmore[5] vultūs[3],
ōrābunt[1] causās[2] melius[3], caelīque[3] meātūs[2]
dēscrībent[1] radiō[4] et[5] surgentia[7] sīdera[8] dīcent[6]:
tū[1] regere[4] imperiō[6] populōs[5], Rōmāne[2], mementō[3]

(hae[1] tibi[3] erunt[2] artēs[4]), pācīque[3] impōnere[1] mōrem[2],
parcere[1] subiectīs[2] et[3] dēbellāre[4] superbōs[5].'

'Others[1] will beat out[2] more gently[3] breathing[4] bronze[5]
(So[1] I believe[2]), will draw[1] living[2] expressions[3] from[4] marble[5],
Will argue[1] cases[2] better[3], and will describe[1] the movements[2] of the sky[3]
With the measuring-rod[4] and[5] tell of[6] the rising[7] constellations[8]:
You[1], Roman[2], remember[3] to rule[4] the peoples[5] with mastery[6]
(These[1] will be[2] your[3] skills[4]), and to impose[1] the custom[2] for peace[3],
To spare[1] the defeated[2] and[3] to conquer[4] the proud[5].'

> **Nota bene**
> **spīrantia** is a form of the present participle **spīrāns** and **surgentia** of **surgēns**. For more information on present participles, see page 87. **mollius** is the comparative form of the adverb **molliter** and **melius** of **bene**. For more information on the comparison of adverbs, see page 129. **mementō** is a form of the imperative of the defective verb **meminisse** (meaning *to remember*). For more information on defective verbs, see page 117. **subiectīs** is a past participle. For more information on past participles, see page 83.

The death of Turnus

You will find Virgil very sympathetic to those who had the misfortune to stand in the way of Aeneas' divine mission. Dido was one example; here, very close to the end of the poem, you get a picture of the hopeless position that local prince Turnus is in, trying to defeat the invader.

29

ac[1] velut[2] in[3] somnīs[4], oculōs[9] ubi[5] languida[6] pressit[8]
nocte[10] Quiēs[7], nēquīquam[1] avidōs[5] extendere[4] cursūs[6]
velle[3] vidēmur[2] et[7] in[8] mediīs[9] cōnātibus[10] aegrī[11]
succidimus[12]; nōn[2] lingua[1] valet[2], nōn[5] corpore[6] nōtae[3]
sufficiunt[5] vīrēs[4] nec[7] vōx[8] aut[9] verba[10] sequuntur[11].

And[1] just as[2] in[3] sleep[4], when[5] gentle[6] Rest[7] has closed[8] the eyes[9]
At night[10], in vain[1] we seem[2] to want[3] to stretch out[4]
Eager[5] movements[6] and[7] in[8] the middle of[9] our efforts[10], weak[11],
We fail[12]; the tongue[1] is of no use[2], known[3] strength[4]
Is not enough[5] for the body[6] and neither[7] voice[8] nor[9] words[10] follow[11].

Nota bene

vidēmur is a form of the deponent verb **vidērī** and **sequuntur** of **sequī**. For more information on deponent verbs, see page 115.

Culture vulture

At its peak the Roman Empire stretched from the Scottish Borders to the Sahara Desert and from the Atlantic Ocean to the Persian Gulf. The system of government required to maintain order across such a vast area was complex and open to abuse. Rome's ruling elite, i.e. the emperor and the Senate, were always on the lookout for men of outstanding ability who could be trusted to govern as their representatives overseas.

In many frontier provinces like Britain, which tended to be more volatile, the emperor himself appointed the governor in charge, known as **lēgātus Augustī** (meaning literally *a deputy of Augustus*). In the other more peaceful provinces, the appointment of governor – known as **prōcōnsul** (meaning literally *in place of the consul*) – was up to the Senate*. In almost all provinces to be governor you had to be a senator who had already achieved the highest offices of state.

The capabilities of a potential governor were displayed through a senatorial career ladder known as the **cursus honōrum** (meaning literally *the course of public offices*). You began in Rome for a year as a **vīgintīvir** (meaning literally *a 20-man*), one of 20 young men in a junior management position. You then went abroad on military service to join a legion as a **tribūnus mīlitum** (meaning literally *an officer of the soldiers*).

Back in Rome, you would be aiming to become a **quaestor** (meaning literally *an investigator*) for a year, a post which involved the management of public money and qualified you for formal entry into the Senate itself where government business was debated. Promotion beyond this meant either becoming a **tribūnus plēbis** (meaning literally *an officer of the people*) or an **aedīlis** (meaning literally *of a building*). Aediles were responsible for the maintenance of public services and amenities.

Only once you had been a **praetor** (meaning literally *someone in command*), a post which involved supervision of the law courts in Rome, could you finally look forward to the command of a legion abroad or the governorship of a province. However, the governorship of some provinces only went to men who had served as **cōnsul** (meaning *a consul*). The consulship was the highest public office of all in Rome and involved presiding over meetings of the Senate and steering government business.

A few provinces were governed by a **praefectus** (meaning *a prefect*), a post open only to non-senators. The most important of these was Egypt, which as Rome's 'bread-basket' was judged too strategic to have a potentially over-ambitious senator in charge. Judaea was also governed by a Roman prefect, the most famous being Pontius Pilate.

* There were exceptions, however. Rather than leaving the choice to the Senate, Trajan himself chose Pliny to be governor of Bithynia in 109 CE. (For more information on Pliny, see page 229.)

Horace

carpe dīem – Seize the day

If you need reminding of the value of a good education, the selection of lyric poetry in this unit will show what an Italian former slave managed to achieve for his son. Having attended the best schools in Rome and Athens, and despite having fought on the wrong side at the battle of Philippi in 42 BCE, Horace rose to become one of the most highly acclaimed poets of the golden age of Augustus – and is now one of the most frequently quoted writers from the Classical world.

Taking the proverbial

Horace's literary criticism is still studied by students of literature today, and you'll discover that some of his original observations have become established sayings.

30 **parturient[2] montēs[1], nascētur[5] rīdiculus[3] mūs[4].**

Mountains[1] will be in labour[2], a laughable[3] mouse[4] will be born[5].

> **Nota bene**
> **nascētur** is a form of the deponent verb **nascī**. For more information on deponent verbs, see page 115.

31 **indignor[1] quandōque[2] bonus[3] dormītat[5] Homērus[4].**

I am offended[1] whenever[2] good[3] Homer[4] nods[5].

> **Nota bene**
> **indignor** is a form of the deponent verb **indignārī**. For more information on deponent verbs, see page 115.

You will find that Horace's letters are also full of clever reflections on contemporary life, like these opening lines addressed to the unknown Numicius.

32 **nīl[2] admīrārī[1] prope[4] rēs[6] est[3] ūna[5], Numicī[7],**
sōlaque[1] quae[2] possit[3] facere[4] et[5] servāre[6] beātum[7].

To wonder at[1] nothing[2] is[3] nearly[4] the one[5] thing[6], Numicius[7],
And the only[1] [thing] which[2] can[3] make[4] and[5] keep[6] [a man] happy[7].

> **Nota bene**
> **admīrārī** is the infinitive of a deponent verb. For more information on deponent verbs, see page 115.

And before long you appreciate how quotable Horace's letters have become.

33 **nātūram[2] expellēs[1] furcā[3], tamen[4] usque[5] recurret[6].**

You will drive out[1] nature[2] with a pitchfork[3], however[4] she will[6] always[5] run back[6].

34 **et[1] semel[2] ēmissum[3] volat[5] irrevocābile[6] verbum[4].**

And[1] once[2] sent out[3] a word[4] is in flight[5] that cannot be called back[6].

> **Nota bene**
> **ēmissum** is a form of the past participle of **ēmittere**. For more information on past participles, see page 83.

35 **scrībimus[3] indoctī[1] doctīque[2] poēmata[4] passim[5].**

Unskilled[1] and skilled[2] we write[3] poems[4] everywhere[5].

> **Nota bene**
> **poēmata** is the accusative plural of the Greek noun **poēma**.

The benefits of fine wine

You are left in no doubt that Horace valued the good things in life. In one of the early Odes, the mythical Teucer has had a glass or two and is encouraging his men as they accompany him into exile from the island of Salamis. They go on to found another Salamis on Cyprus.

36 **'nīl[1] dēspērandum[2] Teucrō[3] duce[4] et[5] auspice[6]: Teucrī[5]**
certus[2] enim[1] prōmīsit[4] Apollō[3]
ambiguam[4] tellūre[2] novā[1] Salamīna[5] futūram[3].'

'Nothing[1] should be despaired of[2] with Teucer[3] as leader[4] and[5]
protector[6]:
For[1] faithful[2] Apollo[3] has promised[4] of Teucer[5]
That in a new[1] land[2] there will be[3] a second[4] Salamis[5].'

> **Nota bene**
> **dēspērandum** is a form of the gerundive of the verb **dēspērāre**. For more information on gerundives, see page 92. **Salamīna** is in the accusative case and **futūram** is part of an infinitive (with **esse** left out) because they are part of reported speech following **prōmīsit**. For more information on reported speech, see page 113.

You will find Horace more urgent here. There is nothing mythical about what he has cause to celebrate in this early Ode: it is 30 BCE and Cleopatra, who had spread terror across the Roman world, was dead.

37

nunc[1] est bibendum[2], nunc[3] pede[5] līberō[4]
pulsanda[7] tellus[6], nunc[8] Saliāribus[10]
ornāre[14] pulvīnar[15] deōrum[16]
tempus[13] erat[12] dapibus[11], sodālēs[9].

Now[1] one must drink[2], now[3] with unrestrained[4] foot[5]
The earth[6] must be struck[7], now[8], comrades[9],
With magnificent[10] feasts[11] it was[12] time[13]
To decorate[14] the couch[15] of the gods[16].

> **Nota bene**
> **bibendum** is a form of the gerundive of the verb **bibere** and **pulsanda** of **pellere**. For more information on gerundives, see page 92. **Saliāribus** is a form of the adjective **Saliāris** (referring to the Salii, who were priests of Mars and famous for their extravagant celebrations).

Odes 3: setting the challenge

The third book of Odes is generally regarded as Horace's most important achievement. Right from the outset you hear him confidently proclaiming himself the champion of a new kind of poetry.

38 **ōdī[1] profānum[2] vulgus[3] et[4] arceō[5];**
favēte[1] linguīs[2]: carmina[3] nōn[4] prius[6]
audīta[5] Mūsārum[8] sacerdōs[7]
virginibus[10] puerīsque[11] cantō[9].

I hate[1] the uninitiated[2] crowd[3] and[4] I keep [it] at a distance[5];
Be reverent[1] with your tongues[2]: songs[3] not[4] heard[5] before[6]
As priest[7] of the Muses[8]
I sing[9] to girls[10] and boys[11].

Nota bene
audīta is a form of the past participle of **audīre**. For more information on past participles, see page 83.

And his is poetry that has clearly made a lasting impression, since you will no doubt recognise the first line of this extract from Wilfred Owen's WWI poem.

39 **dulce[2] et[3] decōrum[4] est[1] prō[6] patriā[7] morī[5]:**
mors[1] et[2] fugācem[4] persequitur[3] virum[5],
nec[1] parcit[2] imbellis[3] iuventae[4]
poplitibus[5] timidōve[6] tergō[7].

It is[1] pleasant[2] and[3] proper[4] to die[5] for[6] your country[7]:
Death[1] even[2] pursues[3] the fleeing[4] man[5],
Nor[1] does it spare[2] of unwarlike[3] youth[4]
The knees[5] or the fainthearted[6] back[7].

Nota bene
morī is the infinitive of a deponent verb and **persequitur** is a form of the deponent verb **persequī**. For more information on deponent verbs, see page 115. **parcit** is from **parcere** and is always followed by the dative case. For more information on the uses of the cases, see the supplement on page 277.

Odes 3: in praise of poetry

One of Horace's most celebrated poems is in honour of an obscure country spring – but listen closely and you will see that in the end it is as much in honour of Horace's own prowess as a poet.

40

ō[1] fōns[2] Bandusiae[3], splendidior[4] vitrō[5],
dulcī[2] digne[1] merō[3] nōn[4] sine[5] flōribus[6],
crās[1] dōnāberis[2] haedō[3],
cui[1] frōns[2] turgida[3] cornibus[5]

prīmīs[4] et[7] venerem[8] et[9] proelia[10] dēstinat[6].
frūstrā[1]: nam[2] gelidōs[10] īnficiet[8] tibi[9]
rubrō[6] sanguine[7] rīvōs[11]
lascīvī[4] subolēs[3] gregis[5].

tē[7] flāgrantis[3] atrōx[1] hōra[2] Canīculae[4]
nescit[5] tangere[6], tū[1] frīgus[4] amābile[3]
fessīs[6] vōmere[7] taurīs[5]
praebēs[2] et[8] pecorī[10] vagō[9].

fīēs[3] nōbilium[4] tū[1] quoque[2] fontium[5],
mē[1] dīcente[2] cavīs[5] impositam[4] īlicem[3]
saxīs[6], unde[7] loquācēs[9]
lymphae[10] dēsiliunt[11] tuae[8].

O[1] spring[2] of Bandusia[3], more splendid[4] than glass[5],
Worthy[1] of sweet[2] wine[3] not[4] without[5] flowers[6],
Tomorrow[1] you shall be presented[2] with a kid[3],
Whose[1] brow[2] swollen[3] with [its] first[4]

Horns[5] forecasts[6] both[7] love[8] and[9] battles[10].
In vain[1]: for[2] the offspring[3] of the playful[4] herd[5]
With red[6] blood[7]
Will stain[8] your[9] cold[10] streams[11].

The fierce[1] hour[2] of the blazing[3] Dog Star[4]
Does not know how[5] to touch[6] you[7], you[1] offer[2] cherished[3] coolness[4]
To bulls[5] weary[6] from the ploughshare[7]
And[8] to the wandering[9] flock[10].

You[1], too[2], will become[3] [one] of the famous[4] springs[5],
With me[1] telling[2] of the holm-oak[3] set on[4] the hollow[5]
Rocks[6], from where[7] your[8] chattering[9]
Waters[10] jump down[11].

Nota bene

splendidior is the comparative form of the adjective **splendidus**. For more information on the comparison of adjectives, see page 22. **cui** is in the dative case because it expresses possession. For more information on uses of the cases, see the supplement on page 277. **flāgrantis** is a form of the present participle **flāgrāns** and **dīcente** of **dīcēns**. For more information on present participles, see page 87. **impositam** is a form of the past participle of **impōnere**. For more information on past participles, see page 83.

Odes 3: claiming the prize

In the final ode of this third book you can see that Horace now feels extremely confident of his place among the greats.

41

exēgī[1] monumentum[2] aere[4] perennius[3]
rēgālīque[6] sitū[7] pȳramidum[8] altius[5],
quod[1] nōn[2] imber[4] edax[3], nōn[5] Aquilō[7] impotēns[6]
possit[8] dīruere[9] aut[10] innumerābilis[11]
annōrum[13] seriēs[12] et[14] fuga[15] tempōrum[16].
nōn[1] omnis[2] moriar[1], multaque[3] pars[4] meī[5]
vītābit[6] Libitīnam[7]: usque[1] ego[2] posterā[5]
crescam[3] laude[6] recēns[4], dum[1] Capitolium[4]
scandet[3] cum[5] tacitā[6] virgine[7] pontifex[2].

I have completed[1] a memorial[2] most lasting[3] than bronze[4]
And more lofty[5] than the royal[6] site[7] of the pyramids[8],
Which[1] no[2] greedy[3] storm[4], no[5] violent[6] north wind[7]
Is able[8] to destroy[9] or[10] the countless[11]
Cycle[12] of the years[13] and[14] flight[15] of the ages[16].
I shall not[1] all[2] die[1], and a great[3] part[4] of me[5]
Shall avoid[6] death[7]: always[1] I[2] shall grow[3]
Fresh[4] from future[5] praise[6], as long as[1] the high priest[2]
Shall climb[3] the Capitol[4] with[5] the silent[6] [Vestal] virgin[7].

Nota bene

perennius is a comparative form of the adjective **perennis** and **altius** of **altus**. For more information on the comparison of adjectives, see page 22. **moriar** is a form of the deponent verb **morī**. For more information on deponent verbs, see page 115.

The golden mean

Horace is famous for advocating 'moderation in all things' and 'a middle way'. This extract from one of his more moralising pieces gives you a flavour of what that meant for a poet who had come so far from such humble beginnings.

42

hoc[1] erat[2] in[3] vōtīs[4]: modus[1] agrī[2] nōn[3] ita[4] magnus[5],
hortus[2] ubi[1] et[4] tectō[6] vīcīnus[5] iūgis[8] aquae[9] fōns[7]
et[10] paulum[11] silvae[12] super[13] hīs[14] foret[3].

This[1] was[2] in[3] my prayers[4]: a measure[1] of land[2] not[3] so[4] large[5],
Where[1] a garden[2] should be[3] and[4] near[5] to the house[6] a spring[7] of running[8] water[9]
And[10] a small bit[11] of woodland[12] beyond[13] these[14].

Nota bene

foret is an alternative form of the third person singular of the imperfect subjunctive of **esse**. For more information on the subjunctive, see page 95.

Culture vulture

The purpose of giving boys an education in Roman times was to teach them the things that made for a cultured and civilised life: essential literacy (in both Latin and Greek), simple numeracy, an appreciation of their Latin and Greek literary heritage, and the art of rhetoric. It wasn't required by law and it had to be paid for, but the advantages of a sound education were widely recognised.

Formal schooling began at about the age of seven, when boys would have started attending the class of a **lūdī magister** (meaning *a master of a school*) in a rented room or public place. Then, once they had achieved a basic level of literacy and numeracy, it was felt by many parents that by the age of eleven their children had learnt enough through formal education and they were directed more specifically towards earning a living, perhaps through an apprenticeship in a trade or business.

Girls were also expected to be able to read and write, but they usually learnt these things within the home from their parents or brothers. The chief goal set for them was to learn the skills of a good home-maker and how to organise a household of slaves (if they were affluent enough to have them) – in preparation for becoming a wife and having a home of their own from the age of 14 or so.

Boys from the wealthier families, however, went on to more advanced schooling run by a **grammaticus** (meaning *a language/literature teacher*). The next four or five years would be spent concentrating on the great works of the literary canon at that time, to the point where the boys had an excellent understanding of Greek, as well as Latin, language and literature.

They started with the *Iliad* and the *Odyssey* of Homer, regarded as the bedrock of that Greek culture and civilisation the Romans admired so much and took so much inspiration from. Then they moved on to the works of the Athenian dramatists of the fifth century BCE – such as Aeschylus' *Oresteia*, Sophocles' *Oedipus Rex* and the *Medea* by Euripides. Latin poetry also featured strongly, including Virgil and Horace himself. (For more information on Virgil, see page 182.)

These works of literature would be read aloud, their grammatical structures analysed, and long passages would be learnt off by heart. Such an approach prepared the boys well if they went on to a third and final stage of formal education, at the school of a **rhētor** (meaning *a rhetoric teacher*). These teachers were often Greek and they trained their students in the art of public speaking, drawing from the celebrated Greek orators who had gone before, such as Demosthenes.

Livy

vae victīs – Down with the defeated

You won't want to use Livy as a guide to finding your way over the Alps, but the extracts in this unit will show you how a Roman historian could use the skills of a poet to impress upon his readers what had made their people great. His monumental history of Rome charts the rise of the city from its legendary beginnings, via the traumas of the Punic Wars, to being the centre of a vast empire during the reign of Augustus.

Romulus and Remus

You discover straightaway that Livy has a very high regard for Rome and its achievements.

43

sed[1] dēbēbātur[13], ut[2] opīnor[3], fātīs[14] tantae[5] orīgō[4] urbis[6] maximīque[8] secundum[10] deōrum[12] opēs[11] imperiī[9] prīncipium[7].

But[1], so[2] I believe[3], the foundation[4] of so great[5] a city[6] – and the beginning[7] of the greatest[8] empire[9] next to[10] the power[11] of the gods[12] – was owed[13] to destiny[14].

Nota bene

maximī is a superlative form of the adjective **magnus**. For more information on the comparison of adjectives, see page 22.

But you also find that he is not afraid to give air to theories that do not always show his legendary forebears in the best possible light. (Romulus and Remus have been cast adrift in a basket to die.)

44

vastae[3] tum[1] in[5] hīs[6] locīs[7] sōlitūdinēs[4] erant[2]. tenet[2] fāma[1] cum[3] fluitantem[9] alveum[10], quō[11] iam[14] expositī erant[13] puerī[12], tenuis[4] in[7] siccō[8] aqua[5] dēstituisset[6], lupam[16] sitientem[15] ex[17] montibus[18] quī[19] circā[21] sunt[20] ad[24] puerīlem[26] vāgītum[25] cursum[23] flexisse[22]; eam[1] submissās[3] īnfantibus[5] adeō[6] mītem[7] praebuisse[2] mammās[4] ut[8] linguā[15] lambentem[13] puerōs[14] magister[9] rēgiī[10] pecoris[11] invēnerit[12] – Faustulō[4] fuisse[3] nōmen[2] ferunt[1] – ab[2] eō[3] ad[6] stabula[7] Larentiae[5] uxōrī[4] ēdūcandōs[8] datōs[1]. sunt[1] quī[2] Larentiam[4] vulgātō corpore[9] lupam[6] inter[7] pāstōrēs[8] vocātam[5] putent[3]: inde[15] locum[10] fābulae[11] ac[12] mīrāculō[13] datum[14].

At that time[1] there were[2] vast[3] wildernesses[4] in[5] these[6] places[7]. The story[1] goes[2] that, when[3] the shallow[4] water[5] had set down[6] on[7] dry land[8] the floating[9] basket[10] where[11] the boys[12] had been exposed[13] already[14], a thirsty[15] she-wolf[16] from[17] the mountains[18] which[19] are[20] roundabout[21] turned[22] [its] course[23] towards[24] the crying[25] of the boys[26]; [and] she[1] offered[2] her lowered[3] teats[4] to the babies[5] so[6] gently[7] that[8] the herdsman[9] of the king's[10] cattle[11] found[12] [her] licking[13] the boys[14] with her tongue[15] – they say[1] his name[2] was[3] Faustulus[4] – [and the boys were] given[1] by[2] him[3] to his wife[4] Larentia[5] at[6] her haunt[7] to be brought up[8]. There are[1] [those] who[2] think[3] that Larentia[4] was called[5] a she-wolf[6] among[7] the shepherds[8] from acting as a prostitute[9]: the reason[10] for the story[11] and[12] the miracle[13] [has been] given[14] from this[15].

Nota bene

fluitantem is a form of the present participle **fluitāns**, **sitientem** of **sitiēns**, and **lambentem** of **lambēns**. For more information on present participles, see page 87. **expositī** is a form of the past participle of the verb **expōnere**, **submissās** of **submittere**, **datōs** and **datum** of **dare**, **vulgātō** of **vulgāre**, and **vocātam** from **vocāre**. For more information on past participles, see page 83. **dēstituisset** is a subjunctive because it is following **cum** (meaning *when*). For more information on When to use the Subjunctive, see page 104. **lupam** and **eam** are in the accusative case and **flexisse** and **praebuisse** are infinitives because they are all part of reported speech following **tenet fāma**; **nōmen** is in the accusative case and **fuisse** is an infinitive following **ferunt**; and **Larentiam** is in the accusative case and **vocātam** is part of an infinitive (with **esse** left out) following **putent**. For more information on reported speech, see page 113. **invēnerit** is a subjunctive because it is expressing a result following **ut**, and **putent** because it is expressing a possibility after **quī**. **ēdūcandōs** is a form of the gerundive of the verb **ēdūcāre**. For more information on gerundives, see page 92.

The rape of Lucretia

You will be gripped by the drama of this vivid scene. Like her husband and her father, you can only watch in awe as Lucretia takes her sense of honour to the extreme after being sexually assaulted by the then king. Their reassurances count for nothing.

45 **dant[3] ordine[2] omnēs[1] fidem[4]; cōnsōlantur[1] aegram[2] animī[3] āvertendō[4] noxam[5] ab[6] coāctā[7] in[8] auctōrem[9] dēlictī[10]: mentem[1] peccāre[2], nōn[3] corpus[4], et[5] unde[6] cōnsilium[7] āfuerit[8] culpam[9] abesse[10]. 'vōs[1]' inquit[2] 'vīderitis[3] quid[4] illī[6] dēbeātur[5]: ego[2] mē[4] etsī[1] peccātō[5] absolvō[3], suppliciō[7] nōn liberō[6]; nec ūlla[1] deinde[6] impudīca[2] Lucrētiae[5] exemplō[4] vīvet[3].' cultrum[1], quem[2] sub[5] veste[6] abditum[4] habēbat[3], eum[8] in[9] corde[10] dēfīgit[7], prōlapsaque[11] in[12] vulnus[13] moribunda[15] cecidit[14]. conclāmat[2] vir[1] paterque[3].**

All[1] in order[2] they give[3] the promise[4]; [and] they comfort[1] [her] sick[2] in mind[3] by turning away[4] the guilt[5] from[6] the one forced[7] onto[8] the author[9] of the crime[10]: the mind[1] sins[2], not[3] the body[4], and[5] where[6] intention[7] was absent[8] blame[9] is absent[10]. 'You[1],' she said[2], 'will have seen[3] what[4] is owed[5] to that man[6]: even if[1] I[2] acquit[3] myself[4] from the sin[5], I do not free[6] [myself] from the punishment[7]; and let not any[1] shameless[2] [woman] live[3] by the example[4] of Lucretia[5] from this[6].' The knife[1], which[2] she had[3] concealed[4] beneath[5] her robe[6], she plunges[7] it[8] in[9] her heart[10], and collapsing[11] under[12] the wound[13] she fell[14] dying[15]. Her husband[1] cries out[2], and her father[3].

Nota bene

cōnsōlantur is a form of the deponent verb **cōnsōlārī**. For more information on deponent verbs, see page 115. **āvertendō** is a form of the gerund of the verb **āvertere**. For more information on gerunds, see page 88. **coāctā** is a form of the past participle of **cōgere**. For more information on past participles, see page 83. **mentem**, **corpus**, and **culpam** are all in the accusative case and **peccāre** and **abesse** are both infinitives because they are part of reported speech following **cōnsōlantur**. For more information on reported speech, see page 113. **debeātur** is a subjunctive because it is expressing a question indirectly after **quid**, and **vīvet** because it is expressing a wish. For more information on when to use a subjunctive, see page 104 **abditum** is a form of the past participle of **abdere** and **prōlapsa** of the deponent verb **prōlābī**.

And you can decide if you think Lucretia's husband Brutus is her equal as he swears revenge on the rapist, Tarquin the Proud, last King of Rome.

46 **Brūtus[4] illīs[1] luctū[3] occupātīs[2] cultrum[8] ex[10] vulnere[11] Lucrētiae[12] extractum[9], mānantem[13] cruōre[14] prae[6] sē[7] tenēns[5], 'per[3] hunc[4]' inquit[1] 'castissimum[6] ante[7] rēgiam[8] iniūriam[9] sanguinem[5] iūrō[2], vōsque[10], dī[11], testēs[13] faciō[12] mē[14] L.[16] Tarquinium[17] Superbum[18] cum[19] scelerātā[20] coniuge[21] et[22] omnī[23] liberōrum[25] stirpe[24] ferrō[26]**

ignī[27] quācumque[28] dēhinc[31] vī[29] possim[30] exsecūtūrum[15], nec[33] illōs[34] nec[35] alium quemquam[36] regnāre[37] Rōmae[38] passūrum[32].'

With them[1] caught up[2] by grief[3], Brutus[4], holding[5] in front of[6] him[7] the knife[8] drawn out[9] from[10] the wound[11] of Lucretia[12] [and] dripping[13] with blood[14], said[1], 'I swear[2] by[3] this[4] blood[5], most chaste[6] until[7] a king's[8] outrage[9], and you[10], gods[11], I make[12] witnesses[13] that I[14] will punish[15] Lucius[16] Tarquinius[17] Superbus[18] along with[19] his wicked[20] wife[21] and[22] their whole[23] issue[24] of children[25] with sword[26], with fire[27], with whatever[28] strength[29] I can[30] hereafter[31], and [I] will suffer[32] neither[33] them[34] nor[35] anybody else[36] to be king[37] in Rome[38].'

Nota bene

occupātīs is a form of the past participle of the verb **occupāre** and **extractum** of **extrahere**. For more information on past participles, see page 83. **mānantem** is a form of the present participle **mānāns** and **tenēns** is also a present participle. For more information on present participles, see page 87. **mē** is in the accusative case and **exsecūtūrum** and **passūrum** are both part of future infinitives of deponent verbs (with **esse** left out) because they are part of reported speech following **iūrō** and **testēs faciō**. For more information on reported speech or deponent verbs, see pages 113 and 115. **possim** is a subjunctive because it is expressing possibility. For more information on when to use the subjunctive, see page 104. **Rōmae** is in the locative case. For more information on the locative case, see page 134.

Horatius holds the bridge

You may already have an image in your mind of the fully-armed Horatius Cocles leaping into the River Tiber, having successfully defended the last bridge against Porsenna's Etruscan army.

47

quae[3] cum[1] in[5] obiectō[7] cuncta[2] scūtō[6] haesissent[4], neque[9] ille[8] minus[10] obstinātus[11] ingentī[14] pontem[13] obtineret[12] gradū[15], iam[1] impetū[5] cōnābantur[2] dētrūdere[3] virum[4], cum[6] simul[7] fragor[8] ruptī[9] pontis[10], simul[11] clāmor[12] Rōmānōrum[13], alacritāte[15] perfectī[17] operis[16] sublātus[14], pavōre[21] subitō[20] impetum[19] sustinuit[18]. tum[1] Cocles[2] 'Tiberīne[5] pater[4]' inquit[3], 'tē[8] sanctē[7] precor[6], haec[10] arma[11] et[12] hunc[13] mīlitem[14] propitiō[15] flūmine[16] accipiās[9].' ita[1] sīc[2] armātus[3] in[5] Tiberim[6] dēsiluit[4] multīsque[7] superincidentibus[9] tēlīs[8] incolumis[13] ad[11] suōs[12] trānāvit[10], rem[15] ausus[14] plūs[17] fāmae[18]

habitūram[16] ad[19] posterōs[20] quam[21] fideī[22]. grāta[3] ergā[4] tantam[5] virtūtem[6] cīvitās[1] fuit[2]; statua[1] in[3] comitiō[4] posita[2]; agrī[2] quantum[1] ūnō[4] diē[5] circumarāvit[3], datum[6].

Because[1] the rest of[2] these things[3] had stuck[4] in[5] his shield[6] [that was] put in the way[7], and he[8] no[9] less[10] resolved[11] was keeping possession of[12] the bridge[13] with his huge[14] stride[15], now[1] they began to try[2] to dislodge[3] the man[4] with an attack[5], when[6] not only[7] the crash[8] of the broken[9] bridge[10] but also at the same time[11] the shout[12] of the Romans[13], raised[14] by the speed[15] of the work[16] having been completed[17], held up[18] their attack[19] with sudden[20] panic[21]. Then[1] Cocles[2] said[3], 'Father[4] Tiber[5], I pray[6] solemnly[7] to you[8], may you receive[9] these[10] weapons[11] and[12] this[13] soldier[14] in your gracious[15] river[16].' In this way[1] thus[2] armed[3] he jumped down[4] into[5] the Tiber[6] and with many[7] spears[8] falling down upon[9] [him] he swam across[10] to[11] his own[12] [men] unharmed[13], having dared[14] a thing[15] [which would be] about to have[16] more[17] repute[18] among[19] his descendants[20] than[21] trustworthiness[22]. The state[1] was[2] thankful[3] for[4] such great[5] courage[6]; a statue[1] [was] set up[2] in[3] the place of assembly[4]; how much[1] land[2] he ploughed around[3] in one[4] day[5], [was] given[6] [to him].

Nota bene

obiectō is a form of the past participle of the verb **obiçere**, **obstinātus** of **obstināre**, **ruptī** of **rumpere**, **perfectī** of **perficere**, and **sublātus** of **tollere**. For more information on past participles, see page 83. **haesissent** and **obtineret** are subjunctives because they both follow **cum** (meaning *because*); **accipiās** is a subjunctive because it is expressing a wish (after the verb **precor**). For more information on when to use the subjunctive, see page 104. **armātus** is the past participle of **armāre** and **ausus** of the semi-deponent verb **audere**. For more information on semi-deponent verbs, see page 116. **superincidentibus** is a form of the present participle **superincidēns**; **habitūram** is a form of the future participle of **habēre**. For more information on present participles or future participles, see pages 87 and 91. **posterōs** is the comparative form of an adjective used here as a noun. For more information on the comparison of adjectives, see page 22. **posita** is a form of the past participle of **pōnere** and **datum** of **dare**.

The war with Hannibal

This is no longer the stuff of legend, even if it didn't happen often. It is 217 BCE and you know the defeat of the Roman army by Hannibal's invading Carthaginians at Lake Trasimene is only too real.

48 **haec[1] est[2] nōbilis[3] ad[5] Trasumēnum[6] pugna[4] atque[7] inter[12] paucās[13] memorāta[8] populī[11] Rōmānī[10] clādēs[9].**

This[1] is[2] the famous[3] battle[4] at[5] Trasimene[6] and[7] a recorded[8] disaster[9] of the Roman[10] people[11] among[12] few[13].

Nota bene

memorāta is a form of the past participle of the verb **memorāre**. For more information on past participles, see page 83.

As you observe the panic in the capital caused by rumours post-Trasimene, the tension is almost palpable.

49 **Rōmae[1] ad[2] prīmum[3] nuntium[4] clādis[6] eius[5] cum[12] ingentī[13] terrōre[14] ac[15] tumultū[16] concursus[7] in[9] forum[10] populī[8] est factus[11]. mātrōnae[1] vagae[2] per[3] viās[4], quae[7] repēns[8] clādēs[9] allāta[10] quaeve[11] fortūna[13] exercitūs[14] esset[12], obviōs[6] percontantur[5]; et[1] cum[2] frequentis[4] contiōnis[5] modō[3] turba[6] in[8] comitium[9] et[10] cūriam[11] versa[7] magistrātūs[13] vocāret[12], tandem[1] haud[2] multō[3] ante[4] solis occāsum[5] M.[6] Pompōnius[7] praetor[8] 'pugnā[12]' inquit[9] 'magnā[11] victī sumus[10].'**

In Rome[1] at[2] the first[3] news[4] of this[5] disaster[6] a rushing together[7] of the people[8] into[9] the forum[10] happened[11] with[12] enormous[13] fear[14] and[15] uproar[16]. Ladies[1] wandering[2] through[3] the streets[4] inquire of[5] [those they are] meeting[6], what[7] [was] the sudden[8] disaster[9] [that had been] reported[10] or what[11] was[12] the fate[13] of the army[14]; and[1] because[2], with the size[3] of a full[4] public meeting[5], the crowd[6], turned[7] towards[8] the place of assembly[9] and[10] the senate-house[11], began to call for[12] the magistrates[13], at last[1] not[2] much[3] before[4] sunset[5] Marcus[6] Pomponius[7] the praetor[8] said[9], 'We have been defeated[10] in a great[11] battle[12].'

Nota bene

Rōmae is in the locative case. For more information on the locative case, see page 134. **factus** is the past participle of the verb **fierī** and **allāta** a form of the past participle of **adferre**. For more information on past participles, see page 83. **esset** is a subjunctive because it is asking a question indirectly following **quae**. For more information on when to use the subjunctive, see page 104. **percontantur** is a form of the deponent verb **percontārī**. For more information on deponent verbs, see page 115. **versa** is a form of the past participle of **vertere** and **victī** of **vincere**. **vocāret** is a subjunctive because it is following **cum** (meaning *because*).

And although far worse was to come at Cannae in 216 BCE, you also remember that Rome did survive. Maharbal's famous words to his brother will have haunted many a victorious general since.

50 **tum[1] Maharbal[2]: 'nōn[5] omnia[7] nīmīrum[3] eīdem[8] dī[4] dedēre[6]. vincere[2] scīs[1], Hannibal[3]; victōriā[6] ūtī[5] nescīs[4].' mora[1] eius[2] dīeī[3] satis[6] crēditur[4] salūtī[7] fuisse[5] urbī[8] atque[9] imperiō[10].**

Then[1] Maharbal[2] [said]: 'Truly[3] the gods[4] have not[5] given[6] everything[7] to the same man[8]. You know how[1] to win[2], Hannibal[3]; you do not know how[4] to use[5] the victory[6].' The delay[1] of that[2] day[3] is believed[4] to have been[5] enough[6] for the safety[7] of the city[8] [Rome] and[9] the empire[10].

Nota bene

dedēre is an alternative form of **dedērunt**, the third person plural of the perfect tense of **dare**. **ūtī** is a deponent verb and is always followed by the ablative case. For more information on deponent verbs, see page 115. **fuisse** is an infinitive because it is part of reported speech following **crēditur**. For more information on reported speech, see page 113.

Culture vulture

The vast majority of the Roman population were ordinary citizens who made up what was known as the **plēbs** (meaning *the masses*). They were the craftsmen and shopkeepers and managers of small enterprises. Many were only able to get temporary employment as casual labourers, and others simply survived on what they could get from patrons or on handouts of free grain from the state.

If you wanted access to any kind of position of authority, you needed a personal fortune of 400,000 sesterces. This would qualify you as a member of the equestrians or the knights, known as the **equitēs** (meaning literally *the horsemen*).

This social class was said to have originated when the kings of Rome needed the more affluent citizens to form a cavalry section to support the foot-soldiers.

The highest privileges, however, were reserved for the **senātōrēs** (meaning literally *the elders*). Their wealth and rank were usually inherited, and these men were in most cases the ones who became consul or provincial governor, or who commanded the Roman legions. But if the **censōrēs** (meaning literally *the valuers*) found out that a man's personal wealth had fallen below 1,000,000 sesterces, he would forfeit his position in the aristocracy.

Most Roman families, whatever their social status, owned at least one slave. Slaves carried out the everyday household tasks such as cooking and cleaning; they were the farmhands and shepherds; and in urban areas they performed most of the heavy manual labour required in the running of public services. However, many slaves were also highly skilled and were engaged in clerical work, book-keeping, teaching, and entertainment.

Slaves came from all over the Roman world, most often after they had been captured as a result of war or piracy. Legally, slaves were not regarded as people but as commodities to be bought and sold. They could not marry, they could not own property, they could not vote, they could not take a case to court. However, they were allowed to move around without restriction, to visit the market and the temples, and to attend public entertainments.

Perhaps as a reward for loyal service, slaves more than 30 years old were sometimes freed by their owners. A freed slave was known as a **lībertus** (meaning *a freedman*) or a **līberta** (meaning *a freedwoman*). The freeing of a slave was known as **manūmissiō** (meaning literally *the sending away from the hand*), and meant that the slave was no longer under the owner's legal control.

Ex-slaves could not join the equestrian or senatorial class, nor could they serve in the army or stand for election, and they did still have to perform certain duties for their former owners; but many of them used the skills they had acquired to good effect, becoming prosperous and respected citizens.

Ovid

et mihi cēdet Amor – And Love shall yield to me

Like Horace, Ovid received a first-rate education in Rome and Athens. In this unit you will find examples of the sparkling wit that marks out his love poetry (begun when he was barely 20 years old), as well as portraits from the epic *Metamorphoses*, a poem which has had more influence on western culture than any other. Unlike Horace, Ovid ended his days in exile, dying in 17 CE at the age of sixty far from the playground of his youth. (For more information on Horace, see page 190.)

Early promise

You will find that no one could write love poetry after Ovid had finished with it. Here he is having a go at Aurora, the goddess of the dawn, who perhaps understandably prefers her young lover Cephalus to her old husband Tithonus. Fine, says Ovid, then stop spoiling my night-time fun by appearing too soon.

51

Tīthōnō[4] vellem[1] dē[5] tē[6] narrāre[3] licēret[2]:
fēmina[3] nōn[1] caelō[5] turpior[4] ūlla[2] foret[1].
illum[3] dum[1] refugis[2], longō[6] quia[4] grandior[5] aevō[7],
surgis[1] ad[5] invīsās[6] ā[3] sene[4] māne[2] rotās[7];
at[1] sī[2] quem[5] manibus[7] Cephalum[4] complexa[3] tenērēs[6],
clāmārēs[1] 'lentē[3] currite[2], noctis[5] equī[4].'

I would like[1] to be permitted[2] to talk[3] to Tithonus[4] about[5] you[6]:
There would not be[1] any[2] woman[3] more shameful[4] in heaven[5].
While[1] you run away from[2] him[3], because[4] [he is] older[5] by a long[6] time[7],
You rise[1] early[2] from[3] the old man[4] to[5] your hated[6] chariot[7];
But[1] if[2] embracing[3] Cephalus[4] whom[5] you were holding[6] in your hands[7],
You would shout[1], 'Run[2] slowly[3], horses[4] of the night[5].'

Nota bene

vellem is a subjunctive because it is expressing a wish; **licēret** is an impersonal verb and is also a subjunctive, as is **foret**. For more information on when to use the subjunctive or impersonal verbs, see pages 104 and 93. **turpior** and **grandior** are comparative forms of the adjectives **turpis** and **grandis**. For more information on the comparison of adjectives, see page 22. **invīsās** is a past participle and **complexa** is a past participle of the deponent verb **complectī**.

For more information on past participles or deponent verbs, see pages 83 and 115. **tenērēs** and **clāmārēs** are both subjunctives because they are part of sentences following **sī**.

Reckless youth

Now Ovid sets out the rules for 'love' as a game, which both sexes can play without getting hurt. You may not be surprised that this very risqué kind of poetry was not viewed favourably by the establishment and was a major factor in Ovid's banishment from Rome.

52 **nec[1] timidē[2] prōmitte[1]: trahunt[4] prōmissa[3] puellās[5];**
pollicitō[5] testēs[4] quōslibet[2] adde[1] deōs[3].
Iuppiter[1] ex[3] altō[4] periūria[5] rīdet[2] amantum[6]
et[1] iubet[2] Aeoliōs[3] inrita[6] ferre[5] notōs[4].
per[5] Styga[6] Iūnōnī[7] falsum[4] iūrāre[3] solēbat[2]
Iuppiter[1]: exemplō[5] nunc[2] favet[3] ipse[1] suō[4].
expedit[1] esse[2] deōs[3] et[4], ut[5] expedit[6], esse[8] putēmus[7];
dentur[3] in[4] antīquōs[5] tūra[1] merumque[2] focōs[6].

And do not promise[1] shyly[2]: promises[3] draw[4] girls[5];
Add[1] any[2] gods[3] you like[2] as witnesses[4] to the promise[5].
Jupiter[1] laughs[2] from[3] heaven[4] at the oaths[5] of lovers[6]
And[1] orders[2] the Aeolian[3] winds[4] to carry[5] [them] to no effect[6].
Jupiter[1] was used[2] to swearing[3] a lie[4] by[5] the Styx[6]
To Juno[7]: he himself[1] now[2] favours[3] his own[4] example[5].
It is useful[1] that there are[2] gods[3] and[4], as[5] it is useful[6], let us believe[7] there are[8];
Let incense[1] and wine[2] be given[3] at[4] the ancient[5] altar-fires[6].

Nota bene

nec prōmitte is an alternative way to express the command **nōlīte prōmittere**. For more information on the imperative, see page 55. **amantum** is a form of the present participle **amāns**. For more information on present participles, see page 87. **favet** is a form of the verb **favēre** and is always followed by the dative case. **expedit** is an impersonal verb. For more information on impersonal verbs, see page 93. **esse** is an infinitive because it is part of reported speech following **putēmus**; **putēmus** and **dentur** are subjunctives because they are expressing wishes. For more information on reported speech or when to use the subjunctive, see pages 113 and 114.

Echo and Narcissus

You will find that Ovid combines drama and playfulness in equal measure throughout the *Metamorphoses*, as every conceivable form of love or lust leads to some fantastic transformation or other. Here the young Narcissus is being spied on in the forest by the obsessive but tongue-tied nymph Echo.

53

forte[2] puer[7] comitum[6] sēductus[1] ab[3] agmine[5] fīdō[4]
dīxerat[8] 'ecquis[9] adest[10]?' et[11] 'adest[14]' responderat[13] Ēchō[12].
hic[1] stupet[2], utque[3] aciem[5] partēs[8] dīmittit[4] in[6] omnēs[7],
vōce[3] 'venī[4]' magnā[2] clāmat[1]; vocat[6] illa[5] vocantem[7].
respicit[1] et[2] rūrsus[3] nūllō[4] veniente[5] 'quid[7]' inquit[6]
'mē[9] fugis[8]?' et[10] totidem[13], quot[14] dīxit[15], verba[12] recēpit[11].
perstat[1] et[2] alternae[5] dēceptus[3] imāgine[4] vōcis[6],
'hūc[2] coeāmus[3]' ait[1] nūllīque[4] libentius[7] umquam[6]
respōnsūra[8] sonō[5] 'coeāmus[11]' rettulit[10] Ēchō[9]
et[1] verbīs[4] favet[2] ipsa[5] suīs[3] ēgressaque[6] silvā[7]
ībat[1], ut[2] īniceret[3] spērātō[5] bracchia[4] collō[6].

Led away[1] by chance[2] from[3] his faithful[4] band[5] of companions[6] the boy[7]
Had said[8], 'Is anyone[9] here[10]?' and[11] Echo[12] had responded[13], 'Here[14].'
He[1] is amazed[2], and as[3] he sends out[4] a piercing look[5] in[6] all[7] directions[8],
He shouts[1] in a loud[2] voice[3], 'Come[4]'; she[5] calls[6] the caller[7].
He looks back[1] and[2] again[3] with no one[4] coming[5], he says[6], 'Why[7]
Do you flee from[8] me[9]?' and[10] he received back[11] the words[12] as many times[13] as[14] he said[15] [them].
He stands still[1] and[2], deceived[3] by the appearance[4] of the other's[5] voice[6],
Says[1], 'Here[2] let's come together[3]' and to no[4] sound[5] ever[6] more willingly[7]
About to reply[8] Echo[9] responded[10], 'Let's come together[11]',
And[1] she backs up[2] her own[3] words[4] herself[5] and having come out of[6] the wood[7]
She began to go[1], so that[2] she might throw[3] her arms[4] around the longed for[5] neck[6].

Nota bene

sēductus is the past participle of the verb **sēdūcere**; **vocantem** is a form of the present participle **vocāns** and **veniente** of **veniēns**. For more information on past participles or present participles, see pages 83 and 87. **dēceptus** is a form of the past participle of **dēcipere** and **spērātō** of **spērāre**; **ēgressa** is the past participle of the deponent verb **ēgredī**; **respōnsūra** is the future participle of

respondere. For more information on deponent verbs or future participles, see pages 115 and 91. **coeāmus** is a subjunctive because it is expressing a wish; **īniceret** is a subjunctive because it is expressing purpose after **ut**. For more information on when to use the subjunctive, see page 104. **libentius** is the comparative form of the adverb **libenter**. For more information on the comparison of adverbs, see page 129.

Now it is Narcissus' turn to become obsessive, as it dawns on him that the gorgeous boy he has seen is his own reflection in a pool.

54

'iste[3] ego[1] sum[2]! sensī[4]; nec[7] mē[8] mea[5] fallit[7] imāgō[6]:
ūror[1] amōre[2] meī[3], flammās[6] moveōque[4] ferōque[5].
quid[1] faciam[2]? roger[3], anne[4] rogem[5]? quid[7] deinde[6] rogābō[8]?
quod[1] cupiō[2], mēcum[4] est[3]: inopem[8] mē[7] cōpia[5] fēcit[6].
ō[1] utinam[2] ā[5] nostrō[6] sēcēdere[4] corpore[7] possem[3]!
vōtum[2] in[3] amante[4] novum[1]: vellem[5], quod[6] amāmus[7], abesset[8]! –
iamque[1] dolor[2] vīrēs[4] adimit[3], nec tempora[6] vītae[8]
longa[5] meae[7] superant[9], prīmōque[11] extinguor[13] in[10] aevō[12].
nec[3] mihi[5] mors[1] gravis[4] est[2], positūrō[7] morte[6] dolōrēs[8]:
hic[1], quī[2] dīligitur[3], vellem[4], diūturnior[6] esset[5]!
nunc[1] duo[2] concordēs[3] animā[7] moriēmur[4] in[5] ūnā[6].'

'I[1] am[2] that one[3]!' I've realised[4]; and my[5] image[6] does not deceive[7] me[8]:
I am inflamed[1] with love[2] of myself[3], I both stir[4] and bear[5] the flames[6].
What[1] should I do[2]? Should I be asked[3], or[4] should I ask[5]? Then[6] what[7]
shall I ask[8]?
What[1] I desire[2], it is[3] with me[4]: plenty[5] has made[6] me[7] poor[8].
O[1] would that[2] I could[3] separate[4] from[5] our[6] body[7]!
A new[1] prayer[2] in[3] a lover[4]: I wish[5] what[6] we love[7] were not there[8]! –
And already[1] suffering[2] saps[3] my strength[4], and long[5] periods[6]
Of my[7] life[8] have not survived[9], and in[10] the prime[11] of life[12] I am
destroyed[13].
And death[1] is[2] not[3] serious[4] to me[5], with death[6] about to lay aside[7] my
sufferings[8]:
This one[1], who[2] is highly prized[3], I wish[4] he were[5] longer lasting[6]!
Now[1] two[2] of the same heart[3] we will die[4] in[5] one[6] breath[7].'

Nota bene

faciam, **roger** and **rogem** are all subjunctives because there is an element of wondering in the questions being asked; **possem** is a subjunctive because it is expressing a wish following **utinam**; **abesset** and **esset** are both subjunctives because they are expressing wishes following **vellem** which is also subjunctive. For more information on when to use the subjunctive, see page 104. **mēcum** = **cum mē**. **amante** is a form of the present participle **amāns**; **positūrō** is a form of the future participle of **pōnere**. For more information on present participles or future participles, see pages 83 and 91. **diūturnior** is the comparative form of the adjective **diūturnus**. For more information on the comparison of adjectives, see page 22. **moriēmur** is a form of the deponent verb **morī**. For more information on deponent verbs, see page 115.

Medea

The character of Medea fascinated Ovid. Here you will catch a glimpse of the agonies of passion, as Medea struggles between love and loyalty after setting eyes on the handsome stranger Jason. He will need help to steal the legendary Golden Fleece from under her father's nose.

55

'excute[1] virgineō[4] conceptās[3] pectore[5] flammās[2],
sī[6] potes[7], īnfēlīx[8]. sī[1] possem[2], sānior[4] essem[3];
sed[1] trahit[4] invītam[5] nova[2] vīs[3], aliudque[8] cupīdo[6],
mēns[9] aliud[10] suādet[7]: videō[1] meliōra[2] probōque[3],
dēteriōra[5] sequor[4]!'

'Shake off[1] the flames[2] that have been kindled[3] in your girlish[4] breast[5],
If[6] you can[7], unfortunate one[8]. If[1] I could[2], I would be[3] more rational[4];
But[1] a new[2] force[3] drags[4] [me] against my wishes[5], and the heart[6] advises[7] one thing[8],
The head[9] another[10]: I see[1] what is better[2] and I approve[3] [it],
I follow[4] the worse[5]!'

Nota bene

conceptās is a form of the past participle of **concipere**. For more information on past participles, see page 87. **possem** and **essem** are subjunctives because they are in sentences following **sī**. For more information on when to use the subjunctive, see page 104. **sānior** is the comparative form of the adjective **sānus** and **meliōra** a comparative form of **bonus**; **dēteriōra** is also a comparative form. For more information on the comparison of adjectives, see page 22. **sequor** is a form of the deponent verb **sequī**. For more information on deponent verbs, see page 115.

Daedalus and Icarus

You can feel the tension mounting as Daedalus and his son Icarus first set out for Athens from the island stronghold of Crete in their doomed bid for freedom on manmade wings.

56

inter[1] opus[2] monitūsque[3] genae[5] maduēre[6] senīlēs[4],
et[7] patriae[9] tremuēre[10] manūs[8]. dedit[1] ōscula[2] nātō[4]
nōn iterum[5] repetenda[6] suō[3] pennīsque[8] levātus[7]
ante[10] volat[9], comitīque[2] timet[1], velut[3] āles[4], ab[11] altō[12]
quae[5] teneram[7] prōlem[8] prōdūxit[6] in[9] āera[10] nīdō[13];
hortāturque[1] sequī[2], damnōsāsque[4] ērudit[3] artēs[5],
et[1] movet[2] ipse[5] suās[3] et[6] nātī[8] respicit[7] ālās[4].
hōs[3] aliquis[1], tremulā[7] dum[4] captat[5] harundine[8] piscēs[6],
aut[9] pāstor[10] baculō[11] stīvāve[14] innīxus[13] arātor[12]
vīdit[2] et[15] obstipuit[16], quīque[2] aethera[5] carpere[4] possent[3]
crēdidit[1] esse[6] deōs[7].

During[1] the work[2] and warnings[3] the old[4] cheeks[5] became wet[6],
And[7] the hands[8] of the father[9] shook[10]. He gave[1] kisses[2] to his[3] son[4]
Never[5] to be sought again[6] and, lifted up[7] on his wings[8],
He flies[9] in front[10], and fears[1] for his companion[2], just as[3] a bird[4], which[5]
Has brought out[6] its tender[7] offspring[8] into[9] the air[10] from[11] a high[12] nest[13];
And he encourages[1] [him] to follow[2], and teaches[3] [him] the fatal[4] skills[5],
And[1] moves[2] his own[3] wings[4] himself[5] and[6] looks back at[7] [those] of his son[8].
Someone[1] saw[2] these[3] [two], while[4] he was catching[5] fish[6] with a quivering[7] rod[8],
Or else[9] a shepherd[10] with a staff[11] or a ploughman[12] leant[13] on the plough-handle[14],
And[15] gaped in astonishment[16], and believed[1] [those] who[2] could[3] fly through[4] the sky[5]
To be[6] gods[7].

Nota bene

maduēre is an alternative form of **maduērunt** (the third person plural of the perfect tense) and **tremuēre** of **tremuērunt**. **repetenda** is a form of the gerundive of the verb **repetere**; **levātus** is the past participle of **levāre**. For more information on gerundives or past participles, see pages 92 and 83. **hortātur** is a form of the deponent verb **hortārī**, and **sequī** is also a deponent verb; **innīxus** is the past participle of the deponent verb **innītī**.

For more information on deponent verbs, see page 115. **possent** is a subjunctive because it follows the relative pronoun **quī** within reported speech; **deōs** is in the accusative case and **esse** is an infinitive because they are part of reported speech following the verb **crēdidit**. For more information on when to use the subjunctive or reported speech, see pages 104 and 113.

Culture vulture

The Romans are famous for the straightness of their roads. Rivers or mountains might force the surveyors to plot a diversion, but they never lost sight of their original target of getting from one town to another by the shortest possible route. They paid considerable attention to achieving a hard, flat surface that would drain effectively. On a good day a traveller could walk 20 miles on a Roman road, more by carriage or by mule.

Originally the purpose of the roads was military, built so that troops could move rapidly about the provinces; but they were also very useful for other forms of state business. The **cursus pūblicus** (meaning literally *the public course*) was an early kind of postal system. Couriers just had to show their **diplōma** (meaning *a letter of introduction*) at a posting station and they were supplied with fresh horses and other assistance. Perhaps 50 miles a day could be covered in this way.

For an empire based around a sea like the Mediterranean, travel by trading vessel was often necessary but dangerous. Even within the sailing season of March to November there were pirates and storms to contend with. You had to negotiate your passage with the captain, wait for favourable weather and provide your own supplies to last the journey, which would be passed mainly on deck since there were no cabins. And no captain would set sail or dock without an animal sacrifice.

The wider the Roman sphere of influence became, aided by new routes overland and across the sea, the more the Romans themselves were exposed to foreign influences. This was particularly true of philosophy and religion. Stoicism was the most popular philosophical system to come out of Greece. Its adherents taught that a virtuous life of self-control and fulfilling one's duty was more satisfying than material wealth and pleasure-seeking – not always a popular notion in imperial Rome.

The cult of the goddess Isis spread from Egypt right across the empire. Associated with new life, particularly the hope of life after death, Isis-worship drew many followers, some of whom went through special initiation ceremonies in order to join what was known as the brotherhood of Isis. One very popular festival, at the beginning of the annual sailing season, involved dedicating a new ship to the goddess in order to ensure safe passage for sea-going travellers over the coming year.

Mithraism originated in Persia. Also offering the promise of life after death, the god Mithras had triumphed over the power of evil in the form of a great bull. Giving specific attention to acts of courage and devotion, the cult of Mithras was particularly popular in military circles and, again, required its followers to undergo secretive initiation rites. And, of course, there was also Christianity which came from the East – and which was legalised by the Emperor Constantine in 313 CE.

Martial

rīdē sī sapis – Laugh if you are wise

If you want a realistic glimpse of everyday life in Rome, the selection of poetry by Martial in this unit will give you a flavour of its inhabitants, and its sights and sounds. Martial came from Spain but spent most of his life in Rome. He wrote a poem commemorating the opening of the Colosseum in 80 CE, but is best known for his witty and satirical epigrams on all aspects of human behaviour.

Talking about marriage

Roman poets depended on patronage to make a living out of their writing. In this epigram, Martial gently flatters his patron and fellow-Spaniard, Terentius Priscus, at the expense of a certain Paula.

57

nūbere[2] vīs[1] Prīscō[3]. nōn mīror[4], Paula[5]; sapisti[6].
dūcere[3] tē[4] nōn vult[2] Prīscus[1]. et[6] ille[5] sapit[7].

You want[1] to marry[2] Priscus[3]. I am not surprised[4], Paula[5]; you've been wise[6].
Priscus[1] does not want[2] to marry[3] you[4]. He[5], too[6], is wise[7].

Nota bene

nūbere refers to the role of the woman in marriage and is always followed by the dative case, while **dūcere** always refers to the role of the man. **vīs** and **vult** come from **velle**.

When you think of a Roman marriage, you probably imagine the husband was always the one in charge. Martial never married, but these epigrams show that he was a very shrewd observer of what could really go on.

58

uxōrem[5] quārē[1] locuplētem[4] dūcere[3] nōlim[2]
quaeritis[6]? uxōrī[4] nūbere[2] nōlo[1] meae[3].
īnferior[3] mātrōna[1] suō[4] sit[2], Prīsce[6], marītō[5]:
nōn aliter[1] fīunt[4] fēmina[2] virque[3] parēs[5].

Why[1] I do not want[2] to marry[3] a wealthy[4] wife[5]
You ask[6]? I do not want[1] to be wife[2] to my[3] wife[4].
Let a married woman[1] be[2] lower[3] than her[4] husband[5], Priscus[6]:
In no other way[1] do a woman[2] and a man[3] become[4] equal[5].

Nota bene
nōlim is a subjunctive form of **nōlle** because it follows **quārē**. For more information on making use of the subjunctive, see page 104. **īnferior** is a comparative adjective. For more information on the comparison of adjectives, see page 22.

59 **īnscrīpsit[5] tumulīs[1] septem[2] scelerāta[4] virōrum[3]**
'sē fēcisse'[7] Chloē[6]. quid[1] pote[2] simplicius[3]?

On the tombs[1] of seven[2] husbands[3] the wicked woman[4] wrote[5]
Chloe[6] 'did this'[7]. What[1] could[2] [be] clearer[3]?

Nota bene
'sē fēcisse' is the usual formula inscribed on a monument by the person who erects it. **pote** is a neuter form of the adjective **potis** (meaning *able*) and the verb in the sentence has been left out.

Love and friendship

When you want to talk about other people and your relationships with them, your emotions can sometimes be very strong. Martial shows his feelings very plainly in these epigrams.

60 **nōn amo[1] tē[2], Sabidī[3], nec possum[4] dīcere[5] quārē[6]:**
hoc[4] tantum[2] possum[1] dīcere[3] – nōn amo[5] tē[6].

I do not love[1] you[2], Sabidius[3], and I can't[4] say[5] why[6]:
I can[1] only[2] say[3] this[4] – I do not love[5] you[6].

Nota bene
tantum is an adverb here. For more information on adverbs, see page 127.

61 **quid[2] mihi[6] reddat[5] ager[3] quaeris[1], Line[7], Nōmentānus[4]?**
hoc[3] mihi[4] reddit[2] ager[1]: tē[6], Line[7], nōn videō[5].

You ask[1] what[2] the farm[3] at Nomentanum[4] gives back[5] to me[6], Linus[7]?
The farm[1] gives back[2] this[3] to me[4]: I do not see[5] you[6], Linus[7].

> **Nota bene**
> **reddat** is a subjunctive because it is part of a question reported indirectly after **quid**. For more information on making use of the subjunctive, see page 104.

Sometimes, however, your friends' characters can be very contradictory, and so can your feelings towards them.

62 **difficilis[1] facilis[2], iūcundus[3] acerbus[4] es[5] īdem[6]:**
nec[3] tēcum[4] possum[1] vīvere[2] nec[5] sine[6] tē[7].

Difficult[1]/easy-going[2], pleasant[3]/disagreeable[4], you are[5] the same[6]:
I can[1] live[2] neither[3] with you[4] nor[5] without[6] you[7].

> **Nota bene**
> **tēcum** = **cum tē**.

Life and death

You will find strong encouragement to 'seize the day' in these closing lines from an epigram written to Martial's elderly patron, Julius Martialis.

63 **nōn est[1], crēde[2] mihī[3], sapientis[4] dīcere[5] 'vīvam[6]':**
sēra[5] nimis[4] vīta[1] est[3] crāstina[2]: vīve[6] hodiē[7].

It's not[1], believe[2] me[3], for the wise[4] to say[5] 'I shall live[6]':
The life[1] of tomorrow[2] is[3] too[4] late[5]: live[6] today[7].

> **Nota bene**
> **crēdere** is always followed by the dative case. **sapientis** is the genitive singular of the present participle **sapiēns**. For more information on uses of the cases, see the supplement on page 277, and on present participles, see page 87.

And you will also find Martial at his gentlest in these lines from an epigram on a dead child.

64 **mollia[5] nōn[1] rigidus[2] caespes[3] tegat[4] ossa[6]; nec[1] illī[2],**
terra[3], gravis[5] fueris[4]: nōn fuit[2] illa[1] tibi[3].

Let not[1] hard[2] turf[3] cover[4] her soft[5] bones[6]; and not[1] to her[2],
Earth[3], will you have been[4] a burden[5]: she[1] was not[2] to you[3].

Nota bene
tegat is a subjunctive because it is expressing a command. For more information on when to use the subjunctive, see page 104.

The Roman emperor

You would want to catch the eye of the emperor, who was the most important patron of all. In these epigrams, Martial showers compliments upon the ruler of the time, Domitian. Laying claim to a revered tradition, Roman emperors also used the names 'Augustus' and 'Caesar'.

65

pars[2] quota[1] Parrhasiae[3] labor[7] est[5] Mareōticus[6] aulae[4]?
clārius[7] in[1] tōtō[2] nīl[6] videt[5] orbe[3] diēs[4].
haec[3], Auguste[2], tamen[1], quae[5] vertice[8] sīdera[7] pulsat[6],
pār[10] domus[4] est[9] caelō[11] sed[12] minor[14] est[13] dominō[15].

What[1] part[2] of the imperial[3] palace[4] is[5] Egyptian[6] work[7]?
In[1] the whole[2] world[3] the day[4] sees[5] nothing[6] more splendid[7].
However[1], Augustus[2], this[3] house[4], which[5] knocks[6] the stars[7] with its top[8],
Is[9] equal[10] to the sky[11] but[12] is[13] smaller[14] than its master[15].

Nota bene
clārius is a comparative form of the adjective **clārus** and **minor** of **parvus**. For more information on comparison of adjectives, see page 22. Parrhasiae is a reference to the legendary King Evander who came from Parrhasia (in Arcadia) and settled on the future site of Rome. **Mareōticus** is a reference to Egypt (from the town of Marea).

66

prīma[1] salūtantēs[6] atque[3] altera[4] conterit[5] hōra[2];
exercet[2] raucōs[3] tertia[1] causidicōs[4];
in[1] quīntam[2] variōs[5] extendit[4] Rōma[3] labōrēs[6];
sexta[1] quiēs[3] lassīs[4], septima[5] fīnis[6] erit[2];
sufficit[4] in[2] nōnam[3] nitidīs[5] octāva[1] palaestrīs[6];
imperat[2] exstructōs[4] frangere[3] nōna[1] torōs[5]:
hōra[2] libellōrum[6] decima[1] est[4], Euphēme[3], meōrum[5],
temperat[4] ambrosiās[5] cum[1] tua[2] cūra[3] dapēs[6],
et[1] bonus[2] aetheriō[5] laxātur[4] nectare[6] Caesar[3]
ingentīque[4] tenet[1] pōcula[3] parca[2] manū[5].
tunc[1] admitte[2] iocōs[3]: gressū[6] timet[3] īre[4] licentī[5]
ad[7] mātūtīnam[9] nostra[1] Thalīa[2] Iovem[8].

The first[1] hour[2] and[3] the next[4] wears out[5] the morning callers[6];
The third[1] keeps busy[2] the hoarse[3] lawyers[4];
Into[1] the fifth[2] Rome[3] continues[4] various[5] tasks[6];
The sixth[1] will be[2] a siesta[3] for the tired[4], the seventh[5] an end[6];
The eighth[1] up to[2] the ninth[3] is sufficient[4] for the shining[5] exercise-ground[6];
The ninth[1] gives the order[2] to squash[3] the piled-up[4] couches[5]:
The tenth[1] hour[2], Euphemus[3], is[4] for my[5] little books[6],
When[1] your[2] care[3] oversees[4] the divine[5] feast[6],
And[1] good[2] Caesar[3] is relaxed[4] with heavenly[5] nectar[6]
And holds[1] a small[2] cup[3] in his great[4] hand[5].
At that time[1] introduce[2] my witty poems[3]: our[1] Thalia[2] is afraid[3] to go[4]
With her cheeky[5] step[6] to[7] Jupiter[8] in the morning[9].

Nota bene

salūtantēs is a present participle referring to the clients who call on their patrons first thing in the morning. For more information on present participles, see page 87. **nitidīs** refers to the gleam of the oil used on the body during exercise. **frangere** gives the impression of couches piled up with cushions being reclined upon. **Euphēmus** supervised Domitian's dinners. **Thalīa** is the Muse of comedy, and the source of Martial's inspiration. **Iovem** is the accusative singular of **Juppiter**, the king of the Roman gods.

Satirical jokes

If you want to make a joke at someone else's expense, these epigrams of Martial show how scathing you can be. Martial was never afraid to name names.

67 **Thāis[1] habet[2] nigrōs[3], niveōs[5] Laecānia[4] dentēs[6].**
quae[1] ratiō[3] est[2]? ēmptōs[3] haec[1] habet[2], illa[4] suōs[5].

Thais[1] has[2] black[3], Laecania[4] snow-white[5] teeth[6].
What[1] is[2] the reason[3]? This one[1] has[2] bought ones[3], that one[4] her own[5].

68 **'Thāida[3] Quīntus[1] amat[2].' 'quam[1] Thāida[2]?' 'Thāida[2] lūscam[1].'**
ūnum[3] oculum[4] Thāis[1] nōn habet[2], ille[5] duōs[6].

'Quintus[1] loves[2] Thais[3].' 'Which[1] Thais[2]?' 'One-eyed[1] Thais[2].'
Thais[1] doesn't have[2] one[3] eye[4], that man[5] two[6].

Thais is not the only one to come in for Martial's acerbic attention. Medical practice in Roman times was notoriously unreliable and prone to quackery and superstition.

69 **languēbam[1]: sed[2] tū[3] comitātus[4] prōtinus[5] ad[7] mē[8]**
vēnistī[6] centum[9], Symmache[11], discipulīs[10].
centum[1] mē[6] tetigēre[5] manūs[2] Aquilōne[4] gelātae[3];
nōn habuī[1] febrem[2], Symmache[3]: nunc[4] habeō[5].

I was feeling weak[1]: but[2] you[3], accompanied[4], immediately[5]
Came[6] to[7] me[8] with a hundred[9] pupils[10], Symmachus[11].
A hundred[1] hands[2] frozen[3] with the north wind[4] touched[5] me[6];
I did not have[1] a fever[2], Symmachus[3]: now[4] I have[5].

Nota bene
comitātus is the past participle of the deponent verb **comitārī**. For more information on past participles or deponent verbs, see pages 83 and 115. **prōtinus** is an adverb. For more information on adverbs, see page 127. **tetigēre** is a shortened form of **tetigērunt** from the perfect tense of **tangere**.

70 **nūper[1] erat[2] medicus[3], nunc[4] est[6] vespillo[7] Diaulus[5].**
quod[1] vespillo[2] facit[3], fēcerat[5] et[6] medicus[4].

Recently[1] he was[2] a doctor[3], now[4] Diaulus[5] is[6] an undertaker[7].
What[1] an undertaker[2] does[3], a doctor[4] had done[5] also[6].

Poets

As a poet, you would be conscious of those who had gone before you. In his own poetry Catullus was witty and frank with his emotions, like Martial. (For more information on Catullus, see page 174).

71 **hērēdem[2] tibi[3] mē[1], Catulle[4], dīcis[5].**
nōn crēdam[1] nisi[2] lēgerō[3], Catulle[4].

I[1] [am] heir[2] to you[3], Catullus[4], you say[5].
I will not believe[1] [it] unless[2] I will have read it[3], Catullus[4].

> **Nota bene**
> **hērēdem** and **mē** are in the accusative case because they are part of reported speech following the verb **dīcis**; the infinitive **esse** has been left out. For more information on reported speech, see page 113.

When you discuss your appreciation of poetry, you are quite likely to come across some people who share the view of Vacerra in this epigram of Martial.

72

mīrāris[1] veterēs[3], Vacerra[4], sōlōs[2]
nec laudās[5] nisi[7] mortuōs[8] poētās[6].
ignōscās[2] petimus[1], Vacerra[3]: tantī[6]
nōn[5] est[4], ut[8] placeam[9] tibī[10], perīre[7].

You admire[1] only[2] the old[3] [ones], Vacerra[4],
And you do not praise[5] poets[6] unless[7] dead[8].
We ask[1] [that] you forgive[2] [us], Vacerra[3]:
It is[4] not[5] worth[6] dying[7] so that[8] I may please[9] you[10].

> **Nota bene**
> **ignōscās** and **placeam** are both subjunctives because they follow **ut**; both verbs are followed by the dative case. The phrase **ut nōbīs** has been left out of the sentence with **ignōscās**. For more information on when to use the subjunctive, see page 104. **tantī** is in the genitive case after **est**. For more information on the use of the cases, see the supplement on page 277.

Culture vulture

With no state assistance to speak of, the patronage system was a key aspect of Roman society. The **patrōnus** (meaning *a patron*) offered help and protection to his **clientēs** (meaning *clients*) in return for various services. The clients called on their patron each morning and accompanied him on his round of business and social calls. The most powerful patron of all was the emperor; everyone else was his client.

The clients might be required to lead the applause after the patron had made a speech, or to campaign for votes on his behalf during an election. As a poet, Martial was expected to praise his patron in his poetry. Romans did not regard this simply as flattery, but as a proper and respectful thing to do.

Through the patronage system, after many years of poverty, Martial was able to afford to buy himself a small house in Rome and a modest farm outside the city at Nomentanum. Eventually he was able to return to his native Spain to live on a farm given him by another (female) patron.

An aspiring poet in Rome who wanted to bring his work to the attention of the public would be prepared to read it aloud to anyone who cared to listen – on street corners, in barber's shops, under a colonnade. In one of his epigrams, Martial complained that a certain Ligurinus badgered him from dawn until dusk with his poetry, and then woke him up again even after he'd gone to sleep.

A **recitātiō** (meaning *a recital*) was a specially organised event during which the poet would give a public reading of his work. Once he had a patron, a writer would give readings of his work to the patron's friends and family, or other invited guests, at the patron's home. He might also read his work to guests gathered in his own home, perhaps as part of a dinner.

Sometimes an **audītōrium** (meaning *a hall for public readings*) was hired for the occasion. At the front were the most distinguished guests on chairs with cushions; wooden benches were set out behind, and perhaps even tiered seating. When everything was ready, the writer stepped forward and delivered a **praefātiō** (meaning *a brief introduction*). Then he sat down to read the work itself.

These public recitations filled a real need at a time when books were not mass-produced or made available digitally. The poet would try to reach as wide an audience as possible, while avoiding the expense and labour of creating large numbers of copies of his work which would have to be produced by hand. The audience, in turn, could sample a writer's work without having to go to the trouble of browsing large and unwieldly scrolls of manuscript at a bookseller's.

Tacitus

sine īrā et studiō – Without anger and bias

In this unit you will get a flavour of a very distinctive storytelling technique. Tacitus was one of the best known public speakers of the late first century CE, and a friend and teacher of Pliny; but we remember him today for his graphic accounts of the intrigues and excesses of Roman imperial life from Augustus' successor Tiberius to Domitian via Nero. (For more information on Pliny, see page 229.)

Calgacus' last stand

This famous and damning indictment of the Romans is put into the mouth of a Caledonian chieftain before a crushing defeat in the battle of Mons Graupius at the hands of Agricola in 84 CE. Agricola was governor of Britain at the time and, you may be surprised to discover, Tacitus' father-in-law.

73

'nunc[1] terminus[2] Britanniae[3] patet[4], atque[5] omne[6] ignōtum[7] prō[9] magnificō[10] est[8]. sed[1] nūlla[2] iam[5] ultrā[4] gēns[3], nihil[6] nisi[7] fluctūs[8] ac[9] saxa[10], et[1] infestiōrēs[2] Rōmānī[3], quōrum[4] superbiam[5] frūstrā[7] per[8] obsequium[9] ac[10] modestiam[11] effugiās[6]. raptōres[1] orbis[2], postquam[3] cuncta[4] vastantibus[7] dēfuēre[6] terrae[5], iam[8] mare[10] scrūtantur[9]. sī[1] locuplēs[4] hostis[2] est[3], avārī[5], sī[6] pauper[7], ambitiōsī[8], quōs[9] nōn[10] Oriēns[11], nōn[12] Occidēns[13] satiāverit[14]: sōlī[1] omnium[2] opēs[4] atque[5] inopiam[6] parī[7] adfectū[8] concupiscunt[3]. auferre[1] trucīdāre[2] rapere[3] falsīs[5] nōminibus[6] imperium[7], atque[8] ubi[9] sōlitūdinem[12] faciunt[11], pācem[13] appellunt[4].'

'Now[1] the boundary[2] of Britain[3] is revealed[4], and[5] everything[6] unknown[7] is[8] as good as[9] glorious[10]. But[1] no[2] nation[3] [lies] beyond[4] now[5], nothing[6] except[7] waves[8] and[9] rocks[10], and[1] the more dangerous[2] Romans[3], whose[4] pride[5] you would run away from[6] in vain[7] by means of[8] submission[9] and[10] respect[11]. Plunderers[1] of the world[2], after[3] the rest[4] of the earth[5] has failed[6] with them destroying[7] [it], now[8] they hunt out[9] the sea[10]. If[1] the enemy[2] is[3] rich[4], [they are] greedy[5], if[6] poor[7], ambitious[8], [they] whom[9] neither[10] the East[11] nor[12] the West[13] will have satisfied[14]: alone[1] of all[2] [men] they covet[3] wealth[4] and[5] poverty[6] with equal[7] desire[8]. To steal[1], to slaughter[2], to plunder[3] they call[4] with false[5] names[6] government[7], and[8] when[9] they make[10] a desert[11], [they call it] peace[12].'

Nota bene
infestiōrēs a comparative form of the adjective **infestus**. For more information on the comparison of adjectives, see page 22. **effugiās** is a subjunctive because it is expressing a possibility. For more information on when to use the subjunctive, see page 104. **vastantibus** is a form of the present participle **vastāns**; **dēfuēre** is an alternative form of **dēfuērunt** (the third person plural of the perfect tense of **dēesse**); **scrūtantur** is a form of the deponent verb **scrūtārī**. For more information on present participles or deponent verbs, see pages 87 and 115.

Most military commanders you could name will have rehearsed their final words to their troops with Calgacus' celebrated closing line in mind – while hoping for a better outcome.

74 **'proinde[1], itūrī[2] in[3] aciem[4], et[6] maiōrēs[8] vestrōs[7] et[9] posterōs[10] cōgitāte[5].'**

'Therefore[1], [you who are] about to go[2] into[3] battle[4], think about[5] both[6] your[7] ancestors[8] and[9] descendants[10].'

Nota bene
itūrī is a future participle from the verb **īre**; **maiōrēs** is a comparative form of the adjective **magnus** used here as a noun. For more information on future participles or the comparison of adjectives, see pages 91 and 22.

The Druids' last stand

It is now 61 CE and Boudicca's 'Celtic Spring' is about to be unleashed in the south-east of England; but here you will find that the new governor of Britain is far away, wanting to prove himself in the wilds of North Wales.

75 **Suētōnius[1] igitur[2] Mōnam[6] īnsulam[5], incōlis[8] validam[7] et[9] receptāculum[10] perfugārum[11], aggredī[4] parat[3]: nāvibus[3] peditēs[1], equitēs[4] vadō[6] secūtī[5] aut[7] adnantēs[8] equīs[9] trānsiērunt[2]. stābat[3] prō[4] lītore[5] dīversa[1] aciēs[2], dēnsa[6] armīs[7] virīsque[8], intercursantibus[10] fēminīs[9]; quae in[4] modum[5] Furiārum[6] veste[3] fērālī[2], crīnibus[8] dēiectīs[7] facēs[10] praeferēbant[9]; Druidēsque[1] circum[2], precēs[5] dīrās[4] sublātīs[7] ad[8] caelum[9] manibus[6] fundentēs[3], novitāte[12] aspectūs[13] perculērunt[10] mīlitēs[11] ut[14] quasi[20] haerentibus[21] membrīs[19] immōbile[17] corpus[18] vulneribus[16]**

praebērent[15]. deinde[1] hortante[3] duce[2] et[4] sē[7] ipsī[5] stimulantēs[6] nē[8] muliebre[11] et[12] fānāticum[13] agmen[10] timērent[9], īnferunt[1] signa[2] sternuntque[3] obviōs[4] et[5] ignī[8] suō[7] involvunt[6]. praesidium[2] posthāc[1] impositum est[3] victīs[4] excīsīque sunt[9] lūcī[5] saevīs[7] superstitiōnibus[8] sacrī[6]: nam[1] Druidēs[2] cruōre[7] captīvō[8] adolēre[5] ārās[6] et[9] hominum[12] fibrīs[13] cōnsulere[10] deōs[11] fās[4] habēbant[3].

Suetonius[1], therefore[2], prepares[3] to attack[4] the island[5] of Anglesey[6], strengthened[7] with inhabitants[8] and[9] a refuge[10] for deserters[11]: the infantry[1] crossed[2] on boats[3], the cavalry[4] following[5] in the shallows[6] or[7] swimming alongside[8] their horses[9]. A hostile[1] battle-line[2] was standing[3] on[4] the shore[5], packed[6] with weapons[7] and men[8], with women[9] running about among[10] [them]; who[1] [were] in black[2] clothing[3] in[4] the manner[5] of Furies[6], [and] with dishevelled[7] hair[8] were brandishing[9] torches[10]; and Druids[1] roundabout[2], pouring out[3] fearful[4] prayers[5] with hands[6] raised[7] to[8] heaven[9], overawed[10] the soldiers[11] by the strangeness[12] of their appearance[13] so that[14] they exposed[15] to wounds[16] a motionless[17] body[18] with limbs[19] as if[20] sticking[21]. Then[1] with their leader[2] encouraging[3] [them] and[4] they themselves[5] urging[6] themselves[7] on so as not[8] to be afraid of[9] an army[10] made up of women[11] and[12] raving[13], they carry onwards[1] the standards[2] and cut down[3] those in the way[4] and[5] envelop[6] [them] in their own[7] fire[8]. After this[1] a garrison[2] was imposed[3] on the defeated[4] and the sacred groves[5] dedicated[6] to barbaric[7] religious rites[8] were cut down[9]: for[1] the Druids[2] used to consider[3] [it] right[4] to make offerings on[5] altars[6] with the blood[7] of prisoners[8] and[9] to consult[10] the gods[11] with men's[12] entrails[13].

Nota bene

aggredī is a deponent verb and **secūtī** is a form of the past participle of the deponent verb **sequī**. For more information on deponent verbs or past participles, see pages 115 and 83. **adnantēs** is a form of the present participle **adnāns** and **intercursantibus** of **intercursāns**. For more information on present participles, see page 87. **dēiectīs** is a past participle from the verb **dēicere** and **sublātīs** from **tollere**; **fundentēs** is a form of the present participle **fundēns** and **haerentibus** of **haerēns**. **praebērent** is a subjunctive because it is expressing purpose after **ut**; **timērent** because it is expressing purpose after **nē**. For more information on when to use the subjunctive, see page 104. **hortante** is a form of the present participle **hortāns** and **stimulantēs** of **stimulāns**; **victīs** is a past participle from **vincere**.

Nero and the Christians

Three years later large parts of Rome are burnt to the ground and you may remember that Nero has to find a scapegoat.

76

sed[1] nōn[2] ope[4] hūmānā[3], nōn[5] largītiōnibus[6] prīncipis[7] aut[8] deum[10] plācāmentis[9] dēcēdēbat[12] infāmia[11] quīn[13] iussum[16] incendium[15] crēderētur[14]. ergō[1] abolendō[3] rumōrī[2] Nerō[4] subdidit[5] reōs[6] et[7] quaesītissimīs[9] poenīs[10] adfēcit[8] quōs[11] per[16] flāgitia[17] invīsōs[15] vulgus[12] Christiānōs[14] appellābat[13]. auctor[1] nōminis[3] eius[2] Christus[4], Tiberiō[11] imperitante[12], per[7] prōcūrātōrem[8] Pontium[9] Pilātum[10] suppliciō[6] adfectus erat[5]; repressaque[1] in[6] praesēns[7] exitiābilis[2] superstitiō[3] rūrsum[5] ērumperat[4], nōn modō[8] per[9] Iūdaeum[10], originem[11] eius[12] malī[13], sed[14] etiam[15] per[16] urbem[17] quō[18] cuncta[19] undīque[24] ātrōcia[20] aut[21] pudenda[22] cōnfluunt[23] celebranturque[25].

But[1] by no[2] human[3] resources[4], no[5] benevolence[6] of the emperor[7] or[8] appeasing[9] of the gods[10] did the disgrace[11] die down[12] but that[13] it was believed[14] the fire[15] had been ordered[16] [by Nero]. Therefore[1] for the rumour[2] needing to be suppressed[3] Nero[4] falsely substituted[5] culprits[6] and[7] punished[8] with the most outlandish[9] penalties[10] [those] whom[11] the people[12] used to call[13] Christians[14], hated[15] because of[16] their foul deeds[17]. The originator[1] of that[2] name[3], the Christ[4], had been put[5] to death[6] by[7] the procurator[8] Pontius[9] Pilate[10], with Tiberius[11] being emperor[12]; and having been put down[1] the deadly[2] superstition[3] had broken out[4] again[5] in[6] the present[7] [time], not only[8] in[9] Judaea[10], the origin[11] of that[12] evil[13], but[14] also[15] in[16] the city[17] [of Rome] where[18] all things[19] hideous[20] or[21] shameful[22] converge[23] from everywhere[24] and are practised[25].

Nota bene

incendium is in the accusative case and **iussum** is part of an infinitive (with **esse** left out) because they are part of reported speech following **crēderētur**; **crēderētur** is a subjunctive because it is expressing doubt following **quīn**. For more information on reported speech or when to use the subjunctive, see pages 113 and 104. **abolendō** is a form of the gerundive of the verb **abolēre**. For more information on gerundives, see page 92. **quaesītissimīs** is a superlative form of the past participle **quaesītus** from the verb **quaesīre** used here as an adjective. For more information on past participles or the comparison of adjectives, see pages 83 and 22. **imperitante** is a form of the present participle **imperitāns** and

praesēns from the verb **praeesse**. For more information on present participles, see page 87. **repressa** is a past participle from the verb **reprimere**; **pudenda** is a form of the gerundive from the verb **pudēre**.

As you continue the story, you find Tacitus as graphic as any Hollywood film-maker.

77

igitur[1] prīmum[3] correptī[2] quī[4] fatēbantur[5], deinde[1] indiciō[3] eōrum[2] multitūdō[5] ingēns[4] haud[7] proinde[8] in[9] crīmine[10] incendiī[11] quam[12] odiō[13] hūmānī[14] generis[15] convictī sunt[6]. et[1] pereuntibus[4] addita[3] lūdibria[2], ut[5] ferārum[8] tergīs[7] contectī[6] laniātū[10] canum[11] interīrent[9], aut[12] crūcibus[14] adfixī[13] aut[15] flammandī[16], atque[17] ubi[18] dēfēcisset[20] diēs[19] in[22] ūsum[23] nocturnī[25] lūminis[24] ūrērentur[21].

Therefore[1] those brought to trial[2] first[3] [were those] who[4] confessed[5], then[1] on their[2] information[3] a huge[4] crowd[5] were convicted[6] not[7] so much[8] on[9] the charge[10] of arson[11] as[12] from the hatred[13] of the human[14] race[15]. And[1] mockeries[2] [were] added[3] to them dying[4], so that[5] covered[6] in the skins[7] of wild animals[8] they died[9] from the mangling[10] of dogs[11], or[12] [were] fastened[13] to crosses[14], or[15] made for setting alight[16], and[17] when[18] the daylight[19] had faded[20] they were burned[21] as[22] a source[23] of light[24] at night[25].

Nota bene

correptī is a past participle from the verb **corripere**. For more information on past participles, see page 83. **fatēbantur** is a form of the deponent verb **fatērē**. For more information on deponent verbs, see page 115. **pereuntibus** is a form of the present participle **periēns**. For more information on present participles, see page 87. **addita** is a past participle from the verb **addere**, **contectī** from **contegere** and **adfixī** from **adficere**. **interīrent** is a subjunctive because it is expressing purpose after **ut**; **dēfēcisset** and **ūrērentur** are also subjunctives in the sentences that follow. For more information on when to use the subjunctive, see page 104. **flammandī** is a form of the gerund of the verb **flammāre**. For more information on gerunds, see page 88.

And he is no less afraid to express an opinion than any contemporary commentator you care to mention.

78 **hortōs[4] suōs[3] eī[5] spectāculō[6] Nerō[1] obtulerat[2] et[7] circense[10] lūdicrum[9] ēdēbat[8], habitū[13] aurīgae[14] permixtus[11] plēbī[12] vel[15] curriculō[17] insistēns[16]. unde[1] quamquam[2] adversus[3] sontēs[4] et[5] novissima[7] exempla[8] meritōs[6] miserātiō[9] oriēbātur[10], tamquam[1] nōn[3] utilitāte[5] pūblicā[4] sed[6] in[7] saevitiam[8] ūnius[9] absūmerentur[2].**

Nero[1] had offered[2] his own[3] gardens[4] for that[5] spectacle[6] and[7] used to exhibit[8] a show[9] at the circus[10], mingled in[11] to the crowd[12] in the costume[13] of a charioteer[14] or[15] standing[16] in a chariot[17]. For which reason[1], although[2] [people were] opposed[3] to those guilty[4] and[5] deserving of[6] the most extreme[7] forms of punishment[8], pity[9] began to rise up[10], on the grounds that[1] they were being killed[2] not[3] for the public[4] good[5] but[6] because of[7] the cruelty[8] of one man[9].

Nota bene

permixtus is a past participle from the verb **permiscēre**; **insistēns** is a present participle. For more information on past participles or present participles, see pages 83 and 87. **meritōs** is a form of the past participle of the deponent verb **merērī** and **oriēbātur** is a form of the deponent verb **orīrī**. For more information on deponent verbs, see page 115. **absūmerentur** is a subjunctive because it is expressing an opinion following **tamquam**. For more information on when to use the subjunctive, see page 104.

Culture vulture

Show business in the Roman world was truly spectacular and came in three principal forms, all of which took place in large specially-constructed public arenas and attracted huge audiences: chariot-racing, gladiatorial shows (often followed by animal hunts) and drama festivals.

The home of chariot-racing in Rome was the Circus Maximus, which could hold 250,000 spectators. Four teams, each with a distinctive colour (blue, green, red, or white), would race against each other over seven laps of the stadium, which was about five miles in total. The most common chariot was pulled by four horses and was known as the **quadrīgae** (meaning literally *with four shafts*).

The Colosseum in Rome was the most famous arena for watching gladiator contests. It was originally called the Flavian Amphitheatre after the two emperors of the Flavian dynasty, Vespasian and his son Titus, who were responsible for its construction. 50,000 spectators could be accommodated here, and it was even possible to fill the arena with water so that mock sea-battles could be staged.

There were two basic types of gladiator, designed to be pitched against each other. The **murmillō** (which was a Greek name for a type of fish) was heavily armed with sword, shield, greaves, and a helmet complete with visor and fish-shaped crest; the **rētiārius** (meaning literally *a man with a net*) simply had a neck-guard, a trident, and a net. Other types used spears, rode horses, or drove chariots.

A popular addition to these spectacles was the **vēnātiō** (meaning *a beast hunt*). Wild animals would be released into the arena and hunted down by other wild animals – for example, hares or deer by dogs; dogs by wolves; wolves by lions. Alternatively, it would be specially trained men armed only with spears: the **bēstiārius** (meaning *a fighter of wild beasts*) might be pitched against wild boar, bulls, or big cats.

Rome had three main theatres, originally intended for performances of tragedy or comedy. However, it wasn't long before pantomime began to take over, with a single actor – or **pantomīmus** (meaning literally *one man miming everything*) – dancing and miming all the roles, with different masks for each character and accompanied by musicians and a chorus to tell the story. Short one-act farces with rustic settings and vulgar humour were also increasingly popular.

Like other Romans who could afford it, the Emperor Nero would have used his own palace gardens for private shows, featuring actors, musicians, and other performers. Recitals would also have been put on – sometimes of the host's own work, however embarrassing that might be for the guests.

Pliny

quid lībertāte pretiōsus? – What is more precious than liberty?

If you want a feeling for the concerns of a Roman aristocrat in the late first century CE, the selection from Pliny's extensive (and carefully edited) correspondence in this unit will not disappoint. A distinguished lawyer and politician, Pliny rose to become consul in 100 CE at the age of 39 and ten years later was sent by the Emperor Trajan to the southern shores of the Black Sea as a provincial governor.

The art of letter-writing

You might identify with Pliny's frustration at his friend's lack of contact; or perhaps with Fabius Justus' struggle to find anything interesting to tell him.

79

C.[1] PLINIUS[2] FABIO[5] IUSTO[6] SUO[4] S.[3]
ōlim[1] mihi[5] nūllās[3] epistulās[4] mittis[2]. nihil[2] est[1], inquis[5], quod[3] scrībam[4]. at[1] hoc[3] ipsum[4] scrībe[2], nihil[6] esse[5] quod[7] scrībās[8], vel[1] sōlum[2] illud[3] unde[4] incipere[7] priōrēs[5] solēbant[6]: 'sī[1] valēs[2], bene[4] est[3]; ego[5] valeō[6].' hoc[1] mihi[3] sufficit[2]; est[5] enim[4] maximum[6]. lūdere[3] mē[2] putās[1]? sēriō[2] petō[1]. fac[1] sciam[2] quid[3] agās[4], quod[5] sine[8] sollicitūdine[10] summā[9] nescīre[7] non possum[6]. valē[1].

Gaius[1] Pliny[2] sends greetings[3] to his[4] [friend] Fabius[5] Justus[6].
For a long time now[1] you send[2] no[3] letters[4] to me[5]. 'There is[1] nothing[2] which[3] I might write[4],' you say[5]. But[1] write[2] this[3] very[4] [thing], that there is[5] nothing[6] which[7] you might write[8], or[1] only[2] that[3] [place] from where[4] our ancestors[5] were accustomed[6] to start[7]: 'If[1] you are well[2], it is[3] good[4]; I[5] am well[6].' This[1] is enough[2] for me[3]; for[4] it is[5] the most valuable[6] [thing]. Do you think[1] that I[2] am playing[3]? I am asking[1] in earnest[2]. Let[1] me know[2] what[3] you are doing[4], because[5] I cannot[6] be in ignorance[7] without[8] the greatest[9] anxiety[10]. Farewell[1].

Nota bene

S. is an abbreviation of the phrase **salūtem dīcit**. **scrībam** and **scrībās** are both subjunctives because they are expressing possibilities. For more information on the subjunctive, see page 95. The second instance of **nihil** is in the accusative case and **esse** is an infinitive because they are part of reported speech after the verb

scrībe. For more information on reported speech, see page 113. **priōrēs** is a comparative adjective used here as a noun and **maximum** is a superlative form of the adjective **magnus**. For more information on the comparison of adjectives, see page 22. **mē** is in the accusative case and **lūdere** is an infinitive because they are part of reported speech after **putās**. **sciam** is a subjunctive after the imperative **fac** (with **ut** left out) because it is expressing purpose, and **agās** because it is asking a question indirectly after **quid**. For more information on when to use the subjunctive, see page 104.

The price of immortality

Caecina Paetus was involved in a short-lived revolt against the Emperor Claudius in 42 CE. He was given the chance to escape the executioner and his wife Arria joined him in a double suicide. Remarkable enough, you will say. But Pliny is even more impressed by Arria's earlier devotion when she had concealed from her sick husband that their son had died.

80 **praeclārum[4] quidem[1] illud[2] eiusdem[3], ferrum[2] stringere[1], perfodere[3] pectus[4], extrahere[5] pugiōnem[6], porrigere[7] marītō[8], addere[9] vōcem[14] immortālem[10] ac[11] paene[12] dīvīnam[13]: 'Paete[1], nōn dolet[2].' sed[1] tamen[2] ista[7] facientī[6], ista[9] dīcentī[8], glōria[3] et[4] aeternitās[5] ante[11] oculōs[12] erant[10]; quō[1] maius[3] est[2] sine[8] praemiō[9] aeternitātis[10], sine[11] praemiō[12] glōriae[13], abdere[4] lacrimās[5] operīre[6] luctum[7], āmissōque[15] fīliō[14] mātrem[17] adhuc[18] agere[16].**

Indeed[1] that[2] [deed] of the same[3] [woman was] remarkable[4]: to draw[1] a blade[2], to pierce[3] her breast[4], to pull out[5] the dagger[6], to offer[7] [it] to her husband[8], to add[9] the immortal[10] and[11] almost[12] godlike[13] saying[14]: 'Paetus[1], it does not hurt[2].' But[1], however[2], fame[3] and[4] immortality[5] for her doing[6] those[7] [things], saying[8] those[9] [things], were[10] [set] before[11] our eyes[12]; because[1] it is[2] greater[3] to hide[4] tears[5] [and] to conceal[6] grief[7] without[8] the reward[9] of immortality[10], without[11] the reward[12] of fame[13], and with your son[14] lost[15] to act[16] as a mother[17] still[18].

Nota bene

facientī is a form of the present participle **faciēns** and **dīcentī** of **dīcēns**. For more information on present participles, see page 87. **maius** is a comparative form of the adjective **magnus**. For more information on the comparison of adjectives, see page 22. **āmissō** is a past participle from the verb **āmittere**. For more information on past participles, see page 83.

You will find Pliny very respectful towards other well-known writers, even the likes of the satirist Martial. (For more information on Martial, see page 214.)

81 **audiō[1] Valerium[2] Martiālem[3] dēcessisse[4] et[5] molestē[7] ferō[6]. erat[1] homō[5] ingeniōsus[2] acūtus[3] ācer[4], et[6] quī[7] plūrimum[11] in[9] scrībendō[10] et[12] salis[13] habēret[8] et[14] fellis[15] nec[16] candōris[18] minus[17]. prōsecūtus eram[1] viāticō[3] sēcēdentem[2]; dēderam[4] hoc[5] amicitiae[6], dēderam[7] etiam[8] versiculīs[9], quōs[10] dē[12] mē[13] composuit[11].**

I hear[1] that Valerius[2] Martial[3] has died[4] and[5] I am taking[6] [it] badly[7]. He was[1] a talented[2], intelligent[3], sharp[4] man[5], and[6] [one] who[7] used to have[8] in[9] his writing[10] a very great deal[11] of both[12] wit[13] and[14] bile[15] and no[16] less[17] fairness[18]. I had seen him off[1] retiring[2] with travel expenses[3]; I had given[4] this[5] out of friendship[6], I had given[7] [it] even[8] for the little verses[9] which[10] he composed[11] about[12] me[13].

Nota bene

Valerium Martiālem is in the accusative case and **dēcessisse** is an infinitive because they are part of reported speech after **audiō**. For more information on reported speech, see page 113. **plūrimum** is a superlative form of the adjective **multus** and **minus** a comparative form of **parvus**; both are followed by the genitive case here. For more information on the comparison of adjectives or the uses of the cases, see pages 22 and 277. **scrībendō** is a form of the gerund of the verb **scrībere**. For more information on gerunds, see page 88. **habēret** is a subjunctive because it is expressing an opinion after the relative pronoun **quī**. For more information on when to use the subjunctive, see page 104. **prōsecūtus eram** is a form of the deponent verb **prōsequī** and **sēcēdentem** is a form of the present participle **sēcēdēns**. For more information on deponent verbs or present participles, see pages 113 and 87.

As the letter about Martial continues, you realise how highly Pliny regarded writing as an art.

82 **meritōne[1] eum[4], quī[7] haec[9] dē[10] mē[11] scrīpsit[8], et[2] tunc[5] dīmīsī[3] amīcissimē[6] et[12] nunc[14] ut[15] amīcissimum[16] dēfunctum esse[17] doleō[13]? dedit[2] enim[1] mihi[3] quantum maximum[4] potuit[5], datūrus[6] amplius[7] sī[8] potuisset[9]. tametsī[1], quid[2] hominī[6] potest[4] darī[5] maius[3] quam[7] glōria[8] et[9] laus[10] et[11] aeternitās[12]? at[1] non erunt[4] aeterna[5], quae[2] scripsit[3]: non erunt[2] fortasse[1], ille[4] tamen[3] scrīpsit[5] tamquam[6] essent fūtūra[7]. valē[1].**

Rightly[1] did I both[2] dispatch[3] him[4] at that time[5] very affectionately[6], who[7] wrote[8] these[9] [things] about[10] me[11], and[12] do I grieve[13] now[14] that as[15] a very dear friend[16] he has died[17]? For[1] he gave[2] to me[3] as much as[4] he could[5], [and] would be about to give[6] more[7] if[8] he'd been able[9]. Although[1], what[2] more[3] can[4] be given[5] to a man[6] than[7] fame[8] and[9] praise[10] and[11] immortality[12]? 'But[1] what[2] he wrote[3] will not be[4] immortal[5]' [you say]; perhaps[1] they will not be[2], but[3] he[4] wrote[5] [them] as if[6] they would be[7]. Farewell[1].

> **Nota bene**
> **eum** is in the accusative case and **dēfunctum esse** is an infinitive (from the deponent verb **dēfungī**) because they are part of reported speech after **doleō**. For more information on reported speech or deponent verbs, see pages 113 and 115. **maximum** is a superlative form and **maius** a comparative form of the adjective **magnus** and **amplius** is the comparative form of the adverb **amplē**. For more information on the comparison of adjectives or adverbs, see pages 22 and 129. **datūrus** is a future participle from the verb **dare** and **fūtūra** from **esse**. For more information on future participles, see page 91. **potuisset** is a subjunctive because it is following **sī** and **essent** because it is following **tamquam**. For more information on when to use the subjunctive, see page 104.

Writing for Tacitus

Pliny's uncle was also a well-known writer who famously met his death outside Pompeii during the eruption of Vesuvius in 79 CE. Tacitus knows that he will get the facts from Pliny who, as you can see, is only too willing to oblige. (For more information on Tacitus, see page 222.)

83

C.[1] PLINIUS[2] TACITO[3] SUO[4] S.[3]
petis[1] ut[2] tibi[4] avunculī[7] meī[6] exitum[5] scrībam[3], quō[8] vērius[11] trādere[10] posterīs[12] possīs[9]. grātiās agō[1]; nam[2] videō[3] mortī[9] eius[8] sī[10] celebrētur[11] ā[12] tē[13] immortālem[4] glōriam[5] esse[6] prōpositam[7]. quamvīs[2] enim[1] pulcherrimārum[5] clāde[4] terrārum[6], ut[10] populī[11] ut[12] urbēs[13] memorābilī[15] cāsū[14], quasi[8] semper[7] victūrus[9] occiderit[3], quamvīs[1] ipse[2] plūrima[4] opera[5] et[6] mansūra[7] condiderit[3], multum[13] tamen[8] perpetuitātī [15]eius[14] scriptōrum[11] tuōrum[10] aeternitās[9] addet[12]. equidem[1] beātōs[3] putō[2], quibus[4] deōrum[7] mūnere[6] datum est[5] aut[8] facere[9] scrībenda[10] aut[11] scrībere[12] legenda[13], beātissimōs[15] vērō[14] quibus[16] utrumque[17].

hōrum[5] in[4] numerō[6] avunculus[2] meus[1] et[7] suīs[8] librīs[11] et[9] tuīs[10] erit[3]. quō[1] libentius[3] suscipiō[2], dēposcō[5] etiam[4] quod[6] iniungis[7].

Gaius[1] Pliny[2] sends greetings[3] to his[4] [friend] Tacitus[5].
You are asking[1] that[2] I write[3] to you[4] about the death[5] of my[6] uncle[7], so that[8] you can[9] pass [it] on[10] more accurately[11] to our descendents[12]. I thank[1] [you]; for[2] I see that[3] eternal[4] fame[5] would be[6] promised[7] to his[8] death[9] if[10] it were celebrated[11] by[12] you[13]. For[1] although[2] he will have perished[3] in the destruction[4] of [one of] the most beautiful[5] places[6], [and will] always[7] [be] as if[8] about to be overcome[9] like[10] the peoples[11] [and] like[12] the cities[13] in a disaster[14] that is remembered[15], [and] although[1] he himself[2] will have founded[3] very many[4] works[5] and[6] things that will last[7], however[8] the everlasting nature[9] of your[10] writings[11] will add[12] much[13] to his[14] immortality[15]. Indeed[1] I think[2] [them] blessed[3] to whom[4] it has been given[5] by the gift[6] of the gods[7] either[8] to do[9] what must be written down[10] or[11] to write[12] what must be read out[13], but[14] the most blessed[15] [are those] to whom[16] both[17] [have been given]. My[1] uncle[2] will be[3] in[4] this[5] number[6] from both[7] his own[8] and[9] your[10] books[11]. So[1] I respond[2] all the more willingly[3], indeed[4] I demand[5] what[6] you are inflicting upon[7] [me].

> **Nota bene**
> **scrībam** is a subjunctive because it is expressing a purpose following **ut** and **possīs** following **quō**. For more information on when to use the subjunctive, see page 104. **glōriam** is in the accusative case and **esse** is an infinitive because they are part of reported speech following **videō**. For more information on reported speech, see page 113. **victūrus** is a future participle from the verb **vincere** and **mansūra** from **manēre**. For more information on future participles, see page 91. **plūrima** is a superlative form of the adjective **multus** and **beātissimōs** of the **beātus**; **libentius** is the comparative form of the adverb **libenter**. For more information on the comparison of adjectives or adverbs, see pages 22 and 129. **scrībenda** is a form of the gerundive of the verb **scrībere** and **legenda** of **legere**. For more information on gerundives, see page 92.

Writing for love

The difference in age between Pliny and his third wife Calpurnia was more than 25 years, but you can see ere how much in love he is.

84

C.[1] PLINIUS[2] CALPURNIAE[5] SUAE[4] S.[3]
incrēdibile[2] est[1] quantō[3] dēsīderiō[4] tuī[5] tenear[6]. in[1] causā[2] amor[4] prīmum[3], deinde[5] quod[6] nōn cōnsuēvimus[7] abesse[8]. inde[1] est[2] quod[3] magnam[5] noctium[7] partem[6] in[9] imāgine[10] tuā[11] vigil[8] exigō[4]; inde[1] quod[2] interdiū[3], quibus[4] hōrīs[5] tē[8] vīsere[7] solēbam[6], ad[16] diaetam[18] tuam[17] ipsī[9] mē[15], ut[11] vērissimē[13] dīcitur[12], pedēs[10] dūcunt[14]; quod[1] dēnique[2] aeger[4] et[5] maestus[6] ac[7] similis[8] exclūsō[9] ā[10] vacuō[11] līmine[12] recēdō[3]. ūnum[1] tempus[2] hīs[4] tormentīs[5] caret[3], quō[6] in[8] forō[9] et[10] amīcōrum[12] lītibus[11] conteror[7]. aestimā[2] tū[1], quae[3] vīta[5] mea[4] sit[6], cui[7] requiēs[8] in[9] labōre[10], in[11] miseriā[12] cūrīsque[13] sōlācium[14]. valē[1].

Gaius[1] Pliny[2] sends greetings[3] to his[4] [wife] Calpurnia[5].
It is[1] unbelievable[2] with how much[3] longing[4] for you[5] I am gripped[6]. By way of[1] reason[2] the first[3] [is] love[4], then[5] because[6] we are not used to[7] being apart[8]. From this[1] is[2] why[3] I spend[4] a large[5] part[6] of the nights[7] awake[8] with[9] the vision[10] of you[11]; from this[1] [is] why[2] during the day[3], in the[4] hours[5] I was used to[6] looking at[7] you[8], my very[9] feet[10] – so[11] it is said[12] absolutely truly[13] – lead[14] me[15] to[16] your[17] room[18]; why[1] finally[2] I withdraw[3] sick[4] and[5] sorrowing[6] and[7] like[8] [one] shut out[9] from[10] an empty[11] threshold[12]. One[1] time[2] is free from[3] these[4] tortures[5], when[6] I am worn out[7] in[8] the forum[9] and[10] by the lawsuits[11] of my friends[12]. You[1] be the judge[2], what[3] my[4] life[5] is[6], for whom[7] [there is] rest[8] [only] in[9] toil[10], [and only] in[11] wretchedness[12] and in cares[13] [is there] comfort[14]. Farewell[1].

Nota bene
tenear is a subjunctive because it is expressing a question indirectly after **quantō**. For more information on when to use the subjunctive, see page 104. **vērissimē** is the superlative form of the adverb **vērē**. For more information on the comparison of adverbs, see page 129. **exclūsō** is a past participle from the verb **exclūdere**. For more information on past participles, see page 87. **caret** is from **carēre** and is always followed by the ablative. For more information on uses of the cases, see the supplement on page 277. **sit** is a subjunctive because it is expressing a question indirectly after **quae**.

Royal birthday message

Trajan specifically chose Pliny to be provincial governor of the financial disaster that was Bithynia (modern-day northern Turkey) because he was good with money. You'll see that he was also good at remembering birthdays.

85 **C.[1] PLINIUS[2] TRAIANO[4] IMPERATORI[3]**
optō[1], domine[2], et[4] hunc[5] nātālem[6] et[7] plūrimōs[8] aliōs[9] quam fēlīcissimōs[10] agās[3] aeternāque[11] laude[12] flōrentem[13] virtūtis[16] tuae[15] glōriam[14] ... quam[1] incolumis[2] et[3] fortis[4] aliīs[6] super[8] alia[9] operibus[7] augēbis[5].

Gaius[1] Pliny[2] to Emperor[3] Trajan[4].
I desire[1], master[2], that you may enjoy[3] both[4] this[5] birthday[6] and[7] very many[8] other[9] as happy as possible[10] [ones] and with everlasting[11] praise[12] for the flourishing[13] fame[14] of your[15] virtue[16] ... as[1] safe[2] and[3] brave[4] [as you are] you will grow[5] with one[6] work[7] upon[8] another[9].

86 **TRAIANUS[1] PLINIO[2]**
agnoscō[1] vōta[3] tua[2], mī[4] Secunde[6] cārissime[5], quibus[7] precāris[8], ut[9] plūrimōs[11] et[12] fēlīcissimōs[13] nātālēs[14] flōrente[18] statū[15] reī publicae[17] nostrae[16] agam[10].

Trajan[1] to Pliny[2].
I acknowledge[1] your[2] wishes[3], my[4] very dear[5] Secundus[6], with which[7] you are praying[8], so that[9] I may enjoy[10] very many[11] and[12] very happy[13] birthdays[14] with the position[15] of our[16] state[17] flourishing[18].

Nota bene

plūrimōs is a superlative form of the adjective **multus** and **fēlīcissimōs** of **fēlīx**. For more information on the comparison of adjectives, see page 22. **agās** is a subjunctive because it is expressing a wish after **optō** and **agam** because it is expressing purpose after **ut**. For more information on when to use the subjunctive, see page 104. **flōrentem** and **flōrente** are forms of the present participle **flōrēns**. For more information on present participles, see page 87. **Secunde** is the vocative case of Pliny's family name, **Secundus**.

Culture vulture

Under the Roman legal system, trial by jury was used to deal with criminal offences such as murder, adultery, fraud, and corruption. Each different type of crime was the responsibility of a particular court known as a **quaestiō** (meaning *a judicial inquiry*). If a civil case was brought, such as a claim for damages, it was tried by a **iūdex** (meaning *a judge*) assisted by a panel of advisors and legal experts.

During the Principate, the emperor himself took an increasing role in the administration of justice. He was advised by men of mainly senatorial rank who were dubbed the emperor's **amīcī** (meaning *friends*) and part of a loosely-constituted body called the emperor's **cōnsilium** (meaning *council*). Pliny was invited to join Trajan's council from time to time, and cases ranged from personal matters between high-ranking officials to disputes on a larger scale from around the Roman provinces.

For men of the senatorial class, like Pliny, success as a lawyer was a significant factor in making a name for themselves and furthering their career. There were no state prosecutors or departments of justice in Roman times, so it was down to private individuals to bring a case before the court – and the more skilful a speaker he was the better. Cicero, the most famous of them all, rose from very humble origins thanks to his mastery as an orator. (For more information on Cicero, see page 158.)

Court cases were often held in the open air with plenty of room for curious onlookers to crowd round, known as a **corōna** (meaning *a circle*). The **praetor** (meaning *a magistrate*) sat on a raised platform and the **iūdicēs** (meaning *the jurors*), who had all been selected by lot, sat on benches lower down. The plaintiff, who could have as many supporters with him as he wished, had the right to speak first, followed by the defendant and his counsel.

The **ōrātor** (meaning *a public speaker*) was the one who presented the case to the jury. As well as a thorough knowledge of legal precedent, he would pay particular attention to the eloquence and emotional power of his speech, including the use of his voice and gestures. His aim was to sway the opinion of his audience, and he often did this more by attacking the reputation of the accused than addressing the charges that been brought.

When the speeches were over, the jurors considered their verdict. They used voting tablets marked 'C' for **condemnō** (meaning *I condemn*) and 'A' for **absolvō** (meaning *I acquit*). The presiding magistrate then delivered his sentence; there was no right of appeal. And although an unscrupulous Roman orator might try to hoodwink a jury, justice usually prevailed thanks to the strength of Roman law itself, which has had a massive influence on many legal systems today.

Part Three

Latin Legacy

What follows is an alphabetical list of some of the many Latin phrases that you are likely to come across in written English or that you will still find used in spoken English today. You will notice how many expressions from Latin are used in legal, medical, and religious contexts, and also as short-hand in various academic subjects. Latin 'i' sometimes changes to 'j' before a vowel.

— A —

ab initiō = from the beginning
Qualified instructors are able to provide ***ab initio*** *training to all students in the university.*

ab ovō 'from the egg' = from the very beginning
NB The main meal of the day in Roman times started with an appetiser such as eggs.
In my opinion this law is unjust because it ***ab ovo*** *violates European law.*

absit ōmen 'may the (evil) omen be absent' = let it not come true
NB 'Absit omen' is used as the title of a chapter in Thackeray's *The Newcomers.*
All that is necessary is that in the event of calamity – ***absit omen*** *– she has a point of recourse in you.*

ab urbe conditā 'from the city having been founded' = from the foundation of the city
NB The 'city' is Rome and the traditional date of its foundation by Romulus is 753 BCE. The phrase is used as the title of Livy's monumental history of Rome, and is often abbreviated in dates to AUC. (For more information on Livy, see page 198.) An alternative way to express it is **annō urbis conditae** 'in the year of the city having been founded'.
My investigations have gone all the way back to the year zero, ***ab urbe condita***.

AD → see **annō Dominī.**

ad hoc 'for this' = for a particular purpose
The National Council has established an ***ad hoc*** *committee to consider this very pressing issue.*

ad hominem 'according to the man' = directed against a person rather than against their arguments; based on, or appealing to, the emotions rather than reason

*People who make this kind of **ad hominem** criticism are simply showing themselves up, aren't they?*

ad īnfīnītum 'to infinite space' = for ever; endlessly
*At the last count three parliamentary committees were looking into the issue, listening to experts opine **ad infinitum** about this and that.*

ad interim = for the meantime
*The district and sessions court has granted **ad interim** bail to the defendant until 19th January.*

ad lib 'according to what was pleasing' = to speak without preparation; as (much as) one pleases; improvised
NB This phrase is an abbreviation of the Latin **ad libitum**.
*I would love the show to be full of mistakes so that I could **ad lib** my way out of a problem.*

ad maiōrem Deī glōriam = for the greater glory of God
NB This phrase is the motto of the Jesuits (or the Society of Jesus) and is often abbreviated to AMDG.
*Schools were founded by the Jesuits and dedicated **ad maiorem Dei gloriam**.*

ad nauseam 'for sea-sickness' = to the point of nausea; to a disgusting extent
*On each occasion the perpetrators are shown on TV news channels **ad nauseam**.*

ad rem 'to the thing' = to the point
*The property tax (an **ad rem** form of wealth taxation) accounted for nearly two-fifths of tax revenue.*

advocātus diabolī = devil's advocate
NB During the examination of the life of a candidate for Roman Catholic sainthood, the church official tasked with arguing against the proposal is the *advocatus diaboli*.
*During the discussion, the **advocatus diaboli** should wait to see if questions arise and, if not, start the discussion.*

aegrotat 'he/she is ill' = sick note
NB This expression is used to describe a certificate that states a student is too ill to take an exam.
*He was unable to complete all the course requirements, apparently due to illness, but was awarded what is known as an **aegrotat** degree.*

aetātis suae 'of his or her age' = at the age of
NB This phrase is often found on tombstones or memorials and can be abbreviated to **aet**.
__Aetatis suae__ 21, Christopher Marlowe was already a cobbler's son with a BA degree.

ā fortiōrī 'from the stronger' = all the more; for a stronger reason
If some elements of K are linearly independent over k(y), they are __a fortiori__ so over k.

Agnus Deī = Lamb of God
NB A description of Jesus Christ central to the Roman Catholic Mass conducted in Latin, and set to music.
Passing insecurities, such as nervous entries in the __Agnus Dei__, were more than atoned for.

alma mater 'nurturing mother' = someone's former university, college, or school
He will compete against his __alma mater__ as a head coach for the first time on Friday night.

alter ego 'my other self' = a second self; a very close and intimate friend
The identity of the local artist's famous __alter ego__ is being kept firmly under wraps.

alumnus 'someone who has been nursed' = a former student
As an __alumnus__ of the school, he said being mentored as an undergraduate student inspired his donation to the Professional Mentorship Programme.

a.m. → see **ante merīdiem**.

AMDG → see **ad maiōrem Deī glōriam**.

amor patriae 'love of the fatherland' = love for one's country; patriotism
It should, however, be indicated that the Christian virtue of Charity may refer also to __amor patriae__, according to a definition of around 1300.

annō Dominī 'in the year of the Lord' = AD
NB Western calendars use the traditional year of the birth of Christ as their starting-point.
They now want __Anno Domini__ (AD) to be replaced with Common Era (CE) in all textbooks.

annō urbis conditae → see **ab urbe conditā**.

annus mīrābilis = a wonderful year
NB The play on this phrase, **annus horribilis** ('a horrible year'), was made famous by Queen Elizabeth II towards the end of 1992.

*The Olympics and the Diamond Jubilee will, God willing, deliver our **annus mirabilis**.*

ante bellum = before the war
NB This expression was particularly used of the American Civil War (1861–1865).
*Life on the Old Plantation in **Ante-Bellum** Days: Or A Story Based on Facts (1911)*

ante merīdiem 'before midday' = in the morning; a.m.
NB 5.30 **ante meridiem** (that's a.m. in case you didn't know), I wasn't bright-eyed and bushy-tailed.

ante mortem = before death
NB This expression is used mainly in legal or medical contexts.
*Like abscessing, uninterrupted periodontitis would eventually have caused **ante-mortem** tooth loss.*

ante prandium 'before the meal' = the Ante Prandium (a grace said before dinner)
NB This expression can also be abbreviated to **a.p.** and used to indicate medication that must be taken before a meal.
*The reading of Grace before a meal (**ante prandium**) is usually the duty of a Scholar of the College.*

apparātus criticus 'critical apparatus' = textual notes (especially variant readings in the scholarly edition of a text)
*In my **apparatus criticus** I cite M, E, and S in every instance.*

ā priōrī 'from the former' = made from deduction
*The book sets out to analyse the notion of **a priori** justification and of a priori knowledge.*

aqua vītae 'water of life' = brandy; spirits
*Scotland's **aqua vitae** is more than just a strong spirit drink.*

arbiter ēlegantiae 'judge of excellence' = arbiter of taste
NB This expression was used by Tacitus to describe Gaius Petronius at the court of Nero – possibly the same Petronius who wrote the *Satyricon*. (For more information on Tacitus, see page 222.)
*In his role as **arbiter elegantiae**, Gore Vidal can write without recourse to preposterous tableaux.*

argumēntum ad hominem → see **ad hominem**.

ars longa, vīta brevis 'art long, life brief' = art is long, life is short
NB Seneca borrowed this expression from the Greek physician, Hippocrates.
*But age will own the bitter truth, / '**Ars longa, vita brevis**.'*

AUC → see **ab urbe condita**.

aut vincere aut morī 'either to conquer or to die' = victory or death
*'Underneath is my motto: **Aut vincere aut mori**,' he said proudly. Of course he was lying through his teeth.*

aurōra austrālis 'southern dawn' = the Southern Lights
*The footage captures the globe's southern lights, **aurora australis**, as they pass over Australia.*

aurōra boreālis 'northern dawn' = the Northern Lights
*Some of what you will witness includes the **aurora borealis** passing over Turtle Island at night.*

avē atque valē = hail and farewell
NB Catullus concluded his poem to his brother who had died abroad with this expression. (For more information on Catullus, see page 174.)
***Ave atque vale**. Hail and farewell. At first sight that sums up a week in which one President stepped up and another stepped down.*

avē Maria = Hail Mary
NB These are the first two words of the traditional prayer to the Virgin Mary, often set to music.
*The Bach/Gounod **Ave Maria** is a popular and much-recorded setting of the Latin text.*

B

beātae memoriae = of blessed memory
NB This phrase is traditionally used on tombstones and memorials.
*Edward is described as **beatae memoriae** but we do not have to believe that the king was dead when the chapter was first written.*

Beāta Virgō = the Blessed Virgin
NB This is the formal Latin description of Mary, the mother of Jesus, in the Roman Catholic Church, and can be abbreviated as **B.V.**
*The same truth is expressed in the well-known antiphon of the Latin church, **Beata Virgo**.*

bis in diē 'two times in a day' = twice a day
NB This expression can also be abbreviated to **b.i.d.** and used to indicate medication that must be taken twice a day.

bis in die (b.i.d.) *Twice daily.*

bis dat quī cito dat 'he gives twice who gives quickly' = the person who pays promptly doubles their payment
NB This proverb is based on a quotation by the Roman dramatist Publilius Syrus.
*The king told the bishop to remind his 'unruly flock' that **bis dat qui cito dat**.*

BV → see **Beāta Virgō**.

C

c., ca. → see **circa**.

camera obscūra 'dark chamber' = camera obscura
NB Another method of producing an image by controlled use of light is camera lucida ('bright chamber').
*Caravaggio is credited with early use of the **camera obscura** technique.*

carpe diem 'enjoy the day' = seize the day; enjoy the pleasures of the moment without concern for the future
NB Horace used this celebrated expression in his first book of Odes. (For more information on Horace, see page 190.)
*The coach is schooling his team with a **carpe diem** talk, not wanting them to assume the same chance will come their way next year.*

casus bellī 'an occasion of war' = an act used to justify a war; the immediate cause of a quarrel
*But the **casus belli** for military strikes that hawks expected to gain from the report is far from clear-cut.*

cavē = beware!
NB Pronounced like the letters KV, this expression was traditionally used as a warning by schoolchildren that a teacher was coming.
*He won't keep **cave**, shirks his turn / And says he came to school to learn!*

caveat ēmptor = let the buyer beware
*Yet, **caveat emptor**: if the buyer did not check what was being sold and did not compute the cost he was paying, he can hardly blame the seller.*

cētera dēsunt 'the rest of the things are failing' = the rest is missing
'In the name of him who is jealous, even to slaying,' said the first ... **CETERA DESUNT**.

cēterīs paribus 'with the rest of the things equal' = other things being equal
Under scientific experiments, the ***ceteris paribus*** *assumption is realised when a scientist controls for all of the independent variables other than the one under study.*

circa = around; about
NB This term is often used with dates or quantities, and abbreviated as **c.** or **ca.**
Vienna ***circa*** *1780: An Imperial Silver Service Rediscovered.*

citius altius fortius = faster, higher, stronger
NB This Latin expression was borrowed from a school in France by Baron de Coubertin to serve as the motto of the modern Olympic Games.
Athletics is the perfect expression of the Olympic motto, ***citius altius fortius***.

Cōdex Iūris Canonicī = the Code of Canon Law
NB This is the official code of canon law in the Roman Catholic Church.
Pope Benedict XV promulgated the ***Codex juris canonici****, a restatement of the church's canon law.*

cōgitō, ergō sum = I think, therefore I am
NB This famous quotation is the Latin original of the basis of the philosophy of Descartes (1596-1650) – *Je pense, donc je suis.*
*It is worthwhile to show what is really wrong with the '****cogito ergo sum****'.*

compos mentis 'having control of the mind' = of sound mind; sane
*To be non-****compos mentis*** *renders a person not legally responsible.*

cōram populō 'in the presence of the people' = before the public; openly
The more openly, ***coram populo****, it is done, the better. Such a trust is sure not to be betrayed.*

Corpus Christī = the Body of Christ
NB The Latin name of the Christian Church's Feast of the Blessed Sacrament on the Thursday after Trinity Sunday.
Corpus Christi *is a popular vacation destination, military town, and thriving seaport.*

corpus dēlictī 'the body of the crime' = the concrete evidence of a crime
NB This is a legal expression describing the facts that constitute an offence, especially the body of a murdered person.
Without the ***corpus delicti****, there is no evidence of a crime, and there can be no criminal proceedings.*

corpus vīle 'a body worth little' = someone or something fit only to be the object of an experiment; experimental material
*Van Diemen's Land is the unfortunate **corpus vile**; and the report on the results is before us in the shape of a petition from its inhabitants.*

corrigenda = things to be corrected
NB This term is used particularly of errors in printed texts for which corrections are supplied.
*If the book already contains a list of **corrigenda**, see whether all the corrections can now be incorporated into the text.*

cui bonō? 'for which good?' = to whose advantage?; who stood to gain?
NB This expression was quoted by Cicero when he was urging the jurors in a court case to vote with this in mind. (For more information on Cicero, see page 158.)
***Cui bono?** China. Sooner or later Berlin will have to grasp the unpalatable reality, that the European Central Bank must be empowered to stand up as the lender of last resort.*

cum grānō salis 'with a grain of salt' = with a pinch of salt; not too literally
*The possibilities for error should not deter you from using census returns; however, just remember, **cum grano salis**, and dig further.*

cum laude = with praise
NB This term is chiefly used in the US to describe the lowest of three designations for above-average achievement in examinations. The others are, in ascending order, **magnā cum laude** and **summā cum laude**.
*The events and characters of 'Murder **Cum Laude**' reveal the ugly reality of Washington politics and one man's aggressive efforts to uncover the truth.*

curriculum vītae 'the course of a life' = curriculum vitae; CV
*The curriculum vitae or **CV** summarises your academic and employment history in a structured form.*

D

dē factō 'on account of the deed' = in fact; in reality
*We can't just continue to build up a **de facto** Guantanamo Bay and that's what we're doing.*

dē gustibus nōn est disputandum 'there should be no arguing about taste' = there's no accounting for taste; each to his own

The Stigler/Becker principle of ***de gustibus non est disputandum*** *is a frequent topic of discussion among economists.*

dē iūre 'on account of the law' = by right; legally
NB This is the legal opposite of the expression **dē factō**.
Dollarisation entails the ***de jure*** *abandonment of a country's own currency.*

dē mortuīs nīl nisi bonum 'concerning the dead nothing unless good' = say nothing but good about the dead
He should have recalled the old Latin tag, ***de mortuis nil nisi bonum****, when he came to relating the evenings he and friends spent.*

dē novō 'concerning the new' = anew; afresh
The researchers used ***de novo*** *design to produce a protein that would selectively bind two separate metals.*

Deō grātiās = thanks be to God
Anyone who says ***Deo gratias*** *is giving thanks to God.*

Deō volente = God willing
NB This expression is often abbreviated to **DV**.
*Announcements for the incoming week (****DV****).*

dē profundīs = out of the depths (of misery or dejection)
NB These are the opening words of Psalm 129 in Latin, used at Roman Catholic funerals. The expression was also used as the title of Oscar Wilde's 1897 lament written from prison.
This work, part of the ***De Profundis*** *series, won the Drawing Prize.*

deus ex māchinā 'the god from the machine' = something introduced into a play to resolve the plot; an unlikely or artificial device solving a difficulty
The new prime minister is not the ***deus ex machina*** *they were expecting.*

Diēs Īrae = the Day of Wrath
NB These are the first words of a famous Latin hymn of the 13th century, describing the Last Judgment, and used in the Roman Catholic Mass for the dead.
Rachmaninoff's dusting off the ***Dies Irae*** *motto in the last movement is an insistent dance of death.*

disiecta membra 'scattered limbs' = scattered fragments (of written works)
Peculiar customs, with some ***disjecta membra*** *upon art conventions.*

DPhil → see **philosophiae doctor**.

drāmatis persōnae 'the persons of the drama' = the list of characters in a play
*The **dramatis personae** still wig up and showboat shamelessly in front of a jury.*

E

ecce homō = behold the man
NB The words of Pontius Pilate to Christ's accusers in the Latin version of the Gospel of John.
*Currently, the museum has a Caravaggio exhibition focusing on his painting, **Ecce Homo**.*

ēditiō prīnceps 'the first edition' = the first printed edition of a work
*So you can read a Chinese writer's latest work in English as if it were the **editio princeps**.*

e.g. → see **exemplī grātiā**.

ēmeritus 'a soldier who has served his time' = retired from office
*Archbishop **Emeritus** Desmond Tutu has declared war on nations reluctant to commit to reducing carbon emissions.*

ē plūribus ūnum = one out of many
NB This expression is closely associated with the Founding Fathers of the USA, being one country made up of many states.
*'In God We Trust'? I'd like to see us get back to the spirit of **e pluribus unum**.*

ER = Queen Elizabeth
NB This abbreviation of **Elizabeth Rēgīna** ('Elizabeth the Queen') is found on most post boxes in the UK, and was used for King Edward before her, **Eduardus Rēx** ('Edward the King').
*The Stamps of **Elizabeth Regina** and the Royal Family.*

errāre hūmānum est = to err is human
NB This proverbial saying is often completed with the words, 'to forgive, divine'.
*'**Errare humanum est**' or more contemporarily put, 'Nobody's perfect'.*

errātum 'fault' = error in a printed work
NB This word's plural, **errāta**, can be used to refer to a list of such errors.
***Erratum** slips (called '**errata** slips' if they list more than one error) are expensive.*

et aliī = and others
NB This expression is abbreviated in English to **et al.**, and is often used in place of a long list of names.
*India ushers in Marks & Spencer **et al.***

et cētera = and the rest of the things
NB This expression is abbreviated in written English to **etc.**
*The Forced Marriage (Protection and Jurisdiction **etc**) (Scotland) Act 2011 comes into effect today.*

et seq. → see **sequēns**.

ex 'out of' = excluding; removed from
NB As well as its usual meaning of 'former', this word can be used in a financial context to indicate something that is not included, or in a commercial context to show at what point a buyer incurs a bill.
*The following FTSE 100 companies will go **ex**-dividend tomorrow, after which investors will no longer qualify for the latest dividend payout.*
*Some tier-two seamless pipe mills in eastern China have raised their **ex**-works prices.*

ex cathedrā 'from the chair' = with authority
NB This expression is often used in religious contexts, referring to a bishop's throne.
*Only when the Pope delivers a pronouncement **ex cathedra** are his words considered infallible.*

exeat 'let him/her go out' = formal leave of absence
*The queen was on an **exeat** from her imprisonment for leading a rebellion against the king.*

exemplī grātiā 'for the sake of an example' = for example
NB This expression is abbreviated in English to **e.g.**
*The shape of the ears (**e.g.** pendulous or floppy ears) can be a predisposing factor in whether some dogs have ear problems.*

exeunt 'they go out' = the stage direction for actors to leave
NB **exeunt omnēs** ('they all go out') is the expression used for all actors leaving the stage, and **exit** ('he/she goes out') for one specific actor.
*The text of the First Folio edition ends with this stage direction: '**Exeunt** Marching'.*

ex librīs 'from the books' = from the library of
NB This expression is often used on bookplates.
*They plan to rename Scarborough Fair with the Latin phrase **Ex Libris**.*

ex officiō 'out of duty' = by right of position or office
*Highland Park is asking high school juniors to apply to be **ex-officio** members of city commissions.*

ex parte 'from a part' = on behalf of one side only
NB This expression is used in legal contexts of an application in a judicial proceeding.
*The Supreme Court of Queensland granted **ex parte** injunctions against Golden Sparrow Pty Ltd.*

ex post factō 'from what was done after' = with retrospective effect
*There was no **ex post facto** violation since the crime was not completed before the effective date of the relevant amendment.*

ex silentiō 'out of silence' = based on a lack of evidence to the contrary
*For many of them, textual silence indicates real absence – a particularly problematic case of an **ex silentio** argument.*

ex tempore 'out of the occasion' = without preparation; impromptu
NB This expression is written as one word in English.
*A movie was screened, followed by quizzes on vocabulary, **extempore** speeches, an etiquette test and role play.*

ex vōtō 'out of a prayer' = an offering made to fulfil a vow
*Anatomical **ex votos** as offerings to a deity out of gratitude for healing were common among many ancient peoples.*

F

facile prīnceps 'easily first' = the obvious leader
*Eratosthenes was one of the most distinguished Greek men of learning, probably ranking next to the **facile princeps** of them all, Aristotle.*

fēcit 'he/she made' = made by
NB This word is sometimes abbreviated to **fēc.**, and was used on works of art next to the artist's name.
*Plate IV: Marine bodies, fossils. De La Rue del. Benard **fecit**.*

felō dē sē 'felon of him-/herself' = suicide
NB The English word 'felon' comes from the medieval Latin **fello** ('a wicked person').
*It contemplated – it could calculate upon – nothing so outrageous as an act of **felo de se**.*

festīnā lentē 'hasten slowly' = more haste, less speed
NB This motto is traditionally associated with the Emperor Augustus.
*We in Europe have the word Americanism; the ancients had **festina lente**.*

fīat lūx = let there be light
NB This expression comes from the Latin version of the creation story in the Book of Genesis.
*The future of Rollins football speaks to the school's motto, **Fiat Lux**, brimming with an expanse of bright positivity.*

Fideī Dēfēnsor = defender of the faith
NB Originally given to King Henry VIII by the Pope, this title is abbreviated on British coins to **FD**.
***Fidei Defensor** Revisited: Church and State in a Religiously Plural Society.*

fīdus Achātes 'faithful Achates' = a faithful friend or companion
NB Achates was the loyal companion of Aeneas in Virgil's *Aeneid*. (For more information on Virgil, see page 182.)
*The Gospel-writer Luke was St Paul's **fidus Achates**.*

flōruit 'he/she flourished' = an indication of the period when a historical figure, whose birth and death dates are unknown, was most active
NB This word is often abbreviated in written English to **fl.**
*Diogenes Laertius (**floruit** third century CE).*

fōns et orīgō = the source and origin
*The **fons et origo** of all reality, whether from the absolute or the practical point of view, is thus ourselves.*

G

genius locī 'the genius of the place' = the guardian spirit of a place; the special atmosphere of a particular place
*To arrive at an understanding of the **genius loci**, we have introduced the concepts of 'meaning' and 'structure'.*

Glōria in excelsīs Deō = Glory to God in the highest
NB These are the traditional opening words of the Greater Doxology of the Roman Catholic Church.
*'Gloria', short for '**Gloria in excelsis deo**', is Poulenc's widely acclaimed interpretation of this beloved Christian hymn.*

Glōria Patrī = Glory to the Father
NB These are the traditional opening words of the Lesser Doxology of the Roman Catholic Church.
*The school's director of music leads the choir in the programme which begins with Bach's '**Gloria Patri**'.*

— H —

habeās corpus 'may you have the body' = the accuser must produce the accused in person
NB The Habeas Corpus Act of 1679 requires that a detainee should appear in person before a court to determine the legality of the detention.
*The question presented here is whether an appearance under a writ of **habeas corpus** constitutes an 'arrest' or a 'summons'.*

hinc illae lacrimae 'hence those tears' = this is the real grievance
NB This proverbial expression comes from the Roman comedian Terence and was quoted by Cicero and Horace. (For more information on Cicero or Horace, see pages 158 and 190.)
***Hinc illae lacrimae**; in plain truth, Honour had as much love for her mistress as most servants have, that is to say.*

hīc iacet = here lies
NB This expression is often abbreviated to **HI**, or written as **hīc iacet sepultus** ('here lies buried') abbreviated to **HIS**, for use on gravestones and memorials, and followed by the deceased person's name.
*The inscription reads '**HIC IACET** PHILIPPVS DE AVBIGNI.'*

horribile dictū = horrible to relate
*What if we allowed the authors and the reviewers to interact with each other and, **horribile dictu**, to know each other's identities.*

I

ibidem = in the same place
NB This word is often abbreviated to **ibid.** and is used to refer to a book, article, chapter, or page previously cited.
Ibid. *may be roman or italic, provided all are treated in the same way throughout the book.*

id est 'that is' = that is to say; in other words
NB This expression is abbreviated in written English to **i.e.**
Do you know when to use e.g. and when to use ***i.e.****?*

Iēsus Nazarēnus Rēx Iūdaeōrum = Jesus of Nazareth King of the Jews
NB This phrase was the inscription placed over Christ's head during his crucifixion, and is often abbreviated to **INRI**.
This is also wrong with the ***INRI*** *that they neatly transcribe as* ***Iesus Nazarenus Rex Iudaeorum*** *that Pilate ordered to be written on the cross.*

ignis fatuus 'foolish fire' = will o' the wisp
Ignis fatuus *is not generally associated with any perceptible warmth.*

ignōrātiō elenchī 'an ignorance of proof' = a supposed refutation of a proposition that only establishes something irrelevant
It is evident that ***ignoratio elenchi*** *may be employed as well for the apparent refutation of your opponent's proposition as for the apparent establishment of your own.*

ignōtum per ignōtius 'the unknown by means of the more unknown' = an explanation that is obscurer than the thing to be explained
He is an incompetent teacher who usually confuses students by resorting to ***ignotum per ignotius****.*

Imp. = Empress; Emperor
NB This was the abbreviation for the Latin word **imperātor** or **imperātrix**.
From 1877 until 1947 British monarchs held the title Emperor (or Empress) of India. This dignity appeared on coins of that era as ***Ind Imp.***

in absentiā = in someone's absence
A Moscow district court refused to issue ***in absentia*** *an arrest warrant for a US citizen on charges of murdering her adopted son.*

in aeternum 'into eternity' = for ever
A single octave leap in the tenor for 'vivet ***in aeternum****' can invest these key words with an indescribable shudder of muted joy.*

in articulō mortis = at the moment of death
In a few cases the man wants to marry ***in articulo mortis*** *or nearly so.*

in camerā 'in a vaulted chamber' = in private
The judge examined ***in camera*** *the State's list of jurors.*

in extēnsō = at full length
I do not deem it necessary to detail my reasons, ***in extenso****, for disbelieving what I am convinced is a vulgar error.*

in extrēmīs 'in the furthest reaches' = in dire straits; at the point of death
This was despite the Home Secretary explicitly saying that, even ***in extremis****, this must not happen.*

īnfrā dignitātem = beneath someone's dignity
NB This expression is abbreviated to **īnfrā dig** in English.
Possibly they find the royals themselves rather ***infra dig*** *– all that Tupperware!*

in locō parentis = in place of a parent
'Our pupils are not obliged to come here, but if they do they must accept that we are ***in loco parentis****.*

in mediās rēs 'into the middle of things' = into the middle of events; into the middle of a narrative
In many ways our understanding occurs ***in medias res*** *– we never quite know everything that happened before.*

in memoriam = to the memory of; in memory of
If only you could see the way the world has changed because of you. ***In Memoriam****: Freddie Mercury.*

in perpetuum 'into perpetuity' = for ever
Parliament has thought proper, ***in perpetuum****, to declare what the common law is and ever has been.*

in persōnam 'against the person' = directed against a specific person or persons
It is possible that East Asiatic could have achieved pure ***in personam*** *jurisdiction over Indomar in this court.*

in propriā persōnā 'in one's own person' = personally
The defendant refused the services of counsel and filed an opening brief ***in propria persona****.*

in rem 'against the thing' = directed against property rather than a specific person
An Admiralty action ***in rem*** *was not at the time of its inception an action between the same parties as an action in personam.*

in rērum nātūrā 'in the nature of things' = in nature; in the physical world
An allegation that the plaintiff is not ***in rerum natura*** *is equivalent to averring that the person named is fictitious.*

in sitū = in position; in its original position
This practical guide covers all aspects of ***in situ*** *hybridization.*

inter alia = among other things
A law was passed, which provided ***inter alia*** *that immigrants settling in the country should be registered.*

inter aliōs = among other people
*Burke, Carlyle, and Macaulay (****inter alios****) help to adorn Mr Wallace's pages.*

inter vīvōs = between living people
If that happened you would really regret having squandered much of it on ***inter vivos*** *gifts and Alaskan dynasty trusts.*

in tōtō = in total; completely; without exception
They think the repeal of the tax increases, ***in toto****, especially those for the wealthy, redounds upon the party.*

in uterō = within the womb; unborn
The agency has noted that there is little research about the potential risk of amalgam ***in utero****.*

in vacuō = in a vacuum; in an empty space
Compton scattering is often used as a generic term for electron-photon scattering ***in vacuo****.*

in vīnō veritās 'in wine there is truth' = a drunken person tells the truth
The oldest of these drugs is alcohol, and its well-known effect has given rise to the aphorism, ***in vino veritas****.*

in vitrō 'in glass' = made to occur outside the body of the organism; in an artificial environment
In vitro diagnostics are tests that can detect diseases, conditions, or infections.

in vīvō 'in a living thing' = occurring in the living organism
We are the undisputed world leader in real time, ***in vivo****, high-resolution micro imaging systems.*

ipse dīxit 'he/she himself said = an arbitrary assertion; an unsupported statement
It is comforting to witness the reality that he who lives by the ***ipse dixit*** *dies by the ipse dixit.*

ipsissima verba 'the very words' = the precise words used by a writer or speaker
The following attempt to reconstruct Amos's ***ipsissima verba*** *does not exhaust the correspondences between the two approaches.*

ipsō factō = by the very fact
No brother shall marry a wife without special consent of the master, upon pain of forfeiting his place ***ipso facto****.*

L

lāpsus linguae = a slip of the tongue
When Marge asks him where he had spent the winter, he commits an incriminating ***lapsus linguae*** *which Marge fails to pick up on.*

lēx locī 'the law of the place' = the law of the country in question
A reading of the relevant cases shows that the ***lex loci*** *rule was discarded mostly to avoid unjust results in particular cases.*

lēx nōn scrīpta 'unwritten law' = common law (derived from precedent)
The ***lex non scripta*** *prevailed before letters were invented.*

lēx scrīpta 'written law' = statute law
Deviations from the ***lex scripta*** *requirement are found in domains other than the prosecution of crimes against humanity.*

lēx tāliōnis = the law of retaliation
The legislation of the Torah is rooted in the concept of ***lex talionis****, or 'an eye for an eye'.*

locō citātō 'in the place cited'
NB This expression is usually abbreviated to **loc. cit.** in the annotations of printed texts to refer to a book previously quoted.
*392. 'Passage to India', **loc. cit.**, p. 379 (did Whitman give the title to EM Forster?).*

M

magnā cum laude → see **cum laude**.

magnificat 'it praises' = Magnificat
NB This expression is a Latin translation of the opening words of the Song of Mary in the Gospel of Luke, and is the title given for its musical setting.
*Choral music with more than 100 singers participating includes the setting of the **Magnificat** by Stanford.*

magnum opus 'a great work' = the greatest single work of an author or artist
*The wheels have begun to turn on the long-awaited screen adaptation of Orson Scott Card's **magnum opus**, 'Ender's Game'.*

malā fidē = in bad faith
*He claimed that the government's notice and subsequent charge sheet against him were served with **mala fide** intentions.*

mare clausum 'a closed sea' = a sea coming under the jurisdiction of one nation
NB The opposite of this legal term is **mare līberum** ('a free sea').
*It is mare liberum in the British seas but **mare clausum** on the coast of Africa and in the East Indies.*

mare līberum → see **mare clausum**.

mare nostrum 'our sea' = the Mediterranean Sea
NB This name was given by the Romans who felt they owned the sea by military and political dominance.
*The cruise, leaving from Genoa will include stops in the **Mare Nostrum** in Cannes, Barcelona, Palma de Mallorca and Valencia.*

māter = mother
*To be a 'university' hospital would further entrench the **Mater** as a necessary part of Queensland's hospital network.*

Māter Dolōrōsa 'sorrowful mother' = the Virgin Mary sorrowing for the dead Christ
NB This expression probably came from a medieval Latin hymn and is often used in art and music.
*The **Mater Dolorosa** has furnished the text to some of the noblest musical compositions by Palestrina, Pergolesi and Haydn.*

māterfamiliās 'mother of the family' = the mother or female head of a household
*As the musical's kitchen **materfamilias** Queenie, Joyce Austin both jigs to 'Can't Help' and leads the foreboding 'Mis'ry Coming'.*

māteria medica 'medical material' = the branch of medical science concerned with the study of drugs used in the treatment of disease
*The National Institute for Food and Drugs Control will participate in Hong Kong's **materia medica** standards project under an agreement signed today.*

mea culpa = my own fault
NB This expression is used as an acknowledgement of guilt, and can be magnified as **mea maxima culpa** ('my very great fault').
*The CEO, in his **mea culpa**, said that 'privacy principles' recently developed by the company were 'written very deeply into our code'.*

medicīnae doctor 'teacher of medicine' = Doctor of Medicine
NB This expression is abbreviated to **MD** to describe the award of a doctorate in medical research.
***MD** ruled dishonourable by College of Physicians.*

mementō morī 'remember that you must die' = a skull, or other object intended to remind someone of the inevitability of death
*Mazziotti's contemporary **memento mori** are made in a variety of mediums from paintings to embroidered textiles.*

mēns rea 'a guilty mind' = a criminal state of mind; criminal intent
*At this point in time, the investigation has to prove that there was no **mens rea** from the defendant, to help her to get acquitted.*

mēns sāna in corpore sānō = a healthy mind in a healthy body
NB This expression originally comes from the Roman satirist, Juvenal.
*The attainment of this will ensure the invaluable blessing of the **mens sana in corpore sano**.*

mīles glōriōsus = a bragging soldier
NB This expression originally comes from the name of a play by the Roman comedian, Plautus.
*We should not take this as an entirely idle vaunt of some **miles gloriosus**.*

mīrābile dictū = wonderful to relate
*The skin can withstand burns, cuts or any other kind of damage – it even repels mosquitoes – and **mirabile dictu!** is also highly sensitive to erotic caress.*

modus operandī 'a way of working' = the way in which something works; a particular way of working
*Their evidence offered a remarkable insight into the **modus operandi** of the world's most powerful media mogul.*

modus pōnēns 'a putting way' = put **p**, get **q**
NB This expression is commonly used in philosophy to make deductions.
For example: If P is true, then Q is true. P is true. Therefore, Q is true.
*The ability to use any argument successfully in **modus ponens** is the primary necessary condition for the argument's logical validity.*

modus tollēns 'a taking way' = take **p**, take **q**
NB This expression is commonly used in philosophy to make deductions.
For example: If P is true, then Q is true. Q is not true. Therefore, P is not true.
*The power and difficulty of **modus tollens** as a reasoning tool is clearly demonstrated in Watson's card-selection experiment.*

modus vīvendī 'a way of living' = a working arrangement between conflicting interests; a practical compromise
*Then come higher hurdles: writing a constitution, electing a president and negotiating a **modus vivendi** with the military.*

mōtū propriō 'of someone's own movement' = on someone's own initiative; spontaneously
*The House of Representatives committee on ways and means will conduct a **motu proprio** investigation.*

multum in parvō 'much in a little' = a great deal in a small space; lots of information in few words
***Multum in Parvo**: An improved grammar of the English language, for the use of schools and academies.*

mūtātīs mūtandīs 'with things changed that must be changed' = with the necessary changes
*Churchill once said he would like to see 'finance less proud and industry more secure'. **Mutatis mutandis**, his words apply today.*

N

NB → see **notā bene**.

nēmine contrādīcente = with no one contradicting; unanimously
NB This legal expression is often abbreviated to **nem. con.**
*Resolved, **nemine contradicente**, that his Majesty's subjects in America owe the same allegiance and are entitled to the same rights.*

nēmō mē impūne lacessit = no one provokes me with impunity
NB This phrase is the motto of the kings of Scotland and of the Order of the Thistle.
*Some may recollect that in former days the national motto, **Nemo me impune lacessit**, was malevolently transferred from the Scotch thistle to a certain cutaneous malady.*

nē plūs ultrā 'not more beyond' = the extreme point; an impassable obstacle
*This house in Beverly Hills is the **ne plus ultra** of a particular kind of Los Angeles fabulousness.*

nihil obstat 'nothing is standing in the way' = there is no obstacle
*The declaration of non-objection or **nihil obstat** is usually the end of the control procedure.*

nīl dēspērandum 'nothing should be despaired of' = do not despair
NB This expression comes from the Odes of Horace. (For more information on Horace, see page 190.)
***Nil Desperandum** is a podcast presenting new works which elucidate Truth, Life, and the Human Condition.*

nōlēns volēns 'unwilling willing' = whether willing or not
*It renders the individual unhappy and uncomfortable by making him **nolens volens** a politician.*

nōlī mē tangere = do not touch me
NB This expression is a Latin translation of the words of the risen Christ to Mary Magdalene in the Gospel of John.
***Noli Me Tangere**, considered to be the greatest Philippine novel, will be launched as a bilingual book for the first time.*

nōlle prōsequī 'to be unwilling to pursue' = the entry made on the court record when the plaintiff or prosecutor abandons a case.
*However, the State later made an entry of **nolle prosequi**, after concluding the indictment was 'vague as to the specific allegations'.*

nōlō contendere 'I do not wish to contend' = a guilty plea made by a defendant to a criminal charge
*Following the progression of the criminal elder abuse case, the nurse eventually entered a plea of **nolo contendere**.*

nōn compos mentis 'not having control of the mind' = not of sound mind; insane
*The man was deemed **non compos mentis** but for the benefit of public safety he was sentenced.*

nōn sequitur 'it does not follow' = a statement having little or no relevance to what preceded it; a conclusion that does not follow from the premises
*He answered a serious question about his depth of knowledge and preparedness for office with a **non sequitur**.*

notā bene = note well
NB This expression is often abbreviated to **NB**.
*This means transferring an obligation of public finance into a monetary phenomenon. **Nota bene**: not of monetary policy!*

nūllī secundus = second to none
*In 1907 the first complete military airship in England was built, which bore the grandiloquent title of **Nulli Secundus**.*

nunc dīmittis 'now you send forth' = Nunc Dimittis
NB This expression is a Latin translation of the opening words of the Song of Simeon in the Gospel of Luke, and is the title given for its musical setting.
*The double bill comprised a Bach cantata and the world premiere of Symonds' **Nunc Dimittis** set to the same text as the Bach.*

— O —

obiit = he/she died
NB This word is often abbreviated to **ob.** and found on gravestones or memorials.
*Under this stone lies the body of Sir John Marshall Kt., **obiit** 21 of January, 1724.*

obiter dictum 'something said in passing' = an incidental remark
*An **obiter dictum** is not a binding precedent but, in the absence of any authority directly on the point, may influence a subsequent decision.*

obscūrum per obscūrius 'the obscure through the more obscure' = an explanation that is more obscure than the thing to be explained
*The learned professor's explanation is a classic case of **obscurum per obscurius**.*

omnium gatherum = a gathering of all sorts; a miscellaneous collection
NB The word **gatherum** is mock-Latin based on the English word *gather*.
*It truly is an **omnium gatherum**, bringing together eight profiles, 11 parodies, 15 short stories, and 37 theatre and movie reviews.*

onus probandī = the burden of proof
*If there be a presumption of law in favour of the pleading of either party, the **onus probandi** is cast upon his adversary.*

opere citātō = in the work cited
NB The expression is often abbreviated to **op. cit.** in the annotations of printed texts to refer to a work previously quoted.
*On relying on German support see e.g. E.C. Jones, **op. cit.**, 132.12.*

opus anglicanum 'English work' = fine embroidery (especially of church vestments)
***Opus anglicanum** was greatly prized for the quality of its work and the delicacy of its coloured figurative subjects.*

ōrā prō nōbīs = pray for us
*Spotless Dove. **Ora pro nobis**. Vessel of Devotion. **Ora pro nobis**. Font of Virginity. Ora pro nobis.*

ō tempora! ō mōrēs! = O the times! O the customs!
NB This expression comes originally from the Roman orator, Cicero. (For more information on Cicero, see page 158.)
***O tempora! O mores!** What new times and customs have we now, with the euro crisis upon us?*

P

p.a. → see **per annum**.

pāce 'in peace' = with due respect to
Pace their opponents, the Hornets' coach will be the first to tell you that play time is over.

parī passū 'with equal step' = at the same speed; side by side
The said 440 shares shall rank ***pari passu*** *with the existing equity shares of the Company in all respects.*

passim 'here and there' = throughout
NB This word is used to indicate that something referred to occurs frequently in the work cited.
For the Scottish connection, see Colley, 'Britons: Forging the Nation', 101–140, and ***passim****.*

paterfamiliās 'father of the family' = the father or male head of a household
This law prohibited lenders – even after the death of the ***paterfamilias*** *– from recovering money lent to sons.*

Pater Noster = Our Father
NB These are the opening words of the Lord's Prayer in Latin.
Paternoster *Square, home of the London Stock Exchange, sits right next to St Paul's Cathedral in the heart of the City.*

pāx vōbīscum = peace be with you
Pax Vobiscum *is the second of a series of religious addresses that began with 'The Greatest Thing in the World'.*

peccāvī = I have sinned
Sir, ***Peccavi****. I am surprised and a little perturbed that no sharp-eyed critic has pounced upon an error which I made.*

per annum 'by the year' = every year; yearly
This latest announcement paves the way for six more terminals of 30 million tonnes ***per annum****.*

per ardua ad astra = through difficulties to the stars
NB This is the motto of the Royal Air Force.
Per Ardua ad Astra*: Seventy years of the RFC and the RAF.*

per capita 'by heads' = individually; per person
*In 1992 income **per capita** in China was $470 and in Africa it was $530.*

per contrā 'by the opposite side' = on the contrary
NB This expression has been commonly used to indicate guarantees in a balance sheet.
*City offices debentures, **per contra**, £300,000; on sundry other contingent liabilities, **per contra**, £257,640.*

per diem = by the day; daily
*For 2010, **per diem** payments of up to $290 are tax-free.*

per mēnsem = by the month; every month
*1857. From the date of arrival in India, the minimum pay of the assistant-surgeon **per mensem** is £25 13s. 3d.*

per prōcūrātiōnem = through the agency of
NB This expression is abbreviated to **per prō** or simply **p.p.** and used when signing documents on behalf of someone else.
*The secretary signed the letter **per pro** the manager.*

persōna grāta = a welcome person
NB This expression is used especially of a diplomat acceptable to the government of the country to which he/she is sent.
*This is another facet of the **persona grata** limitation on immunity for diplomats who misuse their privileges.*

persōna nōn grāta = an unwelcome person
*Cannes says the director is **persona non grata** after his inappropriate remark.*

petītiō prīncipiī 'the begging of the beginning' = begging the question
NB This expression is used to describe a logical fallacy in which the conclusion has been assumed in the premise.
*What we call 'arguing in a circle' is also a **petitio principii**.*

PhD → see **philosophiae doctor**.

philosophiae doctor 'teacher of philosophy' = Doctor of Philosophy
NB This expression is abbreviated to **PhD** or **DPhil** to describe the award of a doctorate in academic research.
*Bank overdraft charges on current accounts are so complicated even a Maths **PhD** student can't always work them out.*

pīnxit 'he/she painted' = painted by
NB This word was sometimes used on paintings next to the artist's name.
It is in the form of a triptych, and bears the inscription : chata ***pinxit****.*

p.m. → see **post merīdiem**.

post bellum = after the war
NB This expression was particularly used of the American Civil War (1861–1865).
*Those years were christened the '****Post-Bellum*** *Pre-Harlem' era by the novelist Charles Chesnutt.*

post hoc, ergō propter hoc 'after this, therefore on account of this' = the fallacy of assuming that a thing which follows another must have been caused by it
The most vulgar form of this fallacy is that which is commonly called ***post hoc, ergo propter hoc****.*

post merīdiem 'after midday' = in the afternoon; p.m.
Edinburgh, 2 October 1648, ***post meridiem****. The brethren present continue the meeting.*

post mortem 'after death' = examination of a dead body to determine the cause of death; analysis or study of a recently completed event
The results of a ***post-mortem*** *examination carried out on the body of a woman discovered in a lake will be released later.*

post scrīptum 'after what has been written' = a postscript
NB This expression is usually abbreviated to **P.S.** at the foot of a letter or email, and can be followed by an additional **P.P.S.** ('a post-postscript').
In ***P.S.****, Megan McMorris collects these sentiments, as an anthology of unsent letters written by a range of women.*

p.p. → see **per prōcūrātiōnem**.

prīmā faciē 'at first appearance' = on the face of it
He told the media outside his office here on Monday that there was no ***prima facie*** *evidence against her.*

prīmum mōbile 'the first moving thing' = prime mover
The real ***primum mobile*** *of the proceedings was the House Representative from Texas.*

prīmus inter parēs = the first among equals
The key decisions have been taken by Angela Merkel and Nicolas Sarkozy – with Germany's chancellor ***prima inter pares****.*

prō et contrā 'for and against' = arguments for and against
NB This expression is abbreviated to **pros and cons**.
*Tests revealed both **pros and cons** to all types of bulbs and found that CFLs have improved but are not quite as bright.*

prō formā 'for the sake of form' = prescribing a set form or procedure; performed in a set manner
*Unaudited **pro forma** financials on a quarterly basis for 2010 and 2011 are presented in the tables below.*

prō patriā = for one's country
*Danny Lopez wrote about what expats in the USA do **pro patria** Philippines and for free.*

prō ratā 'according to a fixed amount' = in proportion
*Distributions are made to shareholders on a **pro-rata** basis (in accordance with the number of shares that are owned).*

prō tempore = for the time being
*Oscar Rios, a four-time mayor, was selected as mayor **pro tempore**, or vice-mayor.*

proximē accessit 'he/she came very near' = the runner-up
*Of Mr Blackmore's own works, we are inclined to think 'The Maid of Sker' a good **proxime accessit**, as the journalists say, to 'Lorna Doone'.*

Q

QED → see **quod erat dēmōnstrandum**.

quid prō quō 'something for something' = a reciprocal exchange; something given in compensation
*For ethical journalists, this isn't a **quid pro quo**: they know they couldn't afford to buy everything they might conceivably write about.*

quis custōdiet ipsōs custōdēs? = who will guard the guards themselves?
NB This expression comes originally from the Roman satirist, Juvenal.
*The bigger question, which I haven't heard the army address, is the old **Quis custodiet ipsos custodes**? Who guards the guards? Or rather, what about the officers?*

quod erat dēmōnstrandum 'which was what had to be proved' = QED
*The results are as pleasing as a perfect equation and the acronym **QED** (**quod erat demonstrandum**), usually appended to the proof of a theorem, would not be inappropriate.*

quod vidē 'see which thing' = a reference to another part of a written text
NB This expression is abbreviated in English to **q.v.**, or to **q.q.v.** if there are more than one.
There was one ***quod vide*** *by the name of his father, the entry for whom I read.*

quot homines tot sententiae 'as many men, so many opinions' = there are as many opinions as there are people
Quot homines, tot sententiae*, so many men, so many minds: that which thou condemnest he commends.*

quō vādis? = where are you going?
NB This expression comes originally from a fictitious question asked by St Peter (fleeing from persecution in Rome) of the risen Christ (who replied that he was going to Rome to be crucified a second time). St Peter returned and was said to have been crucified upside down.
*What are the next important steps to take? In short, '****Quo Vadis****, Graph Theory'?*

q.v. → see **quod vidē**.

R

rāra avis 'a rare bird' = an exceptional person or thing
She's an exquisite creature too, a ***rara avis*** *of the world, a proper princess.*

rē 'from a thing' = concerning; in the matter of
Re*: Your account #: 678 Dear Mr. Denius: Your outstanding balance of $6000 is over 120 days old.*

rectō 'straight' = the front of a sheet of paper; the right-hand page of a book
In the figure, you can see that 'page' 1 (a ***recto*** *page) appears on the right.*

reductiō ad absurdum = reduction to the absurd
Reductio ad absurdum *is a form of argument in which a proposition is disproven by following its implications to a logical but absurd consequence.*

requiēscat in pāce = may he/she rest in peace
NB This expression is often abbreviated to **RIP**.
My beloved cat died yesterday, may she ***RIP****.*

rēs gestae 'things done' = achievements; circumstances that are admissible in evidence because they explain the matter at hand

*This was protected conduct because it was 'part of the **res gestae** of her overarching grievance about dress-code enforcement'.*

rēs ipsa loquitur 'the thing itself speaks' = the matter speaks for itself
*They are insurance contracts; **res ipsa loquitur**. But they are insurance contracts without an insurable interest.*

rēs publica 'the public thing' = the state; the republic
*The founder of the influential **ResPublica** think-tank is one of the inspirations behind the Big Society and mutualism.*

resurgam = I shall rise again
*Was it only fancy that as he turned away a faint music seemed to arise from the ground, forming into the word '**Resurgam**' as it died away?*

rigor mortis 'the stiffness of death' = the rigidity of joints and muscles in a dead body
*If the meat is chilled too rapidly, before **rigor mortis** sets in, for example, the pork chop will toughen irreversibly.*

RIP → see **requiēscat in pāce**.

rūs in urbe = the country in the city
NB This expression comes originally from the Roman satirist, Martial. (For more information on Martial, see page 214.)
*If you look for **rus in urbe**, where will you find it in such perfection as within a mile of the Wellington Statue in almost any direction you please to take?*

S

sānctum sānctōrum = the holy of holies
*The **sanctum sanctorum** was divided from the sanctum by the most precious veil, hung upon four pillars of silver.*

sartor resartus = the tailor retailored
NB This is the title of a book on the philosophy of life by Thomas Carlyle.
*'**Sartor Resartus?** Gorbachev and the prospects for economic reform in Czechoslovakia.'*

schola cantōrum 'a school of singers' = a choir, usually attached to a religious institution
The ***Schola Cantorum*** *represents a culmination of nineteenth-century efforts to improve church music.*

scīlicet 'one may know' = that is to say; namely
NB This word is often abbreviated in English written texts to **sc.**
For him, truth is found primarily in the judgement, ***sc.*** *in an identity of an S and P, where P is contained in the S.*

semper fidēlis = always faithful
NB This expression is the motto of the United States Marine Corps.
Semper fidelis *is the inspiration for this book's unique approach to corporate leadership.*

semper idem = always the same
NB The motto of Queen Elizabeth I was **semper eadem**.
It was ***Semper Idem's*** *recovery which had so fully compensated Doctor Bicknell for the loss of the sailorman.*

Senātus Populusque Rōmānus 'The Senate and the Roman People' = SPQR
NB This abbreviation **SPQR** is still found in Rome today, e.g. on buses and manhole covers.
The game incorporates a few details that help set the mood: the forts have Roman numerals on them and there's an ***SPQR*** *Legion Eagle standard on the board.*

sequēns = following
NB This word is abbreviated in English to **seq.**, or to **seqq.** if there are more than one, and used to indicate a sequence of pages in written texts.
c. Rite of the initiation. S. II, 1, 26 ***seq.****; P II, 2, 5* ***seq.***

sīc 'thus' = used in parentheses to indicate a mistake in a quotation
*I was told that 'we know where you live, so watch out', 'your [****sic****] dead', ... your [****sic****] the minority here!'*

sīc ītur ad astra 'thus there is a going to the stars' = this is the way to glory
NB This expression comes originally from the Roman poet, Virgil. (For more information on Virgil, see page 184.)
Sic itur ad astra*. You never know what is around the corner.*

sīc trānsit glōria mundī = thus passes the glory of the world
NB This expression is used during the coronation of a new Pope while flax is being burned.
Libyagate: ***Sic transit gloria mundi*** *– Viva la revolucion.*

sī monumentum requīris, circumspice = if you seek (his) monument, look around you
NB This is the inscription on the architect Sir Christopher Wren's tomb in St Paul's Cathedral, and also the motto of the State of Michigan.
What would Steve Jobs expect? ***Si monumentum requiris, circumspice***.

sine diē 'without a day' = indefinitely
Ghana's Parliamentary Majority Leader yesterday announced that the House is expected to rise ***sine die*** *on Wednesday.*

sine quā nōn 'without which not' = someone or something indispensable
Growth has become guidepost and grail, the ***sine qua non*** *of economic existence.*

SPQR → see **Senātus Populusque Rōmānus**.

stābat māter 'the mother was standing' = Stabat Mater
NB This is the title of a Latin sequence commemorating the sorrows of the Virgin Mary at the crucifixion, and set to music.
Lovers of choral music will be able to listen to renditions of Haydn's ***Stabat Mater*** *at the concert this Saturday.*

status quō 'the state in which' = the existing state of affairs
We expect the elections on Sunday will maintain the ***status quo*** *in Russia's political landscape without causing any dramatic change.*

stet 'let it stand' = a proofmark that indicates something altered or crossed out should remain uncorrected
*I realised that the text was actually correct, so wrote '****stet****' in the margin to let the typesetter know not to make the correction.*

sub iūdice 'under a judge' = under judicial consideration; undecided
Therefore, will he please explain how the new ***sub iudice*** *resolution differs from the old one?*

sub rosā 'under the rose' = secretly
Most of the gangs' funding came ***sub rosa*** *from the Colombian military.*

sub vōce 'under the voice' = under the specified word
NB The Italian expression sotto voce also literally means 'under the voice'.
This Latin expression is abbreviated in English to **s.v.** and used as a direction in written texts.
As do, e.g., GesB and HAL, ***s.v.*** *8., Konig,* ***s.v.*** *9. With LexHebAram,* ***s.v.*** *11., s.v. 12.*

suī generis 'of his/her/its own kind' = unique
*Look, here's the guy who reinvented the jazz saxophone, playing with unthinkable speed and a **sui generis** rhythmic sense that's near impossible to copy.*

suī iūris 'of his/her/its own right' = legally competent to manage one's own affairs; independent
*The Byzantine Metropolitan Church **sui iuris** of Pittsburgh was established as the Exarchate of Pittsburgh in 1924.*

summā cum laude
See **cum laude**.

summum bonum = the highest good; the supreme good
*To what extent, for example, do they understand that 'confluence' was the **summum bonum** of his art?*

suprā 'above' = see above
NB This word is used to direct to previous material in a written text.
*Mr. Johnson submitted an amendment intended to be proposed by him to the bill HR 2311, **supra**; which was ordered to lie on the table.*

sūrsum corda = lift up your hearts
NB This expression comes from the Latin Eucharist of the Roman Catholic Church.
***Sursum Corda** is a low-rise, HUD-subsidized apartment complex in Washington, DC and consists of 204 units.*

s.v. → see **sub vōce**.

T

tābula rāsa 'a scraped tablet' = the mind in its uninformed original state; a clean slate
*I had all sorts of viral video ideas for him, back when he was a **tabula rasa** and no one knew who he was.*

taedium vītae 'weariness of life' = extreme ennui; inertia
*When ennui befalls me, it's me who refuses everything that could be a gift. **Taedium vitae**, worse than disgust: the lack of taste for anything.*

Tē Deum = Thee, God
NB These are the first words of an ancient Latin hymn sung or recited in the Christian Church as an expression of thanksgiving on special occasions.
Lord draws a sound of striking amplitude from his orchestra, moderating the tension which explodes in the climactic ***Te Deum****.*

tempus fugit 'time flees' = time flies
With an A grade in GCSE Latin, Frank Lampard will be aware of the popular phrase ***tempus fugit****, knowing it refers to the passage of time.*

terminus ad quem 'the end to which' = the aim of something; the finishing time
As we have seen, Kokovtzov was not able to ascertain the ***terminus ad quem*** *of Bahya's dates with any precision.*

terminus ā quō 'the end from which' = the starting point of something
First, he asks what is the ***terminus a quo*** *of creoles; in other words, what are the specific varieties targeted by non-native speakers in the plantations?*

terra firma 'solid land' = firm ground
Cup horse owner hankers for ***terra firma*** *in the next big race of the season.*

terra incognita 'unknown land' = an unexplored or unknown region
For these men devoted to writing, the library was at once the celestial Jerusalem and an underground world on the border between ***terra incognita*** *and Hades.*

tū quoque 'you also' = you, too; you're another
NB This expression can be used by a person accused of a crime implying that the accuser is also guilty of the same crime.
When quantitative easing was sanctioned in 2009, the shadow Chancellor declared it 'the last resort of desperate governments'. ***Tu quoque****, George.*

U

ūberrima fidēs 'the most abundant trust' = utmost good faith
The former Editor of ***Uberrima Fides****, an insurance law journal, he has numerous published articles about debtor and creditor issues.*

ubi suprā 'where above' = in the place above
NB This expression is often abbreviated to **u.s.** and used in written texts.
Parry, ***ubi supra****, though it was repudiated by Coke, CJ, and the remainder of the court.*

u.i. → see **ut īnfrā**.

ultima Thūlē 'the most distant Thule' = the utmost limit; a remote goal
NB Thule was supposed to be the most northerly region in the world.
A cure for spinal cord injury was the ***ultima Thule*** *of hES cell research.*

ultrā vīrēs 'beyond strength' = beyond the legal powers of someone or something
Is governance of the State of Jammu & Kashmir within legal norms or will it be termed ***ultra vires****?*

urbī et orbī = to the city [of Rome] and to the world
NB This expression is used in the Roman Catholic Church of official announcements with universal importance.
I knew people who climbed on their desks to announce ***urbi et orbi*** *that they were leaving the company.*

u.s. → see **ubi suprā** and **ut suprā**.

ut īnfrā = as below
NB This expression can be abbreviated to **u.i.** and is used in written texts.
(Becomes now the genotype of Pealerina Lalicker, 1950, *ut infra*.)

ut suprā = as above
NB This expression can be abbreviated to **u.s.** and is used in written texts.
So, as a general rule, a trustee shall not be allowed to purchase the trust estate, for his own benefit. Green v. Winter, ***ut supra****.*

V

v. → see **versus** and **vidē**.

vāde in pāce = go in peace
*Being duly immured therein, the abbot cast a handful of earth upon him, and said, '****Vade in pace****', which was equivalent to 'Stay there and rot'.*

vāde mēcum 'go with me' = a handbook for ready reference; a guidebook
A ***Vade Mecum****: Or, A Companion for the Unmarried Ladies.*

vae victīs 'woe to the conquered' = down with the defeated
NB This expression originally comes from the Roman historian Livy, quoting the Gauls' chieftain Brennus from the fourth century BCE. (For more information on Livy, see page 198.)
*The promotion will have a charity event in Genoa (their annual **Vae Victis**) to help raise money for the local population.*

valē = farewell
*It is, or used to be in Dean Inge's time, the custom for boys who were leaving Eton to write a **Vale** in Latin elegiacs.*

varia lectiō = a variant reading
NB This expression is often abbreviated to **v.l.**
*Where **v.l.** follows a reading, it indicates that though there is a variant which avoids the linguistic character in question this reading is not to be followed.*

vēnī, vīdī, vīcī = I came, I saw, I conquered
NB This expression is attributed to Julius Caesar after his victory over the king of Pontus in 47 BCE. (For more information on Caesar, see page 158.)
*When Jim walks off the field from his first Super Bowl win, it will be a **veni, vidi, vici** moment.*

venīre faciās 'you must make come' = a writ directing a sheriff to summon suitable persons to form a jury
*The officer receiving such **venire facias** shall serve the same personally upon the jurors and shall make a list of the persons summoned.*

verbum sat sapientī 'a word enough to the wise' = a word is sufficient for a wise person
*I heard the thrifty merchant found that his horoscope foretold rare things of him in Tartary. **Verbum sat sapienti**!*

versō 'turned' = the back of a sheet of paper; the left-hand page of a book
*Sometimes the description is on the **verso** of the first, and the plate on the recto of the second leaf.*

versus = against
NB This word is often abbreviated in English to **v.**
*In this bottom **versus** top clash Doncaster will have to do without striker El-Hadji Diouf, who is missing with a hamstring injury.*

viā 'by way of' = via
Thus, RiRi did perform live for the Grammy Nominations concert, ***via*** *satellite in London!*

via dolōrōsa 'the sorrowful way' = a painful journey; a difficult process
NB This expression is often used to describe the route Christ followed between Jerusalem and Calvary.
We emerged from the tunnels to witness Christian pilgrims singing Latin hymns as they walked Jesus' last steps on the ***Via Dolorosa****.*

via media = a middle way
Via Media*: The necessity of deeper theological reflection for the genuine renewal of the church.*

vice 'with a change' = as a substitute for
'I'll bet he doesn't stay in the first team long' said Clephane, who was now in the bath, ***vice*** *Otway, retired.*

vice versā 'with a change having been turned' = the other way round
It is madness in the NBA now, with reports flying about which agent called which team and ***vice versa****.*

vidē = see; refer to
NB This word is often abbreviated in printed texts in English to **v.**
The bank was issued supervisory instructions ***vide*** *RBI letter dated April 5, 2007, based on its financial position.*

vidēlicet 'one can see' = namely; that is to say
NB This word is often abbreviated in English to **viz.**
Car companies ***viz.*** *Maruti, Toyota, GM and Honda may hike prices by as much as Rs 10000 for small cars.*

vī et armīs 'by force and arms' = violently; forcibly
A trespass committed with force, as, for example, striking another unlawfully, is said to be done ***vi et armis****.*

virgō intacta 'an untouched girl' = a virgin
'Bethulah', on the other hand, seems to denote any woman, young or old, who is ***virgo intacta****.*

vīvā vōce 'with the living voice' = spoken
NB This expression is often abbreviated to **vīvā**, when referring to an oral examination.
*This book can be used for self-assessment through **viva-voce** sessions for revising all that you already know.*

viz. → see **vidēlicet**.

v.l. → see **varia lectiō**.

vōx populī 'the voice of the people' = public opinion
NB This expression is often abbreviated in English to **vōx pop.** when referring to interviews with members of the public.
***Vox Populi** is the fourth collection of interviews, editorials, essays, observations and insight from a highly-respected broadcaster.*

vōx populī, vōx Deī = the voice of the people is the voice of God
*Jeffersonian democracy and other forms of mob rule, the case is closed; the popular will should rule the day, because **vox populi**, **vox dei**!*

VR = Queen Victoria
NB This abbreviation of **Victōria Rēgīna** ('Victoria the Queen') was found on the first stamps and post boxes in the UK.
***Victoria Regina**: an exhibit from the collections of the Kenneth Spencer Research Library.*

Reference Section

Common uses of the cases

Nominative

You use the nominative case where:

- the noun is the subject of the verb

  Sextus rīdet. — Sextus laughs.

- the noun is a complement

  Rōmulus rēx factus est. — Romulus was made king.

- the noun is in apposition to the subject

  Marcus Annius, mercātor Rōmānus, hoc dīcit. — Marcus Annius, a Roman merchant, says this.

For more information on Nouns, see page 2.

Vocative

You use the vocative case:

- to address a person or thing:

  quid accidit, domine? — What happened, master?

For more information on Questions, see page 123.

Accusative

You use the accusative case:

- for the direct object of the verb

  canis baculum petit. — The dog fetches the stick.

- with verbs of teaching and asking which are followed by the accusative of the person and the thing

  puerum litterās docēbō. — I shall teach the boy literature.

- with verbs of naming and making which are followed by accusatives for the same person or thing

  Ancum Martium rēgem populus creāvit. — The people made Ancus Martius king.

- in exclamations
  ō tempora! ō mōrēs! — O the times! O the customs!

- to show extent of space
  mūrus decem pedēs altus est. — The wall is ten feet high.

- to show extent of time
  Trōia decem annōs obsessa est. — Troy was under siege for ten years.

- to show motion to a place or country, usually with a preposition
  ad Hispaniam effūgērunt. — They escaped to Spain.

- to show motion to a town or small island, without a preposition
  Athēnās lēgātī missī sunt. — Ambassadors were sent to Athens.

For more information on Prepositions, see page 132.

Note also **domum** (meaning *homewards*), **rūs** (meaning *to the country*) and **forās** (meaning *outside*).
  forās cucurrērunt puellae. — The girls ran outside.

- for a cognate, that is an object with a similar meaning to the verb
  vītam bonam vīxit. — He lived a good life.

Genitive

You use the genitive case:

- to indicate possession
  domus rēgis. — The king's house.

- to indicate part of a whole (also known as a *partitive genitive*)
  quid novī? — What news?
  plūs cibī. — More food.
  satis pecūniae. — Enough money.

- to indicate a quality, always with an adjective
  magnae auctoritātis es. — Your reputation is great. (*literally* You are of great reputation.)

- as a predicate, where a person represents a quality
  stultī est hoc facere. — It is [the mark] of a fool to do this.

- with superlatives

Indus est omnium flūminum maximum.	The Indus is the greatest of all rivers.

- in front of **causā** and **grātiā** (meaning *for the sake of*)

tū mē amōris causā servāvistī.	You saved me for love's sake.

- with adjectives suggesting knowledge (e.g. **sciēns**), as well as ignorance (e.g. **īnscius**), desire (e.g. **cupidus**), and sharing (e.g. **particeps**)

Verrēs, cupidus pecūniae, ex hērēditāte praedātus est.	Verres, greedy for money, robbed the estate.

- with verbs of remembering (e.g. **meminī**), as well as forgetting (e.g. **oblivīscī**)

mortis mementō.	Remember death.

- with verbs of accusing, convicting, etc.

ante actārum rērum Antōnius accūsātus est.	Antony was accused of offences committed previously.

- to represent value or worth

frūmentum minimī vendidit.	He sold corn at the lowest price.
floccī non faciō.	I don't care a jot.

Dative

You use the dative case:

- for the indirect object of a verb

pecūniam dominō dedit.	He gave the money to his master.

- with verbs of obeying (e.g. **parēre**), as well as resisting (e.g. **resistere**), pleasing (e.g. **placēre**), and ordering (e.g. **imperāre**)

maria terraeque dīs parent.	Land and sea obey the gods.
centūriō mīlitibus imperāvit.	The centurion ordered the soldiers.

- with verb compounds (beginning **ad-**, **ob-**, **prae-**, **sub-**) that suggest helping or hindering – for example **adesse** (meaning *to come to help*), **subvenīre** (meaning *to help*), and **obstāre** (meaning *to oppose*)

Pompeius hostibus obstitit.	Pompey opposed the enemy.

- to indicate possession

  Poppaea amica est Marciae. — Poppaea is Marcia's friend.

- with adjectives meaning 'like' (e.g. **similis**), as well as 'fit' (e.g. **aptus**) and 'near' (e.g. **proximus**)

  fēlēs tigrī similis est. — The cat is like a tiger.

- to indicate a purpose (also known as a *predicative dative*)

  nēmō mihi auxiliō est. — There is no one to help me.

- to show the agent of a gerundive or of a gerund

  omnia erant agenda nōbīs. — Everything had to be done by us.

Ablative Case

You use the ablative case:

- to indicate being in a place, usually with a preposition

  Milō in urbe mansit. — Milo remained in the city.

Note, however, **totā Asiā** (meaning *throughout Asia*) and **terrā marīque** (meaning *by land and sea*).

- to indicate motion from, or down from, a place, usually with prepositions

  dē equō cecidit. — He fell down from his horse.

  praedam ex urbe ornātissimā sustulit. — He stole booty from the very rich city.

Note that prepositions are omitted before the names of towns, small islands, and **domō** (meaning *from home*), **rūre** (meaning *from the country*), and **forīs** (meaning *from outside*).

  domō cucurrērunt servī. — The slaves ran from the house.

- to indicate origin, sometimes with a preposition

  Rōmulus et Remus, Marte nātī. — Romulus and Remus, born of Mars.

  flūmina in Caucasō monte orta. — Rivers rising in the Caucasus mountains.

- to indicate manner (i.e. how something is done), usually with the preposition **cum** (meaning *with*) when there is no adjective, and without **cum** when there is an adjective

  mulierēs cum virtūte vīxērunt. — The women lived virtuously.

summā celeritāte Poenī regressī sunt. — The Carthaginians retreated at top speed.

For more information on Prepositions, see page 132.

- to represent the time when or within which something happens

  hāc nocte Agricola obit. — Agricola died on this night.

  decem annīs Lacedaimoniī nōn haec cōnfēcērunt. — The Spartans did not complete this task within ten years.

- to show material from which something is made

  statua ex aurō facta est. — The statue was made from gold.

- With verbs of depriving, as well as of filling, of needing, and with the impersonal verb **opus est** (meaning *there is a need*)

  aliquem vītā prīvāre. — To deprive someone of life.

  opus est mihi dīvitiīs. — I need wealth.

For more information on Impersonal verbs, see page 93.

- with certain deponent verbs suggesting use (e.g. **ūtī**), abuse (e.g. **abūtī**), accomplishment (e.g. **fungī**), and possession (e.g. **potīrī**)

  vī et armīs ūsus est. — He used force of arms.

For more information on Deponent verbs, see page 115.

- to indicate a cause

  leō fame dēcessit. — The lion died of hunger.

- in what is known as the ablative absolute, where a noun or pronoun is combined with a present, future, or past participle (or another noun or adjective) – all in the ablative – to form an idea independent of the rest of the sentence

  mē dūcente, cīvēs valdē gaudēbant. — With me leading, the citizens were very glad.

  mīlitibus prōgressūrīs, tuba sonuit. — With the soldiers about to attack, the trumpet sounded.

  hīs rēbus dictīs, iuvenis respondēre timēbat. — With these things having been said, the young man was afraid to reply.

  exiguā parte aestātis reliquā, Caesar in Britanniam proficīscī contendit. — With a small part of the summer left, Caesar hurried to set out for Britain.

Common principal parts of verbs

Latin verbs are most usefully listed under four principal parts, from which you will be able to recognise all other forms of the verb. This is how you will find verbs presented in a Latin dictionary.

	Present tense (1st person singular)	Present infinitive	Perfect tense (1st person singular)	Supine
1st conjugation	**amō**	**amāre**	**amāvī**	**amātum**
2nd conjugation	**habeō**	**habēre**	**habuī**	**habitum**
3rd conjugation	**mittō**	**mittere**	**mīsī**	**missum**
4th conjugation	**audiō**	**audīre**	**audīvī**	**audītum**

Over 400 of the most common verbs in Latin are listed below, along with their meaning in English.

There are about 120 regular verbs with their conjugation indicated by a number from 1 to 4 – for example:

accūsō, accūsāre, accūsāvī, accūsātum	accuse	1

There are nearly 300 verbs which are irregular in parts (highlighted in **bold** type), also with a conjugation indicated by a number from 1 to 4 (or M for mixed conjugation verbs) – for example:

abdō, abdere, **abdidī**, **abditum**	hide	**3**

There are also eight fully irregular verbs and their compounds (all highlighted in **bold** type) – for example:

adeō, **adīre**, **adiī**, **aditum**	approach	

And finally the defective verbs (highlighted in **bold** type) are also included – for example:

coepī, **coepisse**, **coeptus**	begin	

For more information on Defective verbs, see page 117.

Principal parts	Meaning	Conj
abdō, abdere, **abdidī**, **abditum**	hide	**3**
abeō, **abīre**, **abiī**, **abitum**	go away	
abiciō, abicere, **abiēcī**, **abiectum**	throw away	**M**
absum, **abesse**, **āfuī**	be away	
accēdō, accēdere, **accessī**, **accessum**	approach	**3**
accidō, accidere, **accidī**	happen	**3**
accipiō, accipere, **accēpī**, **acceptum**	receive	**M**
accūsō, accūsāre, accūsāvī, accūsātum	accuse	1
addō, addere, **addidī**, **additum**	add	**3**
adeō, **adīre**, **adiī**, **aditum**	approach	
adimō, adimere, **adēmī**, **ademptum**	take away	**3**
adiuvō, adiuvāre, **adiūvī**, **adiūtum**	help	**1**
administrō, administrāre, administrāvī, administrātum	administer	1
adsum, **adesse**, **adfuī**	be present	
adveniō, advenīre, **advēnī**, **adventum**	reach	**4**
aedificō, aedificāre, aedificāvī, aedificātum	build	1
afferō, **afferre**, **attulī**, **allātum**	bring to	
afficiō, afficere, **affēcī**, **affectum**	affect	**M**
afflīgō, afflīgere, **afflīxī**, **afflīctum**	afflict/strike	**3**
aggredior, aggredī, **aggressus sum**	attack	**3**
agnōscō, agnōscere, **agnōvī**, **agnītum**	recognise	**3**
agō, agere, **ēgī**, **āctum**	do/drive	**3**
alō, alere, **aluī**, **altum**	feed	**3**
ambulō, ambulāre, ambulāvī, ambulātum	walk	1
āmittō, āmittere, **āmīsī**, **āmissum**	lose	**3**
amō, amāre, amāvī, amātum	love	1
animadvertō, animadvertere, **animadvertī**, **animadversum**	notice	**3**
aperiō, aperīre, **aperuī**, **apertum**	open	**4**
appāreō, appārēre, appāruī, appāritum	appear	2
appellō, appellāre, appellāvī, appellātum	call	1

Principal parts	Meaning	Conj
appropinquō, appropinquāre, appropinquāvī, appropinquātum	approach	1
arbitror, arbitrārī, arbitrātus sum	think	1
arcessō, arcessere, **arcessīvī**, **arcessītum**	send for	**3**
ardeō, ardēre, **arsī**, **arsum**	burn	**2**
armō, armāre, armāvī, armātum	arm	1
ascendō, ascendere, **ascendī**, **ascēnsum**	climb up	**3**
aspiciō, aspicere, **aspexī**, **aspectum**	look at	**M**
attingō, attingere, **attigī**, **attractum**	touch	**3**
audeō, audēre, **ausus sum**	dare	**2**
audiō, audīre, audīvī, audītum	hear	4
auferō, **auferre**, **abstulī**, **ablātum**	take away	
augeō, augēre, **auxī**, **auctum**	increase	**2**
bibō, bibere, **bibī**	drink	**3**
cadō, cadere, **cecidī**, **cāsum**	fall	**3**
caedō, caedere, **cecīdī**, **caesum**	cut/kill	**3**
canō, canere, **cecinī**, **cantum**	sing	**3**
cantō, cantāre, cantāvī, cantātum	sing	1
capiō, capere, **cēpī**, **captum**	take	**M**
cāreō, cārēre, cāruī	lack	2
carpō, carpere, **carpsī**, **carptum**	pick	**3**
caveō, cavēre, **cāvī**, **cautum**	beware	**2**
cēdō, cēdere, **cessī**, **cessum**	give in/give way	**3**
cēlō, cēlāre, cēlāvī, cēlātum	hide	1
cēnō, cēnāre, cēnāvī, cēnātum	dine/have dinner	1
cernō, cernere, **crēvi**, **crētum**	perceive	**3**
cieō, ciēre, **cīvī**, **citum**	rouse	**2**
cingō, cingere, **cinxī**, **cinctum**	surround	**3**
circumdō, **circumdare**, **circumdedī**, **circumdatum**	place round	**1**
circumspectō, circumspectāre, circumspectāvī, circumspectātum	look round	1

Principal parts	Meaning	Conj
circumveniō, circumvenīre, **circumvēnī, circumventum**	surround	**4**
clāmo, clāmāre, clāmāvī, clāmātum	shout	1
claudō, claudere, **clausī, clausum**	close	**3**
coepī, coepisse, coeptus	begin	
cōgitō, cōgitāre, cōgitāvī, cōgitātum	think/consider	1
cognōscō, cognōscere, **cognōvī, cognitum**	get to know/find out	**3**
cōgō, cōgere, **coēgī, coāctum**	force/compel	**3**
colō, colere, **coluī, cultum**	look after/worship	**3**
collocō, collocāre, collocāvī, collocātum	place	1
comitor, comitārī, comitātus sum	accompany	1
commoveō, commovēre, **commōvī, commōtum**	upset	**2**
comparō, comparāre, comparāvī, comparātum	obtain/compare	1
comperiō, comperīre, **comperī, compertum**	discover	**4**
compleō, complēre, **complēvī, complētum**	fill	**2**
compōnō, compōnere, **composuī, compositum**	put together/settle	**3**
comprehendō, comprehendere, **comprehendī, comprehēnsum**	grasp	**3**
concurrō, concurrere, **concurrī, concursum**	run together	**3**
condō, condere, **condidī, conditum**	found	**3**
cōnficiō, cōnficere, **cōnfēcī, cōnfectum**	finish	**M**
cōnfīdō, cōnfīdere, **cōnfīsus sum**	trust	**3**
cōnfirmō, cōnfirmāre, cōnfirmāvī, cōnfirmātūm	strengthen	1
cōnfiteor, cōnfitērī, **cōnfessus sum**	confess	**2**
congredior, congredī, **congressus sum**	meet	**3**
coniciō, conicere, **coniēci, coniectum**	throw	**M**
coniungō, coniungere, **coniūnxi, coniūnctum**	join	**3**
coniūro, coniūrāre, coniūrāvī, coniūrātum	conspire	1
cōnor, cōnāri, cōnātus sum	try	1

Principal parts	Meaning	Conj
cōnsentiō, cōnsentīre, **cōnsēnsī**, **consēnsum**	agree	**4**
cōnsistō, cōnsistere, **cōnstitī**	stand firm/halt	**3**
cōnspiciō, cōnspicere, **cōnspexī**, **cōnspectum**	catch sight of	**M**
cōnspicor, cōnspicārī, cōnspicātus sum	catch sight of	1
cōnstō, cōnstāre, **cōnstitī**	agree	**1**
cōnstituō, cōnstituere, **cōnstituī**, **cōnstitūtum**	decide	**3**
cōnstruō, cōnstruere, **cōnstrūxī**, **cōnstructum**	construct	**3**
cōnsulō, cōnsulere, **cōnsuluī**, **cōnsultum**	consult	**3**
cōnsūmō, cōnsūmere, **cōnsūmpsī**, **cōnsūmptum**	use up	**3**
contemnō, contemnere, **contempsī**, **contemptum**	despise	**3**
contendō, contendere, **contendī**, **contentum**	strive/hurry	**3**
contingō, contingere, **contigī**, **contāctum**	touch	**3**
convenīo, convenīre, **convēnī**, **conventum**	meet	**4**
convertō, convertere, **convertī**, **conversum**	turn	**4**
coquō, coquere, **coxī**, **coctum**	cook	**3**
corripiō, corripere, **corripuī**, **correptum**	seize	**M**
crēdō, crēdere, **crēdidī**, **crēditum**	believe	**3**
crescō, crescere, **crēvī**, **crētum**	grow	**3**
culpō, culpāre, culpāvī, culpātum	blame	1
cunctor, cunctārī, cunctātus sum	delay	1
cupiō, cupere, **cupīvī**, **cupītum**	desire	**M**
cūrō, cūrāre, cūrāvī, cūrātum	look after/supervise	1
currō, currere, **cucurrī**, **cursum**	run	**3**
custōdiō, custōdīre, custōdīvī, custōdītum	guard	4
damnō, damnāre, damnāvī, damnātum	condemn	1
dēbeō, dēbēre, dēbuī, dēbitum	have to/owe	2
dēcidō, dēcidere, **dēcidī**	fall down	**3**

Principal parts	Meaning	Conj
dēcipiō, dēcipere, **dēcēpī**, **dēceptum**	deceive/trick	**M**
dēdō, dēdere, **dēdidī**, **dēditum**	hand over/yield	**3**
dēdūcō, dēdūcere, **dēdūxī**, **dēductum**	bring/escort	**3**
dēfendō, dēfendere, **dēfendī**, **dēfēnsum**	defend	**3**
dēficiō, dēficere, **dēfēcī**, **dēfectum**	revolt/fail	**M**
dēiciō, dēicere, **dēiēcī**, **dēiectum**	throw down	**M**
dēlectō, dēlectāre, dēlectāvī, dēlectātum	delight	1
dēleō, dēlēre, **dēlēvī**, **dēlētum**	destroy	**2**
dēligō, dēligāre, dēligāvī, dēligātum	tie up/moor	1
dēligō, dēligere, **dēlēgī**, **dēlectum**	choose	**3**
dēmōnstrō, dēmōnstrāre, dēmōnstrāvī, dēmōnstrātum	show	1
dēpōnō, dēpōnere, **dēposuī**, **dēpositum**	lay down	**3**
dēscendō, dēscendere, **dēscendī**, **dēscensum**	go down	**3**
dēserō, dēserere, **dēseruī**, **dēsertum**	desert	**3**
dēsiderō, dēsiderāre, dēsiderāvī, dēsiderātum	long for	1
dēsiliō, dēsilere, **dēsiluī**, **dēsultum**	jump down	**M**
dēsinō, dēsinere, **dēsiī**, **dēsitum**	stop/leave off	**3**
dēsistō, dēsistere, **dēstitī**	stop/leave off	**3**
dēspērō, dēspērāre, dēspērāvī, dēspērātum	despair	1
dēstruō, dēstruere, **dēstruxī**, **dēstructum**	destroy	**3**
dīcō, dīcere, **dīxī**, **dictum**	tell/say	**3**
dīligō, dīligere, **dīlexī**, **dīlectum**	love	**3**
dīmittō, dīmittere, **dīmīsī**, **dīmissum**	send away	**3**
discēdō, discēdere, **discessī**, **discessum**	depart	**3**
discō, discere, **didicī**	learn	**3**
dīvidō, dīvidere, **dīvīsī**, **dīvīsum**	divide	**3**
dō, **dare**, **dedī**, **datum**	give	**1**
doceō, docēre, docuī, **doctum**	teach	**2**
doleō, dolēre, doluī	grieve	2
dormiō, dormīre, dormīvī, dormītum	sleep	**4**

Principal parts	Meaning	Conj
dubitō, dubitāre, dubitāvī, dubitātum	doubt	1
dūcō, dūcere, **dūxī**, **ductum**	lead	**3**
edō, edere, **ēdī**, **ēsum**	eat	**3**
efficiō, efficere, **effēcī**, **effectum**	complete	**M**
effugiō, effugere, **effūgī**	escape	**M**
ēgredior, ēgredī, **ēgressus sum**	go out	**3**
emō, emere, **ēmī**, **ēmptum**	buy	**3**
eō, **īre**, **īvī** *or* **iī**, **itum**	go	
ēripiō, ēripere, **ēripuī**, **ēreptum**	snatch away/rescue	**M**
errō, errāre, errāvī, errātum	wander/be wrong	1
ērumpō, ērumpere, **ērūpī**, **ēruptum**	burst out	**3**
excitō, excitāre, excitāvī, excitātūm	arouse	1
exeō, **exīre**, **exiī**, **exitum**	go out	
exerceō, exercēre, exercuī, exercitum	exercise/train	2
exīstimō, exīstimāre, exīstimāvī, exīstimātum	think	1
expellō, expellere, **expulī**, **expulsum**	drive out	**3**
experior, experīrī, **expertus sum**	try/test	**4**
explicō, explicāre, explicāvī, explicātum	explain	1
exspectō, exspectāre, exspectāvī, exspectātum	wait for	1
exuō, exuere, **exuī**, **exūtum**	take off	**3**
faciō, facere, **fēcī**, **factum**	do/make	**M**
fallō, fallere, **fefellī**, **falsum**	deceive	**3**
faveō, favēre, **fāvī**, **fautum**	favour	**2**
ferō, **ferre**, **tulī**, **lātum**	bring/bear	
festīnō, festīnāre, festīnāvi, festīnātum	hurry	1
fīgo, fīgere, **fīxī**, **fīxum**	fix	**3**
fingō, fingere, **fīnxī**, **fictum**	invent	**3**
fīō, **fierī**, **factus sum**	become/happen	
flectō, flectere, **flexī**, **flexum**	bend	**3**
fleō, flēre, **flēvī**, **flētum**	weep	**2**
fluō, fluere, **flūxī**, **flūxum**	flow	**3**

Principal parts	Meaning	Conj
frangō, frangere, **frēgī**, **frāctum**	break	**3**
fruor, fruī, **frūctus** *or* **fruitus sum**	enjoy	**3**
fugiō, fugere, **fūgī**, **fugitum**	flee/escape	**M**
fugō, fugāre, fugāvī, fugātum	put to flight	1
fundō, fundere, **fūdī**, **fūsum**	pour	**3**
fungor, **fungī**, **fūnctus sum**	perform	**3**
gaudeō, gaudēre, **gāvīsus sum**	be glad	**2**
gemō, gemere, **gemuī**, **gemitum**	groan	**3**
gerō, gerere, **gessī**, **gestum**	carry on/wear	**3**
gignō, gignere, **genuī**, **genitum**	produce	**3**
habeō, habēre, habuī, habitum	have/keep	2
habitō, habitāre, habitavī, habitātum	live (in)	1
haereō, haerēre, **haesī**, **haesum**	stick	**2**
hauriō, haurīre, **hausī**, **haustum**	drain away	**4**
horreō, horrēre, horruī	stand on end	2
hortor, hortārī, hortātus sum	encourage	1
iaceō, iacēre, iacuī	lie down	2
iaciō, iacere, **iēcī**, **iactum**	throw	**3**
iactō, iactāre, iactāvī, iactātum	throw	**M**
ignōrō, ignōrāre, ignōrāvī, ignōrātum	not to know of	1
ignōscō, ignōscere, **ignōvī**, **ignōtum**	forgive	**3**
immineō, imminēre	threaten/hang over	2
impediō, impedīre, impedīvī, impedītum	hinder	4
impellō, impellere, **impulī**, **impulsum**	drive on	**3**
imperō, imperāre, imperāvī, imperātum	order	1
incēdō, incēdere, **incessī**, **incessum**	march/stride	**3**
incendō, incendere, **incendī**, **incēnsum**	burn	**3**
incipiō, incipere, **incēpī**, **inceptum**	begin	**M**
incitō, incitāre, incitāvī, incitātum	drive on	1
inclūdō, inclūdere, **inclūsī**, **inclūsum**	include	**3**
incolō, incolere, **incoluī**	live (in)	**3**
īnferō, **īnferre**, **intulī**, **inlātum**	bring against	

Principal parts	Meaning	Conj
ingredior, ingredī, **ingressus sum**	enter	**3**
īnspiciō, īnspicere, **īnspexī**, **īnspectum**	examine/search	**M**
īnstituō, īnstituere, **īnstituī**, **īnstitūtum**	set up	**3**
īnstruō, īnstruere, **īnstrūxī**, **īnstrūctum**	set/draw up	**3**
intellegō, intellegere, **intellēxī**, **intellēctum**	realise	**3**
interficiō, interficere, **interfēcī**, **interfectum**	kill	**M**
intersum, **interesse**, **interfuī**	be among/be important	
intrō, intrāre, intrāvī, intrātum	enter	1
inveniō, invenīre, **invēnī**, **inventum**	come upon/find	**4**
invītō, invītāre, invītāvī, invītātum	invite	1
irrumpō, irrumpere, **irrūpī**, **irruptum**	rush into	**3**
iubeō, iubēre, **iussī**, **iussum**	order	**2**
iūdicō, iūdicāre, iūdicāvī, iūdicātum	judge	1
iungō, iungere, **iūnxī**, **iūnctum**	join	**3**
iūrō, iūrāre, iūrāvī, iūrātum	swear	1
iuvō, iuvāre, **iūvī**, **iūtum**	help	**1**
lābor, lābī, **lāpsus sum**	slip	**3**
labōrō, labōrāre, labōravī, labōrātum	work	1
lacessō, lacessere, **lacessīvī**, **lacessītum**	harass	**3**
lacrimō, lacrimāre, lacrimāvī, lacrimātum	weep	1
laedō, laedere, **laesī**, **laesum**	hurt	**3**
lateō, latēre, latuī	lie hidden	**2**
laudō, laudāre, laudāvī, laudātum	praise	1
lavō, lavāre, **lāvī**, **lautum** *or* **lavātum** *or* **lōtum**	wash	**1**
legō, legere, **lēgi**, **lēctum**	read	**3**
levō, levāre, levāvī, levātum	lighten	1
līberō, līberāre, līberāvī, līberātum	free	1
licet, licēre, licuit	it is allowed	**2**
locō, locāre, locāvī, locātum	place	1
loquor, loquī, **locūtus sum**	speak	**3**
lūdō, lūdere, **lūsī**, **lūsum**	play	**3**
lustrō, lustrāre, lustrāvī, lustrātum	purify/scan	1

Principal parts	Meaning	Conj
mālo, **mālle**, **māluī**	prefer	
mandō, mandāre, mandāvī, mandātum	command/trust	1
maneō, manēre, **mānsī**, **mānsum**	remain/stay	**2**
meminī, **meminisse**	remember	
mentior, mentīrī, mentītus sum	tell lies	4
metuō, metuere, **metuī**, **metūtum**	fear	**3**
minor, minārī, minātus sum	threaten	1
minuō, minuere, **minuī**, **minūtum**	lessen	3
miror, mirārī, mirātus sum	wonder (at)	1
misceō, miscēre, **miscuī**, **mixtum**	mix	**2**
misereor, miserērī, miseritus sum	pity	2
miseret, miserēre, miseruit	it excites pity	**2**
mittō, mittere, **mīsī**, **missum**	send	**3**
mōlior, mōlīrī, mōlītus sum	strive/toil	**4**
moneō, monēre, monuī, monitum	advise/warn	2
morior, morī, **mortuus sum**	die	**3**
moror, morārī, morātus sum	delay/loiter	1
moveō, movēre, **mōvī**, **mōtum**	move	**2**
mūniō, mūnīre, mūnīvī, mūnītum	fortify	4
mūtō, mūtāre, mūtāvī, mūtātum	change	1
nancīscor, nancīscī, **na(n)ctus sum**	obtain	**3**
nārrō, nārrāre, nārrāvī, nārrātum	tell	1
nāscor, nāscī, **nātus sum**	be born	**3**
nāvigō, nāvigāre, nāvigāvī, nāvigātum	sail	1
necō, necāre, necāvī, necātum	kill	1
negō, negāre, negāvī, negātum	refuse/deny	1
neglegō, neglegere, **neglēxī**, **neglēctum**	neglect	**3**
nesciō, nescīre, nescīvī, nescītum	not to know	4
noceō, nocēre, nocuī, nocitum	harm	2
nōlō, **nōlle**, **nōluī**	not to wish/be unwilling	
nōsco, nōscere, **nōvī**, **nōtum** (in perfect tenses translate as 'know')	get to know	**3**

Principal parts	Meaning	Conj
nūntio, nūntiāre, nūntiāvī, nūntiātum	announce	1
obeō, **obīre**, **obīvī** *or* **obiī**, **obitum**	die	
obiciō, obicere, **obiēcī**, **obiectum**	present/put in the way of	**M**
oblīvīscor, oblīvīscī, **oblītus sum**	forget	**3**
obsideō, obsidēre, **obsēdī**, **obsessum**	besiege	**2**
obstō, obstāre, **obstitī**	obstruct	**1**
obtineō, obtinēre, obtinuī, **obtentum**	hold/obtain	**2**
occidō, occidere, **occidī**, **occāsum**	fall	**3**
occīdō, occīdere, **occīdī**, **occīsum**	kill	**3**
occupō, occupāre, occupāvī, occupātum	seize	1
occurrō, occurrere, **occurrī**, **occursum**	meet	**3**
ōdī, **ōdisse**	hate	
offerō, **offerre**, **obtulī**, **oblātum**	present	
oportet, oportēre, oportuit	be proper/ought	2
opprimō, opprimere, **oppressī**, **oppressum**	crush	**3**
oppugnō, oppugnāre, oppugnāvī, oppugnātum	attack	1
optō, optāre, optāvī, optātum	wish/choose	1
orior, orīrī, **ortus sum**	arise	**4**
ōrō, ōrāre, ōrāvī, ōrātum	beg/plead	1
ornō, ornāre, ornāvī, ornātum	decorate/equip	1
ostendō, ostendere, **ostendī**, **ostentum**	show	**3**
pācō, pācāre, pācāvī, pācātum	pacify	1
paenitet, paenitēre, paenituit	it causes regret	2
pandō, pandere, **pandī**, **passum** *or* **pansum**	spread out/extend	**3**
parcō, parcere, **pepercī**, **parsum**	spare	**3**
pāreō, pārēre, pāruī	obey	2
pariō, parere, **peperī**, **partum**	give birth to	**M**
parō, parāre, parāvī, parātum	prepare	1
pāscō, pāscere, **pāvī**, **pāstum**	feed	**3**
patefaciō, patefacere, **patefēcī**, **patefactum**	open	**M**

Principal parts	Meaning	Conj
pateō, patēre, patuī	be open	2
patior, patī, **passus sum**	suffer/allow	**3**
paveō, pavēre, pavī	fear	2
pellō, pellere, **pepulī**, **pulsum**	drive	3
pendeō, pendēre, **pependī**	hang	**2**
pendō, pendere, **pependī**, **pēnsum**	weigh/pay	**3**
perdō, perdere, **perdidī**, **perditum**	lose/destroy	**3**
pereō, **perīre**, **periī**, **peritum**	perish	
perficiō, perficere, **perfēcī**, **perfectum**	complete	**M**
pergō, pergere, **perrēxī**, **perrēctum**	proceed	**3**
permittō, permittere, **permīsī**, **permissum**	allow	3
perstō, **perstāre**, **perstitī**, perstātum	stand firm	**1**
persuādeō, persuādēre, **persuāsī**, **persuāsum**	persuade	**2**
pertineō, pertinēre, pertinuī, **pertentum**	concern	2
perturbō, pertūrbāre, perturbāvī, perturbātum	confuse	1
perveniō, pervenīre, **pervēnī**, **perventum**	arrive at	**4**
petō, petere, **petīvī**, **petītum**	seek/ask	**3**
placeō, placēre, placuī, placitum	please	2
placet, placēre, placuit	it seems good	2
polliceor, pollicērī, **pollicitus sum**	promise	2
pōnō, pōnere, **posuī**, **positum**	place/put	**3**
portō, portāre, portāvī, portātum	carry	1
poscō, poscere, **poposcī**	ask for/demand	3
possum, **posse**, **potuī**	to be able	
postulō, postulāre, postulāvī, postulātum	demand	1
potior, potīrī, potītus sum	gain possession of	**4**
praebeō, praebēre, praebuī, praebitum	show	2
praeficiō, praeficere, **praefēci**, **praefēctum**	put in command of	**M**
praestō, praestāre, **praestitī**, **praestitum**	stand out	**1**
precor, precārī, precātus sum	pray	1
premō, premere, **pressī**, **pressum**	press	**3**

Principal parts	Meaning	Conj
prōcēdō, prōcēdere, **prōccessī**, **prōcessum**	advance	**3**
prōdō, prōdere, **prōdidī**, **prōditum**	betray	**3**
proficīscor, proficīscī, **profectus sum**	set out	**3**
prōgredior, prōgredī, **progressus sum**	advance	**3**
prohibeō, prohibēre, prohibuī, prohibitum	prevent	2
prōmitto, prōmittere, **prōmīsī**, **prōmissum**	promise	**3**
prōvideō, prōvidēre, **prōvīdī**, **prōvīsum**	take precautions	**2**
pugnō, pugnāre, pugnāvī, pugnātum	fight	1
pūniō, pūnīre, punīvī, punītum	punish	4
putō, putāre, putāvī, putātum	think	1
quaerō, quaerere, **quaesīvī**, **quaesītum**	search/look for	**3**
quaeror, quaerī, **quaestus sum**	complain	**3**
quiescō, quiescere, **quiēvī**, **quiētum**	keep quiet	**3**
rapiō, rapere, **rapuī**, **raptum**	snatch/seize	**M**
recipiō, recipere, **recēpī**, **receptum**	recover/take back	**M**
recūsō, recūsāre, recūsāvī, recūsātum	refuse	1
reddō, reddere, **reddidī**, **redditum**	give back/return	**3**
redeō, **redīre**, **rediī**, **reditum**	come back/return	
redūcō, redūcere, **redūxī**, **reductum**	bring back	**3**
regō, regere, **rēxī**, **rēctum**	rule	**3**
regredior, regredī, **regressum sum**	retreat	**3**
relinquō, relinquere, **relīquī**, **relictum**	leave	**3**
remittō, remittere, **remīsī**, **remissum**	send back	**3**
reor, rērī, **ratus sum**	think	2
repellō, repellere, **reppulī**, **repulsum**	drive back	**3**
reperiō, reperīre, **repperī**, **repertum**	find	**4**
resistō, resistere, **restitī**	resist	**3**
respiciō, respicere, **respexī**, **respectum**	look back	**M**
respondeō, respondēre, **respondī**, **responsum**	answer	**2**
restō, **restāre**, **restitī**	remain	**1**
restituō, restituere, **restituī**, **restitūtum**	restore	3
retineō, restinēre, **retinuī**, **retentum**	hold back	**2**

Principal parts	Meaning	Conj
rīdeō, rīdēre, **rīsī**, **rīsum**	laugh	**2**
rogō, rogāre, rogāvī, rogātum	ask	1
rumpō, rumpere, **rūpī**, **ruptum**	burst	**3**
ruō, ruere, **ruī**, **rutum** (*future participle –* **ruitūrus**)	rush/fall	**3**
sciō, scīre, **scīvī**, **scītum**	know	**4**
scrībō, scrībere, **scrīpsī**, **scrīptum**	write	**3**
sēcernō, sēcernere, **sēcrēvī**, **sēcrētum**	set apart	**3**
secō, secāre, **secuī**, **sectum**	cut	**1**
sedeō, sedēre, **sēdī**, **sessum**	sit	**2**
sentiō, sentīre, **sēnsi**, **sēnsum**	feel/perceive	**4**
sepeliō, sepelīre, sepelīvī, **sepultum**	bury	**4**
sequor, sequī, **secūtus sum**	follow	**3**
serō, serere, **sēvī**, **satum**	sow	**3**
serviō, servīre, servīvī, servītum	serve/be a slave	4
servō, servāre, servāvī, servātum	save	1
simulō, simulāre, simulāvī, simulātum	pretend	1
sinō, sinere, **sīvī**, **situm**	allow	**3**
sistō, sistere, **stitī**, **statum**	set up	**3**
soleō, solēre, **solitus sum**	be used to	**2**
sollicitō, sollicitāre, sollicitāvī, sollicitātum	worry	1
solvō, solvere, **solvī**, **solūtum**	loosen	**3**
sonō, sonāre, **sonuī**, **sonitum**	sound	**1**
spargō, spargere, **sparsī**, **sparsum**	scatter/sprinkle	**3**
spectō, spectāre, spectāvī, spectātum	look at	1
spērō, spērāre, spērāvī, spērātum	hope	1
spoliō, spoliāre, spoliāvī, spoliātum	rob/plunder	1
statuō, statuere, **statuī**, **statūtum**	set up	**3**
sternō, sternere, **strāvī**, **strātum**	cover/overthrow	**3**
stō, stāre, **stetī**, **statum**	stand	1
stringō, stringere, **strinxī**, **strictum**	draw tight/tie	**3**
struō, struere, **struxī**, **structum**	build	**3**
studeō, studēre, studuī	study	2

Principal parts	Meaning	Conj
suādeō, suādēre, **suāsī**, **suāsum**	advise	**2**
subeō, **subīre**, **subiī** *or* **subīvī**, **subitum**	undergo	
subveniō, subvenīre, **subvēnī**, **subventum**	help/come to the aid of	**4**
succēdō, succēdere, **successī**, **successum**	go up/relieve	**3**
succurro, succurrere, **succurrī**, **succursum**	help	**3**
sum, **esse**, **fuī**, **futūrus**	be	
sūmō, sūmere, **sūmpsī**, **sūmptum**	take	**3**
superō, superāre, superāvī, superātum	overcome	1
supersum, **superesse**, **superfuī**	survive	
surgō, surgere, **surrēxī**, **surrēctum**	rise/get up	**3**
suscipiō, suscipere, **suscēpī**, **susceptum**	undertake	**M**
suspicor, suspicārī, suspicātus sum	suspect	1
sustineō, sustinēre, sustinuī, **sustentum**	sustain	**2**
tacēo, tacēre, tacuī, tacitum	be silent	2
taedet, taedēre, taeduit, **taesum est**	be tired of	**2**
tangō, tangere, **tetigī**, **tāctum**	touch	**3**
tegō, tegere, **tēxī**, **tēctum**	cover	**3**
tendō, tendere, **tetendī**, **tentum** *or* **tēnsum**	stretch	**3**
teneō, tenēre, tenuī, **tentum**	hold	**2**
terreō, terrēre, terruī, territum	terrify	2
timeō, timēre, timuī	fear	2
tollō, tollere, **sustulī**, **sublātum**	raise/remove	**3**
tonō, tonāre, **tonuī**	thunder	**1**
torqueō, torquēre, **torsī**, **tortum**	twist	2
trādō, trādere, **trādidī**, **trāditum**	hand over	**3**
trahō, trahere, **trāxī**, **tractum**	drag	**3**
trāiciō, trāicere, **trāiēcī**, **trāiectum**	take across	**M**
trānseō, **trānsīre**, **trānsiī**, **trānsitum**	cross over	
tueor, tuērī, tuitus *or* **tūtus** sum	look at	**2**
ulcīscor, ulcīscī, **ultus sum**	punish/avenge	**3**
urgeō, urgēre, **ursī**	press/urge	**2**
ūrō, ūrere, **ussī**, **ustum**	burn	**3**

Principal parts	Meaning	Conj
ūtor, ūtī, **ūsus sum**	use	**3**
valeō, valēre, valuī, valitum	be strong/healthy	2
vastō, vastāre, vastāvī, vastātum	destroy	1
vehō, vehere, **vexī**, **vectum**	carry	**3**
vēndō, vēndere, **vēndidī**, **vēnditum**	sell	**3**
veniō, venīre, **vēnī**, **ventum**	come	**4**
verberō, verberāre, verberāvī, verberātum	strike/beat	1
vereor, verērī, veritus sum	fear	2
vertō, vertere, **vertī**, **versum**	turn	**3**
vescor, vescī	feed on/eat	3
vetō, vetāre, **vetuī**, **vetitum**	forbid	**1**
videō, vidēre, **vīdī**, **vīsum**	see	**2**
vigilō, vigilāre, vigilāvī, vigilātum	stay awake	1
vinciō, vincīre, **vīnxī**, **vīnctum**	bind	**4**
vincō, vincere, **vīcī**, **victum**	defeat/conquer	**3**
vītō, vītāre, vītāvī, vītātum	avoid	1
vituperō, vituperāre, vituperāvī, vituperātum	blame/curse	1
vīvō, vīvere, **vīxī**, **victum**	live	**3**
vocō, vocāre, vocāvī, vocātum	call/invite	1
volō, **velle**, **voluī**	wish/want	
volvō, volvere, **volvī**, **volūtum**	roll	**3**
voveō, vovēre, **vōvī**, **vōtum**	vow	**2**

Answer key

Exercise 1
a) **fēmina** b) **servōs** c) **puerō** d) **templōrum** e) **cōnsulibus** f) **domine** g) **gentēs** h) **ponte** i) **cīvēs** j) **animālibus** k) **exercitum** l) **diēī**.

Exercise 2
a) **fēlīx** b) **alterī** c) **pulchrōrum** d) **prūdentibus** e) **fortēs** f) **miserum**.

Exercise 3
a) **miseriōres** b) **prūdentissime** c) **maiōrēs** d) **altissimō** e) **minōribus** f) **postrēmae**.

Exercise 4
a) **illa** b) **aliquōs** c) **hunc** & **qui** d) **quōrundam** e) **ipsīs** f) **ego** & **tibi** & **iste** g) **eaedem** h) **quō** i) **quōs** & **noster** & **mēcum** j) **eīs** k) **cuius** & **suum** l) **quis**.

Exercise 5
a) **amant** b) **mittit** c) **habeō** d) **audītis** e) **possumus** f) **facis**.

Exercise 6
a) **docē** b) **invenīte** c) **labōrāte** d) **quaere** e) **īte** f) **iacere nōlī**.

Exercise 7
a) **erat** b) **portābāmus** c) **veniēbās** d) **reddēbant** e) **habēbātis** f) **capiēbam**.

Exercise 8
a) **terrēbit** b) **nōlent** c) **inveniam** d) **amābitis** e) **poterimus** f) **mittēs**.

Exercise 9
a) **quaesīvistī** b) **labōrāvimus** c) **audīvit** d) **māluistis** e) **cēpī** f) **docuērunt** g) **portāverimus** h) **vēnerat** i) **voluerō** j) **fēceritis** k) **reddīderant** l) **terruerās**.

Exercise 10

a) **quaeriminī** b) **amābimur** c) **audiēbātur** d) **inventa** e) **lātī** f) **missīs** g) **doctō** h) **lāta es** i) **amātae erāmus** j) **inventus erō** k) **terrēminī** l) **portāre**.

Exercise 11

a) **reddentēs** b) **habentium** c) **praesentī** d) **exiēns** e) **portandī** f) **audiendō**.

Exercise 12

a) **labōrātūrīs** b) **ventūrī** c) **futūrae** d) **ferendō** e) **mittenda** f) **inveniendō**.

Exercise 13

a) **dominum piget** b) **magistrō placuit** c) **nōbīs libuit** d) **mātrem pudet** e) **ancillīs nōn licet** f) **fulgurāvit**.

Exercise 14

a) **labōrem** b) **veniās** c) **audīret** d) **quaeserīmus** e) **īssētis** f) **essent** g) **porter** h) **doceāris** i) **terrērētur** j) **inventae sīmus** k) **captī essētis** l) **facta essent**.

Exercise 15

a) **iacere** b) **mīsisse** c) **ventūrus esse** d) **doctum īrī** e) **portārī** f) **redditae esse**.

Exercise 16

a) **cōnābantur** b) **sequere** c) **gaudēbimus** d) **mentītī estis** e) **verita erat** f) **passus erō** g) **ausa es** h) **secūtūrī sunt** i) **coepī** j) **nōverat** k) **meminerātis** l) **ōdimus**.

Exercise 17

a) **nōn** b) **nūllōs** c) **minimē** d) **nec ... nec** e) **numquam** f) **nūllae ... nōn** g) **nēmō** h) **nē** i) **nec** j) **haud**.

Exercise 18

a) **quō** b) **quot** c) **quid** d) **ubi** e) **cūr** f) **an** g) **quotiēns** h) **nonne** i) **annōn** j) **quis** k) **quandō** l) **discessitne**.

Exercise 19

a) **laetē** b) **quoque** c) **quam celerrimē** d) **iam** e) **facilius** f) **semper** g) **saepe** h) **statim** i) **ācrius** j) **diūtissimē** k) **fortiter** l) **subitō**.

Exercise 20

a) **ad theātrum** b) **in viā** c) **Rōmae** d) **ex ponte** e) **Athēnīs** f) **super montēs in Ītaliam**.

Exercise 21

a) **ubi** b) **dum** c) **simulac** d) **nam** e) **igitur** f) **itaque** g) **et ... et** h) **antequam** i) **aut ... aut** j) **sed** k) **tamen** l) **ut**.

Exercise 22

a) **secunda** & **bis** b) **trēs** c) **prīmus** & **singulum** & **decem** d) **quattuor** e) **ambōbus** f) **ter; sexāgintā** g) **semel** h) **sextae**.

Exercise 23

a) **vīgintī annōs** b) **prīmā lūce** c) **a.d. ix Kal. Mar.** d) **a.d. viii Īd. Apr.** e) **a.d. viii Īd. Oct.** f) **a.d. ii Nōn. Nov.**

Sources and Index

Sources

This list gives the sources for all the original extracts from the **Latin Literature** section.

Referencing conventions will be consistent whatever edition of a particular Roman writer you read; but conventions can differ from author to author and work to work. For example, the source for the Prologue under Virgil is lines 1-7 of Book 1 of the *Aeneid*, and for Livy's Romulus and Remus it is sections 3-4 of Book 1 of the *History of Rome*.

Cicero (pages 158–165)

The case against Catiline – *Against Catiline* 1.1-2
Writing to Atticus – *To Atticus* 5.1-3, 4
Writing to his wife – *To His Family* 14.19, 20

Caesar (pages 166–173)

Preface – *The Gallic War* 1.1
Roman bravery – *The Gallic War* 5.44
Gallic savagery – *The Gallic War* 6.16
The battle of Pharsalus – *The Civil War* 3.91

Catullus (pages 174–181)

A lover's pet – *Poems* 2.1-10, 3.1-4
In love with Lesbia – *Poems* 5, 8.1-2
On Cicero – *Poems* 49
Conflicting emotions – *Poems* 70, 76.13-14, 85
Love for a brother – *Poems* 101

Virgil (pages 182–189)

Prologue – *Aeneid* 1.1-7
The fall of Troy – *Aeneid* 2.40-49
Aeneas and Dido – *Aeneid* 4.569-570, 622-629
Aeneas in the underworld – *Aeneid* 6.86-87, 417-425, 847-853
The death of Turnus – *Aeneid* 12.908-912

Horace (pages 190–197)
Taking the proverbial – *The Art of Poetry* 139, 359; *Epistles* 1.6.1-2, 10.24, 18.71; 2.1.117
The benefits of fine wine – *Odes* 1.7.27-29, 37.1-4
Odes 3: setting the challenge – *Odes* 3.1.1-4, 2.13-16
Odes 3: in praise of poetry – *Odes* 3.13
Odes 3: claiming the prize – *Odes* 3.30.1-9
The golden mean – *Satires* 2.6.1-3

Livy (pages 198–205)
Romulus and Remus – *The History of Rome* 1.3-4
The rape of Lucretia – *The History of Rome* 1.58-59
Horatius holds the bridge – *The History of Rome* 2.10
The war with Hannibal – *The History of Rome* 22.7, 51

Ovid (pages 206–213)
Early promise – *Amores* 1.13.35-40
Reckless youth – *The Art of Love* 1.631-638
Echo and Narcissus – *Metamorphoses* 3.379-389, 463-473
Medea – *Metamorphoses* 7.17-21
Daedalus and Icarus – *Metamorphoses* 8.210-220

Martial (pages 214–221)
Talking about marriage – *Epigrams* 9.5, 8.12, 9.15
Love and friendship – *Epigrams* 1.32, 2.38, 12.46
Life and death – *Epigrams* 1.15, 5.34.9-10
The Roman emperor – *Epigrams* 8.36.3-4, 11-12, 4.8
Satirical jokes – *Epigrams* 5.43, 3.8, 5.9, 1.47
Poets – *Epigrams* 12.73, 8.69

Tacitus (pages 222–228)
Calgacus' last stand – *Agricola* 30, 32
The Druids' last stand – *Annals* 14.29-30
Nero and the Christians – *Annals* 15.44

Pliny (pages 229–236)
The art of letter-writing – *Letters* 1.11
The price of immortality – *Letters* 3.16, 21
Writing for Tacitus – *Letters* 6.16
Writing for love – *Letters* 7.5
Royal birthday message – *Letters* 10.88, 89

Index

A

ablative 8, 25, 32, 130, 133, 152, 154
ablative absolute 83, 88, 91, 282
accusative 8, 93, 152, 154, 278
active 77, 115
adjectives 2, 16, 125
adverbs 124, 127, 150
Aeneas 182, 184, 185, 187, 250
agent 77, 281
agreement 16
Agricola 222
Anchises 186
army 172, 205
articles 2
Athens 190, 206, 211
Atticus 160
Augustus 165, 188, 190, 198, 222

B

Boudicca 223

C

Caesar 163, 166
Calgacus 222, 223
cardinal numbers 146
Carthage 184
case 2, 7
Catiline 158
Catullus 174, 219, 242
cause 106, 282
chariot-racing 227
Christianity 180, 213
Cicero 158, 164, 177, 236, 245, 251, 261
Cleopatra 166, 192
Clodia 174, 175, 178
Colosseum 214, 227
command 104, 108
comparison 22, 107, 129
complement 278
concession 107
conjugations 42, 115, 283
conjunctions 139
consonants ix

D

Daedalus and Icarus 211
dates 153
dative 8, 30, 92, 93, 153, 280
declensions 3, 6, 9, 17
defective verbs 117, 283
demonstrative pronouns 27, 34
deponent verbs 115, 282
determinative pronouns 27, 32
Dido 184, 187
direct object 8, 77, 278
distributive numbers 149
Domitian 217, 222
drama festivals 227

E

Echo and Narcissus 208
education 196

F

fear 107
feminine 2, 3, 5
fifth Declension 14
first and second declensions 17
first conjugation 45
first Declension 10
fourth conjugation 49
fourth Declension 13
future participles 90, 116
future perfect tense 75
future tense 63, 78, 111

G
gender 2, 3
genitive 8, 24, 28, 279
gerundives 92
gerunds 88, 116
gladiatorial shows 227
government 172, 188

H
Hannibal 203
Hercules 185
historic present 45
Homer 182, 190, 197
Horace 190, 206, 243, 251, 259
Horatius Cocles 201

I
imperative 55, 85, 115
imperfect tense 57, 78, 97, 101
impersonal verbs 93
indefinite pronouns 27
indicative 95
indirect object 8, 77, 280
infinitives 42, 89, 97, 101, 110, 116
interrogative pronouns 27, 38
irregular verbs 44, 50, 56, 61, 66, 72, 82, 111, 283
Isis-worship 213

J
Julius Caesar 153, 162, 273

L
Laocoon 183
legal system 235
Lesbia 175
Livy 198, 238, 273
locative 14, 134, 135
Lucretia 199, 200

M
marriage 160, 164, 214
Martial 174, 214, 220, 231, 267
masculine 2, 3, 4
Medea 210
Mithraism 213
mixed conjugation 53

N
negatives 119, 140
Nero 222, 225, 228, 241
neuter 2, 5
nominative 7, 278
nouns 2
numbers 146

O
ordinal numbers 148
Ovid 175, 206

P
passive 73, 77, 101, 112, 115
past participles 83, 101, 112, 116
patronage 214, 220
perfect stem 43, 68, 74, 75, 97, 111, 117
perfect tense 68, 84, 97, 101
person 46
personal pronouns 27
Pharsalus 162, 171, 172
philosophy 212
place 279, 281
Pliny 165, 189, 222, 229, 236
pluperfect tense 74, 97, 101
plural 2, 6
Pompey 162, 166, 171
possession 8, 30, 279, 281
possessive adjectives 31
possessive pronouns 27, 29
prepositions 132
present participles 19, 87, 116

present tense 45, 78, 97, 101
principal parts 43, 283
pronouns 2, 27, 125
pronunciation viii
purpose 89, 105, 106, 281

Q

questions 104, 108, 123

R

reflexive pronouns 27, 31
relative pronouns 27, 36
religion 180, 212
reported speech 108
result 106
roads 172, 212
Rome 174, 180, 184, 186, 188, 189, 190, 198, 200, 204, 205, 206, 207, 212, 214, 218, 221, 225, 227, 228, 238
Romulus 198, 238
root of the verb 43, 45, 78, 89, 92, 97, 101, 111, 112, 116

S

sailing 212, 213
second conjugation 47
second Declension 10
semi-deponent verbs 117
Senate 159, 160, 172, 188, 189, 268
singular 2
slaves 165, 190, 196, 205
social status 205
stem 21
Stoicism 212
stress ix
subject 7, 278
subjunctive 94, 95, 139, 141, 142, 143, 144
supine 83, 84, 91, 112
supine stem 43

T

Tacitus 222, 232, 241
tenses 42, 96
third conjugation 48
third declension 11, 18
time 94, 106, 107, 152, 279, 282
Trajan 189, 229, 234, 236
Troy 179, 182, 183
Turnus 187

V

verbs 42
Virgil 174, 182, 197, 250, 268
vocative 8, 278
vowels viii

W

weather 94
wish 105
would or should 105

About the author

Since graduating in Classics and Oriental Studies from the University of Cambridge, Ben Harris has worked in a number of teaching and publishing roles. He now writes, edits, and commissions learning materials for classical and other languages.

He was co-author (with Lizzy Nesbitt) of the *OCR A2 Latin OxBox CD-ROM* (Oxford University Press 2009) and compiled *Collins Easy Learning French Idioms* (Collins 2010). He currently works part-time at Cambridge University Press, in collaboration with the University of Cambridge School Classics Project in the UK and North America, on the research and development of teaching resources for the study of Latin and Classical Civilisation.

While studying at Cambridge he won the university prizes for classical verse composition, and is the translator into Latin elegiac couplets of Julia Donaldson and Axel Scheffler's worldwide bestselling picture book *The Gruffalo* (Macmillan 2012).

A keen walker and gardener, he lives in Gloucestershire with his wife and two children.